IN SEARCH
OF
ANCIENT ITALY

ROME The Tabularium

In Search of
ANCIENT ITALY

Pierre Grimal

Translated from the French by
P. D. Cummins

 HILL AND WANG · NEW YORK

ENGLISH EDITION © EVANS BROTHERS LIMITED 1964
ALL RIGHTS RESERVED
LIBRARY OF CONGRESS CATALOG CARD NUMBER: 16–18483

FIRST AMERICAN EDITION OCTOBER 1964

PRINTED IN GREAT BRITAIN

CONTENTS

CHAPTER ONE   *The Destruction of the Eternal City*   9

CHAPTER TWO   *The City of Shades*   31

CHAPTER THREE   *Rome and the Archaeologists:*
Archaic Rome   42

CHAPTER FOUR   *Rome and the Archaeologists:*
From the Republic to the Empire   69

CHAPTER FIVE   *The Roman Campagna:*
From Tibur to Ostia   110

CHAPTER SIX   *The Search for Herculaneum, Pompeii, and*
Stabiae   134

CHAPTER SEVEN   *The Discovery of the Etruscans*   163

CHAPTER EIGHT   *The Greek Colonies and Cities*   205

CHAPTER NINE   *What is Rome?*   240

ILLUSTRATIONS

ROME   *The Tabularium*   *Frontispiece*

facing page

View of the Tiber in the Roman Campagna   16

ROME   *Early view of the Roman Forum*   16

ROME   *The lay-out of the Imperial City*   17

ROME   *The Roman Forum as it is today*   32

ROME   *Plan of the Roman Forum*   33

ROME   *The Arch of Titus in the Roman Forum*   48

ROME   *Interior of the Curia in the Roman Forum*   49

ROME   *Forum Boarium. Sta. Maria Egyptiaca*   64

ROME   *Funerary hut-shaped urns*   65

ROME   *Reconstruction of a Palatine hut*   65

ROME   *The interior of the Colosseum*   80

ROME   *South-east aspect of the Colosseum*   80

ROME   *The mouth of the Cloaca Maxima*   81

ROME   *Remains of the Claudian Aqueduct*   81

ROME   *Flavian Palace on the Palatine*   96

ROME   *Trajan's Market*   97

ROME   *Trajan's Column*   112

ROME   *The Temple of Minerva*   113

ROME   *Arch of Titus*   128

ROME   *Sarcophagus with sculptures depicting a battle between Roman soldiers and barbarians*   128

ROME   *Aerial view of the Baths of Caracalla*   129

ROME   *The Via Appia*   144

ROMAN CAMPAGNA   *Horace's villa*   145

TIVOLI   *Hadrian's villa*   145

OSTIA ANTICA | *View of the street leading to the Porta Laurentina*   160

PALESTRINA | *Detail of the Nile Mosaic*   161

POMPEII | *The Temple of Apollo*   176

POMPEII | *The House of the Faun*   177

POMPEII | *The Colonnade surrounding the Forum*   177

POMPEII | *The Via Stabia*   192

POMPEII | *The House of the Moralist*   192

SICILY, TAORMINA | *View of the Greek theatre*   193

SICILY, SYRACUSE | *The Roman amphitheatre*   208

CERVETRI | *Aerial view of the Etruscan Necropolis*   209

CERVETRI | *Interior of the Regolini-Galazzi Tomb*   209

SICILY, PIAZZA ARMERINA | *Detail of a mosaic*   224

FLORENCE | *Archaeological Museum. The Chimaera*   224

SICILY, PIAZZA ARMERINA | *Detail of a mosaic*   225

SICILY, AGRIGENTE | *View of the so-called Temple of Concord*   248

SICILY, SELINONTE | *Remains of the Temples*   248

PAESTUM | *The Temple of Poseidon*   after 248

PAESTUM | *Interior of the Temple of Poseidon*

SICILY | *Two of the metopes found at Selinonte*

The Warrior of Capestrano   249

For permission to reproduce the photographs in this book the publishers are indebted to the following:

Istituto Geografico de Agostini, Novara; Aldo Martello, Milan; Alinari, Florence; Anderson, Rome; E.N.I.T., Rome; Fotocielo; Fototeca Unione, Rome; Gabinetto Fotografico Nazionale, Rome; Federico Arborio Mella, Milan; Hachettes; Budot-Lamotte; Photo Club du Livre Français; Viollet; Walter Dräyer; Keystone Press.

CHAPTER ONE

The Destruction of the Eternal City

THE ALMOST TOTAL DESTRUCTION of Rome from age to age, the creative destruction, as it were, that continuously replaced the old with the new—this is one of the paradoxes, and by no means the least, of the Eternal City. After Royal Rome, founded towards the middle of the eighth century B.C., Republican Rome gradually arose from the ashes of the conflagration lit by the Gauls at the beginning of the fourth. Republican Rome gave way to the 'modernized' Rome of Sulla the Dictator; Augustan Rome replaced Nero's 'New City'.¹ From antiquity right up to our own times, change succeeded change, and every era, every régime has left its imprint on the Rome of today.

Inevitably, the ceaseless building on the fatal hills led to the destruction and increasing diminution of the heritage of the past. At no period in its history did the inhabitants of Rome consider the city as completed, and as the population figures rose, so the rhythm of its growth was accelerated. New quarters were added, the existing quarters replanned. Not a single monument was regarded as sacrosanct, not even the Temple of Vesta, not even the Temple of Jupiter Capitolinus, the symbol and guarantee of the Republic. The Temple of Vesta, the hearth of the Roman people where the Sacred Fire was kept alight, the repository of the relics on whose safety the fate of Rome depended, was, with its atrium, the House of the Vestals, several times rebuilt, transformed, and embellished. Only the ground on which the Temple of Jupiter Capitolinus stood was respected; the Temple itself was looked upon as no more than the provisional dwelling-place of an invisible and eternal being.

One might have supposed that such a notoriously conservative people as the Romans would have preserved their city from sweeping changes, but no. Senators, when they became aediles or censors and assumed the responsibility for public works, abandoned their diehard traditions, and unhesitatingly introduced the most radical innovations. It is significant that the first basilica—that is, the first portico entirely surrounded by walls designed to protect the citizens from the vagaries of the weather (up to then, their only

meeting-place had been the open Forum)—owed its origin to
Cato, the censor who has gone down to posterity as the reactionary
of reactionaries. Yet Cato, the sworn enemy of all that was Greek,
made no bones about borrowing from Eastern architects the plan
for a building that had never been seen before on the banks of the
Tiber.

The first destroyers of Ancient Rome were the ancient Romans
themselves. The cataclysm which buried the Campanian cities in
A.D. 79 was not as fatal to Pompeii, Herculaneum and Stabiae as
was the mere continuance of life in the capital.*

Almost invariably, victorious generals grown rich with spoils
undertook on their triumphal return to Rome the restoration or
the enhancement of one or more public monuments. In the majority of cases the materials with which they had been built were
utilized for the main structure, but the walls rarely conformed to
their original state. The old methods had given way to more
modern techniques, the stone used in their construction was no
longer in favour. As Rome's might increased, as more and more
territory was conquered and subdued, new quarries were opened
up which provided a superior type of stone better adapted to
durable building.

For centuries the Romans had been content to use the local tufa,
of which there was an abundance—there was a quarry close to the
Capitol, for instance. This dark-grey volcanic stone, cappellaccio,
was extremely friable and did not weather well; apart from the fact
that ample supplies were available close to the building sites,
its one advantage lay in the fact that it was easily worked. Cappellaccio was used for the earliest fortifications—the famous Servian
Wall, the subject of so many studies and still in many respects a
teasing mystery. Because of the fragility of the stone, however, the
blocks were relatively small.

At the close of the fifth century B.C., the capture of the city of
Fidenze situated some seven miles north of Rome made a more
durable type of volcanic stone available to architects. Barely a
hundred years later the fall of Veii made it possible to open up new
quarries north of Rome in the region of Prima Porta on the left
bank of the Tiber. This yellowish tufa, grotta oscura has mainly
been found by archaeologists in the later sections of the Servian
Wall, but it appears to have been in general use until the beginning

*This is equally true of Naples.

of the first century B.C., when it was gradually replaced by an even better-class stone such as that quarried on the banks of the Anio. Whenever a monument was reconstructed or restored, the material then in fashion was used. The original stone vanished from sight; the blocks from walls that were pulled down were either relegated to the foundations or were utilized for the shell of new walls and were cased in or refaced with the stone that happened to be the vogue. Thus, every trace of the original building was lost. Even if certain sections of the old walls were left standing, the dimensions of a monument were frequently increased; this led to extensive alterations, and to demolition work, sometimes on a considerable scale, at the expense of the houses in the vicinity.

All the scrap material that these reconstructions and restorations yielded was re-utilized; usually, it was simply put together to form a series of layers fairly deep in the ground; these layers, by raising the level of the soil and draining it, acted as damp-courses, quite an asset in a city in constant danger of floods, and whose low-lying quarters were quagmires for centuries. So it came about that at a very early date the subsoil of Rome became a veritable graveyard of doomed monuments, a graveyard where archaeologists continually discover vestiges of the remote past and of later ages. An abandoned city left to decay finally collapses on its own ruins, and each phase of its history can be read in more or less regular layers, but no soil has been so continuously disturbed, dug up, re-dug, overturned, re-overturned, as that of Rome, and so it is by no means uncommon to find the foundations of Imperial or later buildings in a Republican layer.

The restorations and reconstructions of isolated monuments had only a limited importance and the problems they posed would have been solved by the patience and ingenuity of archaeologists had not Ancient Rome suffered a series of natural disasters which disrupted the life of the city and brutally changed its face.

While we have no records of all the fires and floods that ravaged Rome, we know that some of them caused massive damage in several quarters and practically wiped them out. From the brief references in Livy and Tacitus, we can form an idea of the magnitude of these catastrophes. The fire of 213 B.C., for instance, reduced all the buildings between the Aventine and the Capitol to ashes.[2] A few years later, the Forum quarter suffered so severely that it had to be entirely rebuilt.[3] The debris was cleared away, the site levelled, but the old foundations were left *in situ* and those of the new buildings superposed. The architects, however, did not adhere strictly to the original plan, and as they had not thought it necessary to retain certain features of the locality, many of the street names soon became meaningless. Archaeologists have found this a source of inextricable confusion. Not infrequently, they come across two descriptions of a particular monument, or particular quarter that are entirely contradictory, but this does not mean that one of them is incorrect. What it does mean is that in the period between the earlier and the later description the monument or the quarter underwent radical modifications.

Owing to the essentially changing character of Roman urbanization, it is dangerous to draw hasty conclusions from the appearance of a site. A classic example of this occurred in the nineteenth century, when certain archaeologists, basing their conviction on the fact that the Palatine is an almost regular quadrilateral, rashly asserted that Royal Rome had been a square city, built on the same grid plan as the *terremare*, the fortified villages of Emilia. This bold statement was completely disproved not so long ago when it was pointed out that the Palatine had been squared by the feverish spadework of the levelling-out that had taken place in the Imperial epoch. Previously, the Palatine had been a succession of irregular heights.

NERO'S BONFIRE

In A.D. 64, on June 18th, the anniversary day and month of the conflagration lighted by the Gauls in 300 B.C., the most famous of all the fires that ravaged Rome suddenly broke out. It began in the vicinity of the Circus Maximus, not far from where the Colosseum now stands, feeding, as Tacitus tells us, on the inflammable material of the shops: oil, tar, and pitch for the nearby shipyards. Fanned by a strong southerly wind, the flames swept unimpeded through the Circus, devastated the plebeian quarters of the Aventine, and spread as far as the Temple of the Moon on the slopes of the hill overlooking the Tiber. On the north they enveloped the heights of the Palatine and, simultaneously, the Forum, setting ablaze the Temple of Jupiter Stator, whose barely recognizable foundations can be seen near the Arch of Titus, the Regia, the sacred edifice built, according to tradition, by King Numa Pompilius, and the Temple and Atrium of Vesta. Unexpectedly, the wind changed direction and drove the flames north-east to the Caelian heights, and then they swept on unchecked till they reached the Esquiline, whose groves acted as a natural fire-break. At the end of the sixth day the fire appeared to have been mastered, but all at once it flared up again in the region of the Campus Martius and at the foot of the Quirinal, where it engulfed the villa of Tigellinus, the Emperor's favourite. When the fire finally burnt itself out, only four of the fourteen districts of Rome were left unscathed; seven had suffered severe damage, the remaining three had been completely obliterated.

According to popular rumour, Nero himself had set Rome ablaze; he was actually at Antium when the fire broke out, but the moment the fearful tidings reached him, he hastened back to Rome. Nero's guilt is far from being established; the energetic measures he took to put out the fire, the fact that his own palace was destroyed, seem to indicate that the accusation was unjust. An equally disastrous fire devastated Lyons in the following year, but the blame for this conflagration was not laid at Nero's door. But whether or not the Emperor lighted the celebrated bonfire, the damage it created was so widespread that the city had to be almost entirely rebuilt.

The amount of debris that had to be cleared away was formidable. Work began without delay, and ships were requisitioned to transport the heavy wreckage to Ostia, where, well offshore, it was heaved overboard into deep water. In 1877, an excavation in the vicinity of the Colosseum revealed quite by chance that the debris had raised the level of the soil by more than sixteen feet whereas, on this same site, from Nero's time to our own, the level has not been raised by more than nine feet—the figures speak for themselves.[4] The palace built by Nero on the Palatine, known as the Domus Transitoria because it communicated with Diocletian's Palace and the Gardens of Maecenas on the Esquiline (the etymology, however, remains very doubtful), had been so severely damaged by the fire that a new imperial residence had to be constructed. The gutted shell of the Domus Transitoria was pulled down, and over its foundations those of the new palace were laid. Today, laid bare by the deep excavations beneath Domitian's Palace, we can see the apartments that were buried under the new foundations; they are almost intact, and it is astounding that instead of being incorporated into the later imperial residence, they were consigned to oblivion. Nero's celebrated Golden House, built on the Caelian after the great fire, was doomed to disappear in the not-so-distant future; Titus razed it to the ground in order to lay the foundations of his thermae.

In spite of all the precautions taken by Nero, the ban on inflammable building materials, the increase of the city's water supplies, the multiplication of its fountains, the wider streets that replaced narrow, tortuous alleys, Imperial Rome suffered other serious fires. We know from the ancient historians that three times in the next three centuries, flames swept through the Forum. The first of these fires occurred in A.D. 80, during the reign of Titus. The second broke out in A.D. 191, when Commodus was Emperor, and was particularly disastrous; the House of the Vestals, for instance, was so severely damaged that it had to be rebuilt. It was enlarged and embellished, and it is this House of the Vestals that we see today.

The third fire, that of A.D. 283, when the imperial crown rested on the head of Carinus, created such havoc on both sides of the Forum that a formidable task awaited Diocletian, and after Diocletian, Maxentius. They had to rebuild the Curia (the excavations and restorations of recent years have given us back the Curia almost intact), the west wall of the Basilica Aemilia, and almost the whole of the Basilica Julia, as well as other important buildings. Some of the reconstructions, notably that of the Curia, were faithful enough, but in many instances strange liberties were taken with the past. During the reign of Maxentius, for example, Hadrian's Temple of Venus and Rome which had had a timbered roof was vaulted with stone in accordance with the style of the day.

THE ROME OF THE BARBARIANS

If scarcely a trace of Royal Rome remained at the time of Augustus, little was left of Augustan Rome at the date when the Barbarians occupied Latium. The classic Rome of Horace and Virgil lay in fragments beneath the new paving, and although the old names persisted, all but a few had become meaningless. In what had formerly been the patrician quarter, the magnificent houses of the wealthy families had been replaced by public buildings for the plebs: thermae, theatres, amphitheatres, circuses, stadia. The Palatine had become an exclusively imperial domain with a vast and complex agglomeration of palaces.

No siege, no invasion, inflicted such damage on Ancient Rome as the Emperors themselves. Personal vanity, followed by the need to woo the people and hasten the process of economic revolution, led to the work of destruction. The aspect of various quarters was completely altered by the continual erection of new buildings; to create space, the existing monuments were demolished and their material and the ornaments that had enhanced them were used elsewhere. The medallions of the Arch of Constantine, for instance, were undoubtedly removed from two, possibly three other arches; the circular medallions of hunting scenes, were taken from an arch erected in honour of Hadrian. The great panels in the attic belonged to an arch raised to commemorate the victories won by Marcus Aurelius in the campaign of A.D. 172–176 against the Huns and Sarmatians. Shamelessly, Constantine, the conqueror of Ponte Milvius, appropriated for himself the glories of the past, and to sate his mania for building, treated Rome as a vast quarry.

With the decline of the Empire, Rome suffered the lot that had befallen the provincial cities. The waning prosperity, the constant threat of Barbarian invasions had the effect of lowering the standard of building; fortifications were hastily run up with the cheapest materials, houses that conformed outwardly with the luxurious traditions of the past were erected with as much speed and as little cost as possible. Whatever lay nearest at hand was utilized: the stones of conveniently situated temples and tombs were incorporated into Hadrian's Wall, and to adorn the first Basilica of St. Peter (Caligula's private circus in the imperial gardens on the Vatican disappeared beneath its foundations), columns, capitals, and parts of architraves were taken from here, there, and everywhere. The fact that these borrowed items of architecture were completely out of keeping with the new building and that inscriptions were still partly legible on many of them, was totally disregarded.[5]

Constantine's architects followed the example of those who had long been in the habit of helping themselves to the material they needed for the reconstruction of temples. The Temple of Saturn, for instance, has obvious disparities which can only be explained by a reconstruction effected in the fourth century B.C. The columns do not correspond with their bases, the Ionic capitals bear no relation to the columns. The Column of Phocas is another example of this borrowing. In A.D. 608 Smaragdus, the Byzantine Exarch of

Italy, desirous of honouring the Emperor who was then reigning over Byzantium, expropriated a column from some other monument, and contented himself by surmounting it with a statue of Phocas and a suitable inscription.

ROME, THE INEXHAUSTIBLE QUARRY

Two centuries of continuous building and rebuilding had resulted in such a vast accumulation of every kind of material that to import stone and marble from a distance had become a needless expense. In any case, the marble-cutters had lost their skill, and more pleasing effects could be obtained by making use of marble that had already been worked. At the close of the fourth century B.C., the temples of the gods, deprived of their revenues, ceased to be places of worship. As it was impossible to maintain them, they gradually began to deteriorate; the roofs fell in, the walls cracked wide. The statues, ornaments, and reliefs, however, were rescued —in other words, they were removed and set up elsewhere, for as they no longer possessed any religious significance, they did not risk the anathema of the new God. The temples, stripped of their beauty, shunned as the haunts of evil spirits, were left to decay for two and a half centuries; they had no place in Christian Rome.

During these 250 years, however, a few public buildings were taken over by the Christians and transformed into churches. Apart from certain inevitable mutilations, these christianized edifices were so carefully maintained that it has been comparatively easy for archaeologists to reconstruct their original aspect. A notable example of this translation is the Curia; in A.D. 630, during the reign of Honorius, it became the church of S. Adriano and remained a place of worship until 1935.

Pope Alexander VII undoubtedly removed the magnificent bronze gates of the Curia to the Lateran. Despite the fact, however, that the three great windows of the façade, whose austere rhythm is so characteristic of imperial architecture, were bricked up, that a narthex giving access to the main entry was almost certainly built, and that the original decorations of the interior were overlaid with pious frescoes, the Curia remained essentially unchanged.[6] One of its annexes, the Secretarium, the repository of the archives, was also transformed into a church and consecrated to Sta Lucia and S. Martino. It was restored by Peter of Cortona in 1640, and it is this church that we see today; sooner or later,

View of the Tiber in the Roman Campagna. (From a lithograph of 1818)

ROME   Early view of the Roman Forum. (From an engraving of 1824)

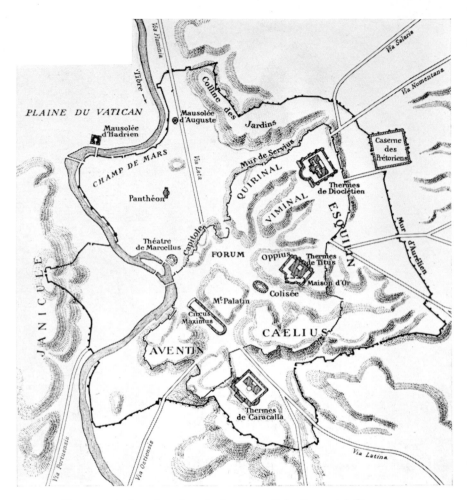

ROME   Reconstruction showing the lay-out of the Imperial City

however, the ancient building hidden beneath the trappings of far later centuries will undoubtedly be revealed.

FROM PAGAN TEMPLE TO CHRISTIAN CHURCH

It was not till the beginning of the seventh century that Pope Boniface IV began to transform temples into churches. In 609, the Pantheon, ceded to him at his request by Phocas, was Christianized and consecrated to the Virgin. The Pantheon, even though it was assured of protection, suffered cruel mutilations. Fifty years after its consecration, Constans II stripped it of its gilt-bronze tiles, and at the time of the Great Schism, during the period when the Orsini were at war with the Colonnas, it was used as a fortress. An agglomeration of wretched buildings arose between its columns and along the outer walls. Finally, round about 1444, Pope Eugenius IV neutralized the Pantheon. The sordid mass of structures that had been run up was demolished, the porticoes were unblocked, and the beauty of its original paving was revealed. Because it was greatly admired by the Romans, and because it was transformed into a church, the Pantheon exists to this day.

The list of churches that were formerly temples is fairly long.[7] One of the most remarkable of these is S. Stefano Rotondo on the Caelian. According to tradition, it displaced Nero's Macellum Magnum, but archaeological analysis has revealed nothing to justify so early a date. It may be, however, that the foundations are Neronian; material of this period may have been used in the course of a reconstruction in the fourth century A.D. We know from the circular shape of this church that it was originally a temple.

There is another circular church in the Forum Boarium, also named S. Stefano Rotondo, but to distinguish it from the church on the Caelian, it is also called S. Stefano delle Carrozze and Sta Maria del Sole. The ancient temple is easily recognizable. We do not know for certain to what deity this small sanctuary was dedicated, but in all probability it was Hercules Custos, whose cult was particularly strong in the locality. It is extremely fortunate for us that it was christianized, since it led to the preservation of one of the gems of Augustan architecture.

Quite close to S. Stefano delle Carrozze stands Sta Maria Egyptiaca. Consecrated in A.D. 872, the church did not acquire its present name until the fifteenth century. Originally, it was a small Syllanian temple, probably dedicated to the sea-god Portunus.

Restored in 1925, the little sanctuary, whose shape has remained almost unchanged, is a perpetual reminder of the days of Cicero's youth. We are fortunate indeed that it has survived when so much of the past lies in ruins.

Sad to relate, the numerous other temples in the quarter did not escape destruction. The neighbouring church of Sta Maria in Cosmedin, built in the sixth century on the site of the Statio Annonae, some of whose pillars it incorporated, was responsible for the disappearance of one of them. When the church was being restored by Pope Adrian I at the close of the eighth century a great monument in travertine was demolished and its materials used to enlarge the apse. Probably this monument was another temple dedicated to Hercules Custos. (It has also been suggested that the monument was the Temple of Ceres.) As late as the fifteenth century a circular temple dedicated to Hercules Triumphans adjoined Sta Maria in Cosmedin; it was demolished by Pope Pius IV, and only a few pictures by artists of the day remind us of its existence.[8]

Some distance from Sta Maria Egyptiaca and Sta Maria in Cosmedin is S. Nicola in Carcere. On this site, there originally stood three ancient temples, generally believed to have been dedicated respectively to Janus, Juno Sospita, and Spes. While they have been identified, the superposing of later buildings has made it extremely difficult to form a clear picture of them.

These few instances of the transformation of temples into churches are sufficient to prove that this process was not, as has been alleged, destructive, but quite the reverse; indeed, the earlier a temple was christianized, the better it fared, for at least it enjoyed a relative measure of protection.

PILLAGES AND VANDALISM

Pope, in his celebrated Epistle to Addison, has this to say about the monuments of Ancient Rome:

> Some felt the silent stroke of mouldering age,
> Some hostile fury, some religious rage;
> Barbarian blindness, Christian zeal conspire
> With papal piety and Gothic fire.

Pope is both harsh and unjust. While a certain amount of destruction is attributable to 'Christian zeal', 'religious rage' was mainly directed against the idols. Furthermore, these idols were rarely smashed to pieces; the gods and goddesses were removed, and duly translated into saints and martyrs, set up elsewhere.

Pope is equally unjust to the Barbarians who came to plunder the city, not to lay it waste. In A.D. 408, Alaric and his Goths were massed at the gates of Rome, and in order to raise the 5,000 gold *libri* which he demanded, the Romans were forced to strip the massive gold from their statues and melt down those which were cast in the precious metal. Two years later Alaric and his hordes ransacked the city; for three days they rushed through the streets pillaging and looting, setting ablaze the houses near the Porta Salaria and burning to the ground the imperial villa in the Gardens of Sallust on the Porta Collina. Probably the Aventine which, a couple of centuries ago, had become the patrician quarter, suffered most.[9] Rome itself, however, was barely scarred.

In the year A.D. 455, it was the turn of Gaiseric and his Vandals to sack the city; they swept from the south and burst in through the Porta Portuensis on the right bank of the Tiber. The Vandals were far more systematic than the Goths; they had assembled a fleet to bear their booty to Africa and spared neither the temples nor the imperial palaces. They stripped the gilt-bronze tiles from the roof of the Capitolium, and the treasures of Jerusalem fell into the hands of Genseric, who for some mysterious, superstitious motive bore them off to Carthage. For fourteen days the Vandals methodically pillaged Rome, bearing off all of value that had escaped the notice of Alaric. When they had thoroughly combed the city they withdrew, and for the next fifty years Rome was left in peace.

During the second half of the fifth century the process of its self-destruction slowly continued. True, in A.D. 458 the Emperor Majorianus issued an edict which forbade citizens to demolish ancient monuments in order to make use of their materials, but the edict remained a dead letter. Certainly, it was no easy matter to compel them to respect temples which had been stripped of their ornaments and which, for lack of funds to maintain them, had fallen into decay. The temptation to appropriate columns and architraves that were so conveniently on hand for the churches that were being built proved irresistible. For the Church of S. Pietro in Vinculi, raised by the Empress Eudoxia, twenty Doric columns were borrowed from a nearby sanctuary—an instance of the liberties that were taken with the heritage of the past.

ROME, TOO VAST, BECOMES AN EMPTY FRAME

When Theodoric entered Rome at the beginning of the sixth century the damage that had been done, while it was very considerable, was not irreparable, and the Emperor immediately took steps to put it right. The first buildings he restored were the theatres, amphitheatres, and circuses which played such a prominent part in the life of the late Empire; at the same time, the drainage system and aqueducts were overhauled, and special magistrates were appointed to a water board. Traces of the repairs carried out by Theodoric, can still be seen, and it would appear that after they had been effected, the art treasures which had been successfully hidden from the Goths and Vandals were replaced in their former settings. We know from Procopius that many masterpieces of sculpture were to be seen in Rome at this time, notably Myron's Cow in the Temple of Peace. The Romans continued to pray to the ancient Janus of the Argiletum, whose temple, restored by Nero, had remained intact. The statues of the Parcae still lined the Comitium, and this quarter was familiarly known as the Three Fates. Not all Rome's prized possessions had vanished, there were many treasures to be had for the taking. Constans II, for instance, while on a visit to Rome in 633, helped himself to a considerable number of bronze statues and carried them off to Constantinople. This was barefaced theft, for Constans could not put forward the excuse that the statues were the rightful plunder of war.

Already Rome had become a half-empty frame, too vast for its shrinking population which was to diminish still more in the sixth century when one of the city's life-lines was cut. Vitiges and his Goths besieged Rome in 537 and again in 538, when, as Procopius tells us, he hit on the stratagem of diverting the water from the aqueducts. Vitiges believed that this would lead to an early surrender, but the effects were not as serious as he had hoped; there were plenty of springs and wells in Rome, and the people had always used the water of the Tiber. But with the cutting of the aqueducts, the imperial baths could no longer function. If it is true that for six centuries the thermae had been the centre of social life, the so-called villas of the plebs, then an entire aspect of ancient Roman civilization vanished for good.

Gradually, large tracts within the city walls became uninhabited. The imperial parks, the gardens of the wealthy patrician families were left untended, and because of the ever-present danger from Barbarians and lawless brigands, the land around Rome was no longer cultivated. Furthermore, as the aqueducts had ceased to function and the drainage canals had not been maintained, produce from the farms and market-gardens which had been the main source of Rome's food supplies dropped to almost nothing. Famine and sickness stalked through the streets and malaria, which in a mild form had been prevalent in the past, became a virulent plague. For centuries, it was the scourge of the Campagna, killing off so many of the inhabitants that the landscape took on the melancholy and desolate air which romantic travellers were to find so enchanting.

Because of the total cessation of maintenance work, the floods of the Tiber became more disastrous than ever. During the late Empire special magistrates had been appointed whose duty it had been to see that the banks were kept in good order and that the river bed was regularly dredged, and as long as these precautions were observed the surplus water drained away fairly rapidly. But when these measures were neglected and it became the custom to dump all the city's filth and rubbish into the Tiber, the river frequently became choked up, its course was diverted, and inundations became more and more frequent. The flood of 856, during the papacy of Benedict III, did very considerable damage. The Campus Martius was completely submerged and the water rose to the first floors of the houses. The Forum Romanum, the Velabrum and the arena of the Circus Maximus were also flooded, and when the water had receded, it was found that the houses in the vicinity were no longer safe and their inhabitants had to be evacuated. The ooze, the mud, the debris that each flood left in its wake raised the level of the soil a little higher, and so the monuments of the past were gradually burried more and more deeply.

THE FORMATION OF MEDIEVAL ROME

After the aqueducts had been cut, the fountains of hillside villages soon ran dry, and the inhabitants had left their homes in increasing numbers to huddle together in swarms in the low-lying quarters of Rome. The misery they suffered from floods can well be imagined, for the Campus Martius was now the most densely populated quarter of Rome. Religious communities installed themselves on the Palatine. At the close of the seventh century the church and monastery of S. Cesario occupied part of the hill, while on the eastern slope there was another monastery known as the Palladium. Two fortresses flanked the Palatine; the first, near the Arch of Titus, was used as the repository for the ecclesiastical records, while the second, buttressed by the Septizonium of Septimius Severus, had been entrusted to the Frangipani for the city's defence. We see that the popes had retained their hold on the most sacred hill of all; since the Emperor of Byzantium was only the nominal suzerain of Rome, the Palatine had become the symbol of their temporal power.

It was only after the city had fallen to the Saracens in 846 that the extension of the existing fortifications to the region of the Vatican was begun. The main system of defence was the Aurelian Wall, some sections of which had been demolished while others could not be manned owing to the accumulation of rubble on either side of the bastions. In 848, on the order of Pope Leo IV, the building of a new wall round the Lion City commenced. Completed in 852, it was twelve feet high and defended by round towers. The keypoint for the new system was the Mausoleum of Hadrian, which had been converted into a small stronghold. From the time of Leo IV, Rome ceased to be the Imperial City centred round the Palatine and the Capitol; with the rise of the Papacy, the whole axis had shifted. The focal points were henceforth the west and the north, and before long, the patrician quarters, the Esquiline, the Aventine and the Palatine, were deserted. Corporations installed themselves in some of the public buildings; the Forum Transitorium, close to Trajan's Forum which the population still used, was taken over by the butchers, who held their elections there; because of its great length, the rope-makers occupied the Basilica Julia in the Forum Romanum; the candle-makers grouped themselves together beneath an ancient portico we cannot identify with any degree of certainty; the limestone-burners, who fed their kilns with broken statues and marble fragments of every description (they even went to the length of demolishing monuments that were still intact), took up their quarters in the Circus Flaminius south of the Campus Martius.

Dotted amongst the ruins of the deserted quarters, rose the strongholds of the barons. In addition to holding the fortress flanking the Palatine on the south, the Frangipani had established themselves in the Colosseum and in the Forum Boarium, where they held the Arch of Janus Quadrifons, and they had also fortified the Arch of Titus and the Arch of Constantine. During the period of the Great Schism anarchy was rife, and the barons seized every strategic point. Rome bristled with towers. The Colonnas occupied the Mausoleum of Augustus in the Campus Martius and the Temple of the Sun on the west slope of the Quirinal. The Crescenzi held the thermae of Severus Alexander, also in the Campus Martius, the Orsini Pompey's Theatre, the Faffi the Theatre of Marcellus, the future site of the Savelli palace.

Naturally, military occupation caused serious damage to certain of these major monuments. The arches of the Theatre of Marcellus, for instance, were bricked up. The Frangipani not only bricked up the four arches of Janus Quadrifons but raised the attic by surmounting it with a brick story with slit look-out windows at the top. If, as sometimes happened, a fortress failed to hold out, it was besieged for the second time by the furious citizens. In 1167 the plebs, who blamed the Colonnas for the defeat inflicted on the Romans by the armed band from Frascati, stormed and took the Mausoleum of Augustus, and vented their rage on the hapless monument. The work of destruction continued until the massive remains that were still standing resisted every effort to batter them down.

THE PILLAGE OF THE PAST

Far more insidious, far more destructive in the long run than the violence of the mob, were the depredations of marble-cutters and limestone-burners, who treated the city as an inexhaustible quarry. At the beginning of the eighteenth century, when Rome was threatened by a Lombard invasion, the example for this kind of pillage was set by no less a personage than the occupant of the Papal Chair, who ordered, at the expense of the ancient monuments, the limestone needed for repairing and strengthening the fortifications. A law had been passed making the stripping of marble from tombs a capital crime, but it was never enforced. In flagrant cases the guilty parties were fined, but a blind eye was turned on the small fry whose daily pilferings proved far more catastrophic than the less frequent hauls of the large-scale operators. In any case, the authorities could not possibly guard all the mausoleums scattered about on private estates; hence the societies formed to protect them were often granted special concessions. In 1426, for example, the ruins of the Basilica Julia in the Forum Romanum were conceded to one such society with permission to 'crush and extract from the foundations of the temple [*sic*], the calciferous stones concealed therein and fabricate limestone from the aforesaid stones', on condition that Cardinal Giacomo Isolani should be given a half-share of the profits.

In this systematic pillaging of Rome statues were particularly sought after, since they produced limestone of excellent quality; those made of precious marbles from the east were the most highly prized. We can imagine all that has been irretrievably lost to us as a result of this vandalism. It was not until the pontificate of Paul III—that is to say, round about 1560—that it was checked. From this time on any who were found guilty of consigning antiquities to the lime-kilns were sentenced to death. A good many statues were certainly preserved by this measure, but the stripping of monuments continued, and innumerable inscriptions that would have helped us to solve countless enigmas vanished in the lime-kilns. The sixteenth-century scholar who mentions an idol discovered on the Quirinal remarks that 'it was no doubt sent to the kiln to dry out the moisture at the back.'

The mania for building that possessed the Romans from the fifteenth century onwards increased the demand for limestone, consequently the destruction of the ruins was accelerated. We can tell how rapid this process was by comparing with earlier accounts the description by that Florentine worthy, Poggio Bracciolini, of his ramble through Rome in the year 1447.

Poggio and his friend Antonio Lusco rode through the city and jogged up the Capitol. Antonio, weary of horseback, suggested that they should climb to the top on foot, and the two friends made the ascent to what they called the 'Tarpeian Citadel'—in other words, the southern summit, or to be more exact, the Capitolium. Here they decided to rest: 'We sat with our backs turned on the approach to a vast marble door and a few scattered columns.' These ruins were undoubtedly all that was left standing of the Temple of Jupiter Capitolinus—ruins that were still recognizable at this era. Within a short time, however, they were destined to vanish. It comes as no surprise to learn that in 1661 gangs of labourers were hard at work removing calciferous stones from the Capitolium. The great marble door mentioned by Poggi, was demolished during the pontificate of Paul II (hence, before the close of 1649), as we know from the map drawn by Francesco di Giorgio Martini. In less than twenty years the last vestiges of the major temple of Rome had been swallowed up by the vast building site into which the city had been transformed.

With the dawn of the Renaissance the genius of the classic writers was once more admired and revered, and one might have expected to find an equal reverence displayed for the monuments of the past associated with men who on paper at least were eulogized as demigods. But this was not the case. The antique was merely a curiosity, and was only given some attention if it was considered to be beautiful, precious, or rare. Poggio and his friend seem to have been transported by a curious kind of satisfaction as they contemplated the shipwreck of Rome: 'Oh mother of illustrious men, emperors and leaders, nurse of all the virtues, begetter of just laws, example of every perfection,' Poggi apostrophized the city, 'today thou art but a plaything of fortune. Not only art thou deprived of thy empire, thy majesty, but thou art reduced to the most abject servitude. Stripped of thy beauty, thou hast indeed sunk low, and only when we ponder over thy downfall can we glimpse the grandeur, the glory, that once were thine.'

Poggio and his contemporaries took a kind of sour pleasure in despairing of Rome in such lofty sentiments, since they were not unmixed with a slighting reference to the Vatican régime. The discredit into which the Papacy had fallen made the contrast between the brilliance of the past and the sordidness of the present even more acute. Men were free to dream of the grandeur of Ancient Rome, but they could no longer cherish the hope—the hope that haunted so many imaginations in medieval times—of bringing that grandeur back to life, or even of finding it amongst the ruins.

A SHORT HISTORY OF THE COLOSSEUM

Perhaps the simplest way of conveying an idea of the vicissitudes that befell the ancient monuments is by following those of the most famous, the most popular of them all, the Flavian Circus, called by the people of Rome from the twelfth century, if not earlier, the Colosseum. The source of this popular appellation is thought to be the Colossus of Nero, transformed by the Flavians into a statue of the Sun, which towered up in the vicinity of the Circus and had given its name to the quarter.

During the Empire, apart from a few fires caused by lightning, the Colosseum suffered no harm, and such repairs as had been necessary had been carried out by Severus Alexander, Gordian III and Decius. The last restorations of which we have authentic evidence were effected by Theodoric, of whose energetic measures for the good of the State we have already spoken. Of what befell the Colosseum in the centuries that followed, history is silent. It was a familiar landmark to the travellers passing through Rome, and we find mention of it in the itineraries designed for pilgrims, but Roman citizens shunned it, believing it to be the haunt of evil spirits. The bloody spectacles that were staged there in the past may have given rise to this superstition, but it is far more likely that the deserted corridors, the vast, empty *cavea* peopled, under the ghostly light of the moon, with a host of phantasms, inspired this terror of the Colosseum, for it was generally believed that it had originally been a temple dedicated to the powers of darkness. Tradition has it that the Flavian Amphitheatre was the first pagan sanctuary, just as the Church of St. Peter's was the first Christian basilica. It was not surprising, then, that the Devil had chosen the Colosseum for the celebration of his sabbaths.

This dread of the Colosseum may have protected it to some extent, but it did not prevent it from falling into profane hands. As has already been said, the Frangipani occupied it for military purposes, but when, in 1244, they wished to cede half of it to the Annibaldi who were in the service of the Emperor Frederick II, Pope Innocent IV refused to give his consent, reasserting the rights of the Church over a monument that was part of the patrimony of Rome, and reminding the Frangipani that it had only been ceded to a lay family. This was quite true, but the fact was that the Church only laid claims to monuments of strategic worth; the Colosseum came into this category, hence the Papal intervention.

In 1231 an earthquake caused the collapse of some twenty columns of the façade. Probably the stonework exposed on the south-west to the full violence of wind and rain, had been weakened and had ended by crumbling away. Right up to the end of the nineteenth century, in that section of the Colosseum facing the Lateran, the remains of houses built by the

Frangipani in the sound parts of the structure were still to be seen.

At the close of the thirteenth century, the Frangipani were forced to abandon their fortress, and the Colosseum passed into the hands of the Annibaldi. On this occasion the Pope was powerless to protest. Subsequently, the Emperor Henry VII took possession of it for a brief spell, after which the Colosseum became once more the property of the Senate and the Roman people. In 1321, to recall the *venationes*, a wild-beast hunt on a grand scale was staged in the Amphitheatre, but during the course of this bloody spectacle so many noble young Romans were killed that its evil reputation was confirmed—undoubtedly it was a place accursed. Once again the Colosseum was abandoned, avoided by all but those who had been conceded the right to cart away the fallen stones for building purposes. Quite apart from its sinister atmosphere, an earthquake in 1349 brought down another twenty columns, and prudence alone dictated that no further use should be made of the Amphitheatre.

A violent dispute had broken out between the Frangipani and the Municipality, each side claiming the monopoly of exploiting the ruins. The Frangipani were bent on acquiring free, gratis, and for nothing the material needed for the palace they were building, while the Municipality was equally determined to retain for its sole use these highly convenient reserves. Meanwhile, the citizens, quite indifferent to the battle that was raging, busied themselves profitably in the Colosseum, surreptitiously extracting the lead that had been used to seal in the crampons; the scars left by these depredations are still visible today, and we would search the Amphitheatre in vain for a crampon whose lead had been overlooked.

Since the Colosseum could no longer be used as a fortress, the Municipality handed it over to various charitable organizations. In 1381 it served as an annexe of the Lateran Hospital. In 1431 the monks of Sta Maria Nuova (now Sta Francesca Romana) incorporated it into their garden, but the people of Rome, determined to retain possession of the famous ruin, tore down the offending wall. Very likely, it had been erected by the monks at the instigation of Pope Eugenius IV, who may conceivably have cherished the hope that a high wall would protect the Colosseum from private marauders. All the concessions previously granted were revoked, but when Nicholas V ascended the Papal Throne in 1447, the depredators returned in force, and removed all the marble and travertine that they could get at with reasonable ease. Ten years later gangs of labourers tore up the marble slabs originally intended for the ornamentation of the benches and now destined to cover the steps of St. Peter's.

The pontificate of Paul II (1464–1471) was equally disastrous for the Colosseum; the entire southern section was turned into a quarry to provide the material needed for the construction of the Palazzo San Marco (now the Palazzo Venezia). Cardinal Alessandro Farnese also exploited the 'quarry', and much of the stone and marble of the Palazzo Farnese (the present French Embassy) originated from the Colosseum.

During the pontificate of Sixtus V, the Colosseum was in dire peril, since the Pope avowed that he intended to demolish 'all those unsightly ruins whose material will be used to restore those worthy of restoration'. Pope Sixtus V had set his heart on modernizing Rome, and on making manifest the triumph of Christianity over paganism by the creation of a network of roads radiating from Sta Maria Maggiore—processional highways along which the cross could be carried in splendour. His grandiose scheme, while it certainly laid the foundation of romantic Baroque Rome, led to fearful destruction. The Septizonium of Septimius Severus was completely demolished, and the touching mausoleum of Caecilia Metella on the Appian Way narrowly escaped the same fate. Domenico Fontana, the favourite architect of this energetic Pope, had the idea of transforming the Colosseum into a centre for the wool industry which Sixtus V was anxious to establish in Rome, but fortunately it came to nothing.

The pressure of work ordered by the Pope was such that the Colosseum was spared, but every monument that stood in the path of the new roads was ruthlessly pulled down.

After the death of Sixtus V, the Colosseum, too massive to be demolished, became a safe refuge for beggars, outlaws and the riff-raff of the city. Even as late as the nineteenth century it was unwise to venture after dark into its labyrinth of arcades, the shadowy setting of a clandestine Court of Miracles. In the hope of preventing this assortment of cut-throats from camping in the Colosseum, Pope Clement IV walled up the lower arches, but this had no effect. A few years later Benedict XIV conceived the idea of consecrating the Amphitheatre. Accordingly, it was dedicated to the Passion; fourteen chapels formed a majestic Via Crucis, and in the centre of the *cavea*, a great crucifix was solemnly erected. The credit for clearing away most of the debris from the Colosseum (the earthquake of 1703 had been responsible for the major part of the rubble) goes to Pope Pius VII, on whose orders a massive buttress was constructed to consolidate that part of the Amphi-theatre which had been weakened by the shock. This buttress, described by Nibby as 'worthy to rank with the finest work of the Empire', was completed under the supervision of the architect Valadier during the pontificate of Leo XII.[10] Henceforward, the Colosseum took its place as an historic monument, and was regarded with pride as part of the patrimony of Rome.

In most respects, the history of the Colosseum is almost identical with that of all the ancient monuments of Rome; the Flavian Amphitheatre, however, was saved by its very massive-ness. Indeed, its structure was so solid that the damage caused to it by earthquakes was relatively slight; furthermore, it contained such a wealth of material that the depredations of stone-cutters and quarrymen made little impression on the whole. The more vulnerable monuments, however, did not fare as well. Many which had survived almost unharmed the worst years of the Medieval Age were mercilessly demolished at the dawn of the Renaissance.

The Temple of Venus was exploited in much the same way as the neighbouring Colosseum. For the vestibule of St Peter's alone, materials were expropriated from the most varied sources: the Capitolium, Caesar's Forum, the Portico of Octavia in the Forum Holitorium, the Baths of Caracalla, to mention but a few. Architects engaged in restoring ancient churches helped them-selves freely to porphyry columns and precious marbles, as well as to the stones required for the walls. Marble-cutters became adept at transforming gods and goddesses into saints. Obelisks that had been raised in the squares of ancient Rome were taken down and erected on other sites. The city was tidying up its ruins, and had no scruples about removing and re-utilizing anything and every-thing that would enhance its renascent splendour.

Nevertheless, the balance sheet did not record a total loss. The interest of architects was awakened by the ancient monuments whose ruins became, as it were, a kind of school where they learnt many valuable lessons. The dome of the Pantheon, the vaulted roof of Constantine's Basilica in the Forum inspired the genius of such masters as Bramante and Michelangelo. Treasures from other Italian cities were gathered together in Rome, and with the passing of time, the marvellous works of art that had miraculously survived all the looting and destruction found their way to the Vatican museums. But the topographical reality of Ancient Rome had become no more than a dim memory, and it was left to archaeologists to retrace lineament by lineament, with infinite patience, the true face of the city.

CHAPTER TWO

The City of Shades

AS THE ANCIENT MONUMENTS were gradually buried in their own ruins, covered with thick layers of sand left by the floods, the memory of them began to fade from men's minds. The old names were retained, but as many of these had lost their meaning, the citizens of Rome invented others, descriptive of this or that locality. Legends grew up round the ghostly palaces, and certain great figures of the past, grown to superhuman proportions, returned to haunt the living.

First and foremost, there was Nero—Nero, so adored by the plebs that they had refused to believe in his death; Nero, most hated and execrated of all the emperors after the triumph of Christianity. No wonder that he was cast in the role of arch-fiend in the pagan hell, no wonder that his name was irrevocably linked to so many ancient monuments. But there were other prodigious shades: Cicero and Pontius Pilate, Augustus and Agrippa, Marcus Aurelius and Nerva shared pride of place with St. Peter and St. Paul; St. Stephen and St. Lawrence ranked with Simon Magus and Catiline.

The churches had become the principal landmarks of Rome, for the ancient names had fallen into disuse. Quarters were called after the industries that were carried on there (the Quarter of the Lime-kilns, and so on), or after the corporations that had installed themselves in the locality—the Basilica Julia, for instance, was known as the Temple of the Rope-makers. Streets were similarly renamed. (Many of these names survive to this day, and are mainly to be found in the Campus Martius and in the vicinity of the Capitol.) Castles and fortresses helped to create the new toponymy, changing names when they passed to another branch of the family or were acquired by fresh owners. So the ancient names, like the ancient monuments, were gradually buried. Many had been dropped and others distorted and corrupted out of all recognition. The confusion created was such that from age to age the features of Ancient Rome became increasingly obscured. How to find a way through this labyrinthine chaos? This was one of the first problems with which the archaeologists of the nineteenth century were to wrestle.

THE ARIADNE THREAD

Certain texts are extant which give us an approximate idea of the extent to which Roman toponymy was invaded by legendary and fanciful nomenclature—texts that have acted in some degree as a guiding thread. After Italy's unification in 1870, when, for the first time, the Eternal City became the object of scientific research, the systematic study of these manuscripts, particularly those written during the Medieval Age and the Renaissance, was begun. Some time later, the first digs were carried out in Rome, but for a considerable period the study of these documents was the principal, if not the only, channel of investigation, for it happened far too frequently that the results of excavations remained unpublished for years. The Ariadne thread was mainly provided by three manuscripts: the Einsiedeln Itinerary (written by a Swiss monk, it forms part of a collection of manuscripts in Switzerland's Einsiedeln Museum); the Itinerary of Benedict, drawn up by Pope Celestinus II when he was a canon of St. Peter's (he was elected to the Papal Throne in 1143); and finally, the *Mirabilis Urbis Romae*, a compilation which appeared in the thirteenth century, but which in all probability had been put together towards the middle of the twelfth, at any rate in its original form.

The Einsiedeln Itinerary, contemporary with Charlemagne's reign and based on a fourth-century map designed, no doubt, for the use of pilgrims, provides a picture of ninth-century Rome. We note that the ancient names of places and buildings are generally correct. These names are landmarks on the eleven routes that cross the city diametrically from gate to gate; it is significant, however, that even at this early date, identification had become difficult. For instance, the Stadium of Domitian (the present Piazza Navona, which has preserved the Stadium's elongated shape) in the Campus Martius is called the Circus of Flaminius, an understandable mistake, since, in addition to the fact that the two were similar in shape, the latter had given its name to the entire quarter. There is a single reference to the Capitol, but no attempt is made to distinguish the buildings that adorned it, indeed, only the church of SS. Sergius and Bacchus (close to the Temple of Concord) and oddly enough, the Umbilicus Romae, the small Servian

ROME   The Roman Forum as it is today. (See plan facing page 33)

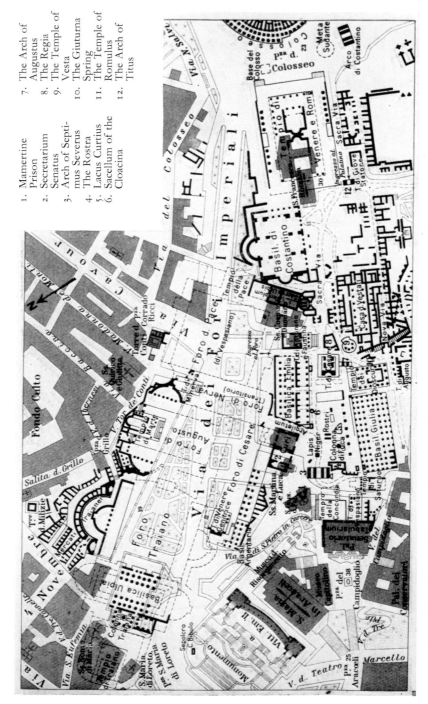

7. The Arch of
   Augustus
8. The Regia
9. The Temple of
   Vesta
10. The Giuturna
    Spring
11. The Temple of
    Romulus
12. The Arch of
    Titus

1. Mamertine
   Prison
2. Secretarium
   Senatus
3. Arch of Septi-
   mus Severus
4. The Rostra
5. Lacus Curtius
6. Sacellum of the
   Cloacina

ROME   Plan of the Roman Forum and the Imperial Fora

pyramid that supposedly marked the centre of Rome and the Empire, are considered noteworthy. The Curia figures merely as the church of S. Adriano into which it had been transformed. The Forum Romanum is mentioned as briefly as the Capitol; its name is given and nothing more, from which we infer that the recollection of the ancient monuments which had stood there in the past had already almost faded from men's minds. The imperial thermae and theatres are correctly designated, as is Trajan's Market, which, as we know, remained in use for a long period of time. Trajan's Baths, however, rightly identified in one Itinerary appear in another as Trajan's Palace. This was a mistake typical of an age when there was a tendency to believe that any ancient building of considerable size had originally been a palatium, the private residence of an emperor or a celebrity.

The Einsiedeln Itinerary mentions a palace belonging to Pontius Pilate adjacent to the churches of Sta Pudenziana and Sta Maria Maggiore, but we have not the slightest idea to what ancient building this refers. It also draws attention to a palace owned by Nero situated between the churches of S. Cosmo and S. Damian (in the immediate vicinity of the Basilica of Constantine) and that of S. Pietro in Vincoli on the Esquiline which pilgrims could see on their left from a considerable distance away. In all probability, the palace in question was in actual fact the Basilica of Maxentius.

This particular quarter was so steeped in memories of Nero that consciously or unconsciously, the Anonymous of the Itinerary may have been affected by them. Beneath the sandalled feet of the pilgrims lay the vast vestibule of Nero's Golden House; the propylaeum had at one time been adorned by a colossus whose features strongly resembled those of the sadistic Emperor, and this had been quite enough for popular imagination to stamp the name of Nero indelibly on the entire locality. A residence on the Vatican hill came to be known as another of Nero's palaces for much the same reason; this building was associated in the minds of the people with the memory of Christians martyred in the Emperor's gardens.

When the Anonymous gives the current name of an ancient monument, we see what fancies have been woven round it. Almost certainly the edifice bordering on the Palatine and immediately to the west of the Arch of Constantine, to which he attaches the curious name of Testamentum (in medieval Latin, a book) was none other than the Septizonium. In point of fact, the Septizonium was not unlike an open book, and no doubt pilgrims, gazing up at the mysterious monument that adorned the propylae of the Servian palace, imagined that here, before their eyes, was the grimoire (book of magic spells), of the sorcerer-kings. Because of its illusory resemblance to a book, the Septizonium was sometimes called the Septifolium—the Seven Pages. Possibly something of its significance may have conveyed itself to the more perceptive, for the Septizonium was, in fact, a monument of an astrological and sacred character, and had been designed by its architects as a symbol of the seven zones of the cosmos over which the emperor-cosmocrator reigned.

With the passing of the centuries, more and more monuments came to be known by names which popular fancy dictated. From the Itinerary of Benedict, compiled only some two hundred years after the Einsiedeln Itinerary, we see how rapidly the darkness of night is closing in on Ancient Rome. Fantastic identifications have multiplied; on the Vatican hill, there is an imaginary Tomb of Romulus, and in the Forum Holitorium, an equally imaginary Mausoleum of Cicero, as well as a Temple of the Sibyl.

The Itinerary of Benedict brings home to us the fact that twelfth-century Rome, with its simplified pattern of residential quarters and ecclesiastical preserves, could not even grasp the complexities of the urbanization of Ancient Rome, the characteristic features of which had been lost and forgotten. False etymology blurred the past still more. For instance, a mausoleum on the border of the Via Triumphalis is described in the Itinerary of Benedict as 'the Obelisk of Nero'. (Actually, the tomb was pyramidal, but popular terminology did not bother with such nice distinctions.) The Obelisk of Nero was more familiarly known as the Terebinth Tomb; in all probability, terebinth is a corruption of *tibertinum*—made of travertine stone. The mausoleum was subsequently demolished, and its materials used elsewhere, but the terebinth legend persisted and was perpetuated by Antonio Filarete, who adorned one of the panels of the bronze gates of St. Peter's with a turpentine tree.

By the twelfth century, then, Antiquity had become a kind of wonderland of the gigantic, the ridiculous and the sublime. The names of many of the deities of Ancient Rome had been forgotten, others appeared in a mangled form. These last suggest that inscriptions were very imperfectly deciphered. There is mention, for instance, of a goddess Nervia whose temple had formerly stood in Caesar's Forum. Nervia, is of course, simply Minerva, the first three letters of whose name were not legible, as the inscription had been mutilated. This inscription, incidentally, provides us with some valuable information; it confirms the existence of the Chalcidicum Minerva, an annexe added to the Curia in the Augustan era.

The Itinerary of Benedict relates in all seriousness the most arrant nonsense—of an edifying nature, of course. Here is one example. At one time there was a reservoir on the Esquiline known as the Lacus Orphei because of the legend of Orpheus depicted on its fountain. This name persisted till medieval times and was in fact extended to the whole district, as we know from the Einsiedeln Itinerary, which mentions the church of Sta. Lucia-in-Orphea (also spelt Orphtea). The Itinerary of Benedict solemnly recounts the story associated with the Lacus Orphei. A fearful basilisk had taken up its abode by the fountain, and during the demon-haunted hours, it retired to a cave; its reek, its noisome breath instantly killed those who crossed the threshold of its lair. Every year, on a certain day, a procession bearing aloft an image of the Saviour, made its way to the accursed spot to exorcise the monster.

Many more such legends appear in the pages of the *Mirabilis*. One of them relates the story of the two temples raised by Romulus in the garden of one of his palaces. He dedicated them respectively to Piety and Concord, and in the first or second of these sanctuaries, placed a golden statue, declaring that it would remain standing until the day when a virgin was delivered of a child. 'And on the day when Mary was delivered of the infant Jesus, even as Romulus had predicted, the statue fell.'

The *Mirabilis* contains the following story about the Pantheon:

In the days of consuls and senators, the Prefect Agrippa, with four legions, subjugated the Swabians and Saxons. Now in the Temple of Jupiter and Moneta on the Capitol, there were effigies of all those rulers whose countries had become subject to the Empire, and each of these effigies had about its neck a bell. Scarcely had Agrippa returned to Rome than the bell around the neck of the King of Persia began to ring, and thus the Senate knew that he was about to rise against Rome. Therefore, the Senate besought Agrippa to go to Persia and crush the rebellion, but he, weary of wars and conquests, asked that he might delay his decision for three days. The Senate granted his request, and in the solitude of his room, Agrippa sat pondering until sleep overcame him. Then, in a dream, a strange woman appeared to him, and said: 'Thou art sorely troubled, Agrippa,' and he made reply: 'Yes, lady.' Then the apparition said: 'Be of good courage, for I will grant thee victory over the Persians if on thy return thou wilt build for me a temple such as I desire.' Whereupon, she showed him a temple shaped like the Pantheon. 'Who art thou, lady?' Agrippa asked in great amaze, and she answered: 'I am Cybele, Mother of the Gods.' So Agrippa went to Persia and put down the insurrection, and when he returned to Rome, he raised the Pantheon to the goddess. And to do her greater honour, he covered the roof with gilt-bronze tiles and set a golden statue of her on the dome.

We would be quite wrong to place any credence in this story, even when stripped of its fantastic details. True, Agrippa fought in the East, but the Pantheon was never dedicated to Cybele, and no statue of the Mother of the Gods was raised on its dome—indeed, it is not at all certain that the original Pantheon had a dome. There is only one reliable item in the account: the Pantheon was, as we know, roofed with gilt-bronze tiles, the tiles stripped off by Constans II. Stories of this kind obviously spring from imperfectly digested information. Its writer appears to have been struck by the name Pantheon, which he interprets correctly, and also by the fact that Boniface IV, when he transformed the Pantheon into a church, dedicated it to the Virgin, Mother of all the Saints. This was quite enough for our anonymous author to dream up an analogy. 'All the saints' corresponds with 'all the demons', in other words, all the pagan gods, hence it follows that the Virgin Mary, Mother of the Saints, corresponds with Cybele, Mother of the Gods. From this story, it is clear that at the time of the *Mirabilis* information regarding the ancient monuments of Rome was no longer obtained in the traditional manner by word of mouth, but was acquired from literary sources and written up with more or less skill.

This fact is not without importance. Somewhat paradoxically, the *Mirabilis* may be considered as a first attempt in a new field, as heralding the dawn, as it were, of a science of Roman topography, provided, of course, that we are prepared to admit that a science is defined, not by its failure or success, but by its aims and methods. Plainly, the anonymous writers of the *Mirabilis* possessed a fairly accurate knowledge of historical facts; they knew, for instance, that August 1st was the anniversary of the taking of Alexandria by Octavian, and that when he became Emperor he changed his name by the will of the people to Augustus. They were also acquainted with the fact that while consuls were elected in the summer, they did not assume office until the first day of the new year, but the statement that the elections were held in the Temple of Mars (in the Forum of Augustus?) is quite incorrect, and the description given in the *Mirabilis* of the accompanying rites is unmitigated nonsense. Occasionally, the writers mention the sources of their information; most of it appears to have been drawn from Ovid's *Fasti*, but a certain amount was taken from Suetonius, particularly from his *Lives of the Caesars*. From the time of the *Mirabilis*, there was a wide breach between textual knowledge and topographical reality—a breach that present-day scholars, despite all their efforts, have not invariably succeeded in closing.

THE ROME OF THE HUMANISTS

When the humanists of the Renaissance embarked on the attempt to replace the history of Rome in a juster perspective, they found themselves confronted with a chaotic mass of myths, beliefs, and affirmations, all the more difficult to dispose of because amongst so much that was so palpably false, amongst all the distortions, there were recollections of the past which were of genuine value. It would have been strange indeed if the Roman people who had lived for generation after generation amid the mute witnesses of their former glory had not retained a few fragments of the truth. But until the dawn of the era of excavations that were to lay bare beneath the ruins the level of the ancient city, the face of Rome remained veiled with a tissue of legends.

It would take too long to chronicle step by step the efforts made from the beginning of the sixteenth century by Marliani and the first archaeologists to penetrate the mystery. We shall therefore pass on to the nineteenth century and see to what conclusions 300 years of archaeological research had led when, in 1819, Antonio Nibby's book *The Forum Romanum, The Sacred Way, and the Flavian Amphitheatre* appeared. Up to this time, archaeologists had concentrated mainly on the identification of the ruins that were still standing, a task which they carried out with increasing exactitude, and on the study of their architecture from which they learnt many a practical lesson. Excavations were few and far between; occasionally a few ardent spirits would organize a dig, but such explorations were only partial and carried out in the most haphazard way. True, shortly after Carlo Fea was appointed Director of Antiquities in 1801, he initiated a series of excavations in that section of the Forum Romanum adjacent to the Arch of Septimius Severus, but up to 1819 when Nibby's book was published, the results had been disappointingly slender. Nibby's *magnum opus* can justly be considered as the last topographical synthesis prior to the total re-thinking necessitated by the later discoveries in the Forum.

Nibby's hypotheses are not without interest, since they represent the advanced opinions of the day. He was thoroughly familiar with all the documentary evidence, hence his theories are soundly based, but it is instructive to note into what gross errors he was led by too rigid adherence to these texts, by his failure to recognize the fact that each individual text contained only a fraction of the truth and so merely held good for a particular moment in the history of Rome.

For his reconstruction of the Forum, Nibby started off with Dionysos of Halicarnassus, who tells us that it was 'a plain extending between the Capitol and the Palatine', and with Vitruvius, who states that the fora of Ancient Rome were rectangular and were 'almost four times as long as they were wide'. From these texts, Nibby concluded that the Forum Romanum was a rectangle oriented exactly north-south. His first point of reference was the Mamertine prison, within whose grim walls, according to tradition, St. Paul had been incarcerated; for this reason, its site had been remembered through the ages. Nibby then proceeded to argue thus: while the Temple of Antonius and Faustina (incorporated into the church of S. Lorenzo in Miranda but easily identifiable because of the imperial inscription of the architrave) did not, as we know from the Regiones, form part of the Forum, an Arch of Fabius which stood immediately in front of the Temple, *was* included in it, as we learn from all the ancient texts.

Nibby concluded, therefore, that a straight line traced from west to east between the Mamertine and the approach to the Temple would allow him to determine the actual width of the Forum. Placing his reliance on the mathematical formula of Vitruvius, he constructed, between the Capitol and the Palatine, a kind of rectangle whose southern limit coincided with a line that joined the church of S. Theodore with that of the Consolation—in other words, Nibby's rectangle, as we know today, went far beyond the Forum, extending to the middle of the Velabrum.

Nibby's geometry barely took into account the ruins that were then standing—in fact, they were made to fit in with his reconstruction! The truth was that for years, the Vitruvian 'religion' had had a vitiating effect on its devotees who looked upon each article of his *Treatise on Architecture* as if it were gospel. It never occurred to this body of the faithful that Vitruvius's account of the origins of Rome, the foundation of a colony on virgin soil, bore no approximation whatsoever to the slow process of evolution that ultimately gave rise to Rome. Romulus did not trace with mathematical exactness the ideal lines of his city; the statements made by Vitruvius must be confronted by facts and criticized in their light—they cannot possibly be taken as a point of departure.

Nibby attached extraordinary labels to the ruins included in his fantastic reconstruction of the Forum Romanum. For instance, he attributed the three exquisite columns of the Temple of Castor— the columns which make up the characteristic landscape of the Forum—to the Graecostasis, a simple platform where foreign ambassadors waited to be admitted to the Senate, and whose site has not yet been located.

His *naïvete* was extreme, as the following shows. 'Is it not possible', he writes, 'that one of the Jani once stood where the Column of Phocas now stands? Since I cannot prove it, however, I have placed this Arch of Janus in the vicinity of the Basilica Aemilia.' One would have supposed that this would have aroused misgivings in his readers, but no. Only a few years later, although excavations on this site had disclosed nothing, the Forum guides drew the attention of visitors to an entirely imaginary Temple of Janus, pointing to an unidentified ruin that faced the Basilica. Despite all its glaring errors, Nibby's reconstruction of the Forum Romanum survived for more than a century.

The identification of ruins on the slopes of the Capitol was equally inaccurate. The Temple of Saturn became the Temple of Fortune; the Temple of Vespasian figured as the Temple of Jupiter Tonnans. At the opposite extremity, the Temple of Vesta was removed to the site of S. Theodore simply because, like the Temple of Vesta, this church was round!

True, topographers had sped the Temple of Vesta on many a journey in the past. In the sixteenth century, for instance, it had travelled to Sta Maria del Sole in the Forum Boarium, the only circular church that was known at the time. This error is worth recalling, since it persists to this very day; it is by no means unusual to find Sta Maria del Sole figuring as the Temple of Vesta in pictorial albums of Rome. A century and a half of scientific research has not succeeded in exorcizing the shades that haunt the Tiber, the shades that continue to weave a fabled past for Rome.

The Forum Romanum is pretty well known to modern archaeologists, and Nibby's errors have been practically eliminated. The knowledge gained has come mainly from a century of excavations,[1] but though most of the ruins have been identified, there are still many problems to be solved. Every year new hypotheses are advanced on minor discoveries: a magistral tribunal, a *puteus* (a small circular altar erected by the Romans on the spot where a thunderbolt had fallen), the exact line of a road, and often the analysis of later finds throws doubt on conclusions that had previously seemed certain.

The science of Roman topography is a solidly interlocking system, and the merest trifle, the totally unexpected appearance of a pillar, the non-appearance of a wall on a site where a wall had been confidently expected, is enough to precipitate a crisis. Archaeologists find themselves faced with the realization that they have been too hasty in arriving at this or that conclusion, that they have placed too much reliance on this or that similarity, and are forced to revise their opinions. There is no help for it: they must go back to the beginning, reassemble the facts one by one, and throw out all those pieces of the jigsaw which had seemingly fitted so conveniently into place. The future becomes clouded with an uncomfortable doubt: if what appeared true yesterday turns out to be false today, will those certainties, those fragmentary truths that have been so hardly won from the dark night, prove equally false tomorrow?

IMAGINATION, MOTHER OF ERRORS

Oral information about the past is generally not to be trusted in Rome. The temptation to invent a dramatic titbit for the delectation of tourists often proves too much for some guides, and even, it must be admitted, for a few archaeologists. Ever since Winckelmann, Ficorini, and Braci set the example it has been customary for them to act as *ciceroni*, and in this role they have occasionally been guilty of embroidering the past.

On the Palatine there is a subterranean passage, the Crypto-Porticus, dimly lit at infrequent intervals from above. Its eerie gloom plays tricks with the imagination, indeed it induced in the eminent archaeologist, R. Lanciani, the following flight of fancy:

On January 24th A.D. 41, a scene of horror took place in the dark corridor: the murder of the Emperor Caligula. Whoever will endeavour to picture in his mind all the revolting details of that death as described by Flavius Josephus, will hear echoing again in the long, vaulted crypt the last cries of the frantic young prince, fallen on his knees, and trying to avert with his feeble hands the last implacable blows of his assassins.[2]

This picture of a pathetic young stripling unable to defend himself against his butchers is rather surprising to those who recall Suetonius's portrait of Caligula: 'of more than common height, bladder-pale, gross, his face naturally hideous made even more so by the grimaces he practised before the glass to inspire awe and terror in the breasts of all'. Even more surprising, however, is the fact that the 'dark corridor' did not even exist at the time of Caligula's murder! It was built some twenty years later to connect Nero's Domus Transitoria with the Palace of Tiberius on the Esquiline.

There is a moral here for archaeologists who are wrestling with the problems posed by the resurrection of Rome: they must resist the temptation to dramatize even the most insignificant ruin in order to lend it importance, and while we are on this subject, they must also refrain from advancing flimsy hypotheses, from over-hasty, and therefore incorrect, identifications. These are the pitfalls that lie in their path, pitfalls they must take care to avoid.

Even after its destruction, Ancient Rome lived on, secretly and compulsively in the minds of men. The image of the Queen of Cities, sometimes grossly, sometimes more subtly distorted, has never been pinned down, but has changed from age to age. As the ruins that haunt her shades, as the countless faces she has been lent through the centuries testify, Rome is the creatrix of myths. Rome, the many-faced—surely one of the most fascinating, the most amazing of all the faces she has worn is that which after seventy-five years of research is slowly being revealed to us.

CHAPTER THREE

Rome and the Archaeologists: Archaic Rome

ANCIENT ROME WAS NEVER to be re-created. The dream so dear to the humanists (a dream that has haunted many minds) of re-discovering the integral remains of the sacred city, of restoring its monuments and bringing to life its streets, squares and temples, was only a chimera. The glory and the grandeur can never be re-created; apart from all the irreparable destruction, too much of the Rome that was lies buried, perhaps for ever, beneath the modern city.

THE AGE OF SCIENTIFIC RESEARCH

Shortly after the unification of Italy in 1870, Rome was replanned, and we cannot blame the architects for being more concerned with creating a capital worthy of their renascent country than with the preservation at all costs of the ruins of the past. Thanks to rescue digs, a few vestiges were saved, a little more knowledge was gained. Sketches were made of a number of sites, but hardly any of these was published; some still await publication, the rest have been lost. Often archaeologists would arrive on a site only to find that gangs of labourers had forestalled them; the terrain had to be written off as a total loss.

Nothing could be saved in the great peripheral zones, the Esquiline, the Suburra, the Campus Martius; but the heart of Ancient Rome: the Forum, the Palatine, the area between the Capitol and the foot of the Quirinal, the Colosseum, the first stretch of the Appian Way, was scheduled as an archaeological preserve. Thus a reasonable compromise between the needs of the expanding city and the claims of archaeology was arrived at, and due respect paid to the relics of the past. What a pity it is, though, that the Capitol was excluded. The palaces, the Ara Coeli and other ancient churches were left standing, but the colossal monument to King Victor Emmanuel II swallowed up a vast area of the ancient Citadel and made excavations on this paritcular part of the Capitol impossible. This is regrettable, for they would undoubtedly have yielded the most precious results.

With the unification of Italy the temporal power passed from the Church to the State, which appointed Pietro Rosa as Director of Antiquities. Rosa, who had held a similar appointment under Napoleon III and whose work had been crowned with a large measure of success, selected as his collaborators Pellegrini, Brizio, and most fortunate choice of all, Rodolfo Lanciani. Shortly after he had begun to work with Rosa, Lanciani became secretary of the Municipal Archaeological Commission; for the next fifty years, he took part in all the researches carried out in almost every quarter of Rome.

The first, somewhat scanty, reports of the excavations in Rome appeared fairly regularly in the *Bolletino delle Archaeologica Municipale* and also in *Notizie degli Scavi di Antiquita communicate alla Reale Accademia di Lincei*, whose pages were devoted to accounts of all the explorations in Italy. (The *Notizie degli Scavi* had replaced the *Instituto di Corrispondenza Archaeologica*, of which more will be found in a later chapter.) The *Bolletino* and *Notizie degli Scavi* were published without a break for seventy-five years. Both these publications, which still bring out special issues, have been of inestimable service to the study of Ancient Rome.

Each of the various archaeological bodies in Rome, the English, French, Swedish and Rumanian Schools, the German Institute, the American Academy, made its own individual contribution. Regular reunions were held for members of all these institutions who discussed the latest discoveries, expressed their views on this hypothesis and that, compared notes and checked classifications. For some time, these meetings were discontinued, but they have now been resumed, and very useful they are, for in a sense they form a kind of university that is all the more alive because it dispenses with rules and regulations.

New theories are continually being advanced, and much hard, plodding work has to be done by those archaeologists who confine their activities to re-examining and rearranging the data that has been acquired. Periodically, it is essential to draw up classifications, inventories, and provisional syntheses which, as all are aware, only contain part of the truth and leave much to chance, since they depend on outside circumstances for confirmation and completion; excavations may never bring the missing factors to light, but very occasionally they emerge from a totally unexpected source. Hence it follows that the picture of a vanished Rome that this book endeavours to portray—or rather as much of the picture

(43)

that fifty years of uninterrupted research have allowed us to glimpse—is unavoidably incomplete, unavoidably open to doubt. All that can be said is that it will be a little nearer to the truth than others painted in the past. Admittedly there are still parts of the city that are totally unknown, but even so, the unfinished canvas has its value, for it reflects the progress that has been made, and will, it is hoped, lead to a better understanding of that pheno-menon in human, as well as in historical terms: the grandeur and greatness of Ancient Rome.

ROYAL ROME: THE ILLUSIONS

For many years no doubts arose as to the accuracy of the accounts by classic writers of the origins and foundation of the Urbs. Re-search into the early history of Rome was confined to the attempt to identify among the ruins vestiges of the age of kings. Poggio Bracciolini, as he meditated on the city's degradation, doubted whether he could discern more than a few monuments of the Republican era, let alone any that went back to Royal Rome.[1] Poggio's doubt did not go far enough, for in his day, the only buildings which could be seen from the Capitol were those which had been erected during the Empire.

Other visitors to Rome were far less circumspect than Poggio. The Reverend Edward Burton, who spent a year in the city (1818–19) unhesitatingly ascribed the Mamertine Prison, the Servian Wall (or rather, such remains of the wall as were then visible) and the Cloaca Maxima (the great drain running through the Forum Romanum and debouching into the Tiber in the Forum Boarium) to Royal Rome.[2] The reverend gentleman's conviction was shared by many; indeed, it had been expressed by Montesquieu in his *Considérations sur les Causes de la Grandeur de la Décadence des Romains*. A prison, a wall, a sewer—what a pitiable summing up of the genius of an emergent people, what a tawdry crown to award them. We can see how low the Romans ranked in the eyes of the men of the day in comparison with the Greeks—all that they were given credit for was a sewer! They were denigrated to such an extent, in fact, that when it is pointed out with perfect truth that Royal Rome never possessed the marvellous sewage system with which it has been credited, it is tantamount to rehabilitating the Romans!

We know today that even this simplified picture of Royal

Rome was incorrect. Had Montesquieu, the Reverend Edward Burton and the rest been familiar with Plautus, they would have been acquainted with the true history of the Cloaca Maxima. Originally it was a stream running through the Forum Romanum, a stream that remained in its natural state right up to the third century B.C. Almost certainly it had to be completely or partially covered in during the year 179 B.C., when work on the Basilica Aemilia began. The actual construction of the Cloaca Maxima, however, only dates back to 33 B.C., when Agrippa was aedile. It was not a sewer in the modern sense of the word, that is to say it was not an artificial underground conduit that discharged the filth of the city into the Tiber, but a drainage canal that carried off the water from the low-lying quarters of Rome. The main branch which had been channelled north of the Forum drained the Argiletum (there had once been a claypit in the vicinity, hence its name), carrying away the water that flowed from the Quirinal and the Viminal; a secondary branch close to the Temple of Saturn at the mouth of the small valley between the Capitolium and the Citadel, drained the Capitol. It was not until the quarters through which it ran became densely populated that the Cloaca Maxima was used as a sewer. Neither the canalized stream that flowed through the Circus Maximus and drained the valley between the Palatine and Aventine, nor the similarly canalized rivulet that drained the Palus Caprae, the Marsh of the Goat, were used for this purpose, indeed, during the Augustan era, the latter was a favourite swimming-place for the young men of the day. It might have been supposed that the early Romans would have preoccupied themselves with problems of hygiene for their rapidly expanding city, but no. Not until very much later when the drainage system and cesspools proved totally inadequate was any concern shown for these vital matters.

The Moderns who attributed the Cloaca Maxima to Royal Rome, relying on the somewhat vague evidence of Livy which they did not attempt to confirm, made the singular mistake of crediting the Roman masons of the seventh century B.C. with quite incredible skill. As can be seen in the Forum Boarium, the vault of the Cloaca Maxima consists of three concentric arches put together without mortar. Such an advanced technique presupposes a long period of evolution—it could not possibly have made its appearance in such a perfected form out of the blue. Moreover, the arches of sixth- and fifth-century Etruscan tombs (some archaeologists date these tombs considerably later) were rudimentary.³ This is an important point, for, thanks to the work of nineteenth-century archaeologists, it is now generally accepted that the Etruscans were the master-builders and that it was from these people that the Romans learnt the art of construction.

The factual history of Rome and its earliest monuments only goes back to the fourth century B.C.; prior to this date, all certainty ceases, and it was once the common opinion that attempts to probe deeper into the past could only be made via the dangerous road of conjecture. In the middle of the nineteenth century, to the dogmatic assertions of those historians who relied solely on literary evidence and had little or no knowledge of archaeological data, were added those of the hypercritics. It seemed to have been demonstrated conclusively that prior to the fourth century B.C. nothing could possibly be established. The accounts by Livy, Dionysos of Halicarnassus and Plutarch of events that, according to them, had taken place before this date could be written off; they were either repeats of incidents that had occurred during a later era or entirely mythical.

ROYAL ROME: THE FACTS

During the last twenty-five years of the nineteenth century, when the controversy was at its height, archaeology whose results up to then had seemed to be negative, began to make a positive contribution. Since the study of texts had proved so misleading, archaeology had become the one hope of the traditionalists who had refused to budge an inch: surely if the ruins of the past could be brought to light, they would help to dispel all this doubt. Thus spurred on and encouraged, archaeologists immediately set forth on the dangerous road and attacked head-on the most difficult problem of all: the problem of the origins of Rome.

What they first uncovered, however, was not archaic Rome. Lanciani tells us that 'no sooner had a tiled paving, a brick or marble floor been laid bare, no matter whether these were Imperial, Byzantine or Medieval, than the authorities immediately ordered the digging to stop.'⁴ In these conditions, as permission to carry the excavation to deeper levels was refused, it was extremely difficult to find the answers to the questions of the historians. In the Forum Romanum the paving that had been disengaged went back to the fourth century B.C.; almost the whole of the Palatine was covered by the foundations of the imperial palaces. Thus restricted, where could archaeologists look for traces of Romulus and his successors? Fortunately, the difficulties did not damp their enthusiasm. There were spaces between the now sacrosanct paving of the Forum where they were free to excavate to deeper levels. Following the example set by the discoverers of Mycenae (this was the period when the revelation of the Mycenean civilization was forcing Hellenists to discard all their previous theories), Roman archaeologists carried out scientific stratigraphical excavations in these zones in the Forum, and before long their patience was rewarded.

THE DISCOVERIES IN LATIUM

At the beginning of the nineteenth century, chance had led to a discovery in Latium of the utmost importance in its prehistory, and but for which the results of the excavations in the Forum would, as we shall see, have lost much of their significance and value. This stroke of good fortune occurred in the spring of 1817 on the shores of Lake Alba in the heart of Latium. Peasants cutting trenches to plant a vineyard in the pastureland of Pascolare di Castello cut through a thick layer of lava and uncovered a necropolis. There came to light, miraculously preserved, terracotta vases, *dolia*, in each of which was a cinerary urn. The urns were shaped like huts and had remained inviolate; they contained the ashes of the dead and the funerary furnishings: *fibulae* and other ornaments of bronze and amber. Here was the revelation of the earliest Latial civilization.

The full importance of the discovery was not immediately realized. For years a controversy raged backwards and forwards over the mysterious objects, and it was not until 1867 that an official expedition was dispatched to the site. The team, which included such eminent archaeologists as Ponzi, Di Rossi, and Pigorini, soon uncovered another section of the necropolis. It was clear that the *dolia* and sherds of pottery were not migratory—i.e. they had not been washed to this spot by the rains—but that this was a genuine deposit which opened up undreamt of perspectives on the prehistory of Latium. The harvest of pottery was far more abundant than that of 1817. From the fragments, it was possible to ascribe an approximate date to the necropolis: between the

close of the ninth and the close of the eighth century B.C.[5] Archaeologists were now in possession of data that would enable them to
interpret correctly the discoveries that were to be made a few
years later in Roman soil.

THE NECROPOLIS OF THE SACRED WAY

In April 1902 G. Boni, Director of Antiquities of the Forum and
the Palatine, initiated a stratigraphical excavation south-west of the
Temple of Antoninus and Faustina in the narrow strip verging on
the Sacred Way. Some seventeen feet below the paving of the
latter, he had the good luck to discover a necropolis comparable
in every respect with the necropolis of Latium. In the deepest
layers were cremation graves; the cinerary urns in the earthenware
dolia were hut-shaped like those found in Latium. (These hut-
shaped urns were to serve in future as the classic type of cinerary
vase.) In the layers immediately above were other graves, mainly
inhumation *fossae* in which were tufa sarcophagi, coffins of
hollowed-out oak trunks, or the skeletons of bodies that had been
laid in the ground with no protective covering. In every case, the
funerary furnishings were intact, and from the sherds, it was possible to establish the approximate dates of the graves.

After some hesitation, it is now generally accepted that the
earliest graves go back to the eighth century B.C. (They may be
slightly later than the earliest graves in the Latium necropolis,
but this is difficult to prove.) The later graves only go back to the
close of the seventh century B.C.

As soon as the first graves were identified, the traditionalists
uttered a shout of triumph. Here at last was proof that the site of
the future city had been inhabited at a very early date—round
about the date, in fact, when, according to Livy, the Urbs was
founded. The occupants of the graves could be none other than
the Companions of Romulus, those hardy adventurers who quitted
their native Latium and installed themselves on the Palatine. The
classic annalists were vindicated: Livy was right, the hypercritics
were wrong!

Interesting though they were, however, Boni's researches by
no means justified such bold conclusions. His identifications of
the various strata left considerable room for doubt, and in addition, the poverty of some of the material, the continuous distur-
bance of the soil of the different levels from the days of Antiquity

ROME   The Arch of Titus in the Roman Forum

ROME   Interior of the Curia in the Roman Forum

should have been quite enough to temper the enthusiasm. Furthermore, Boni's full report of the excavations was never published as promised, and the results could only be evaluated by studying all his material in the Forum Museum. Such a study undertaken of recent years by the Swedish archaeologist, Einar Gjerstad[6] has confirmed the fact that there were two great periods of burial and has allowed a chronology of outstanding importance to be established.

From the time of Boni it was accepted that the necropolis of the Sacred Way was the cemetery of Palatine Rome, the Urbs of Romulus. In the days of Antiquity, in fact, the burial of the dead within the precincts of the living was strictly prohibited. Was it not natural, then, to assume that the Romans of the Palatine had established their necropolis in the uninhabited valley that was later to become the Forum? Was it not equally logical to conclude that throughout the eighth century, this necropolis had been used exclusively by the Romans and that, at the beginning of the seventh century, a people who practised inhumation had settled in the vicinity? Did there not appear to be evidence of this in the accounts by classic annalists of the Rape of the Sabine Women? Hungry for wives, the Companions of Romulus swooped down on the Sabines and carried off the eligible girls; their menfolk, vowing vengeance, set out to rescue them, but the brides, evidently delighted with their new-found husbands, flung themselves between their menfolk and imposed peace. Later on the two peoples had united; Latins and Sabines reared their families on Roman soil and rubbed shoulders in the Senate. Was it not possible, then, that the juxtaposition of cremation and inhumation graves in the Sacred Way necropolis was accounted for by the juxtaposition of these peoples? Was it not possible that the Sabines who inhumated their dead had, like the Latins, made use of the necropolis? When the expanding city invaded the valley of the Forum, the Sacred Way necropolis had been abandoned; it was undoubtedly covered in and transformed into a building site when the various villages on the hills merged together and the 'Greater' Rome was born.[7]

Apart from a few minor variations, these were the conclusions to which Boni's discovery of the Sacred Way necropolis led. Unfortunately they had been drawn mainly from probabilities and traditions, and the only certainty was represented by some twelve

graves in a few metres of ground. It was assumed far too readily
that what Boni had laid bare was only a segment of a vast necropolis that had extended over the whole valley, and although there
was no more than a single fact to go on, this produced the rashest
generalizations.

Five years after the discovery of the Sacred Way necropolis a
stroke of good fortune revealed the existence of other graves on
the Quirinal on the site where the Ministry of Agriculture now
stands. These were inhumation *fossae* and similar in every respect
to those of the Sacred Way; they contained the same ceramics, the
same funerary furnishings, the same sarcophagi.

We can imagine the importance attached to this new find. 'We
were right!' cried the traditionalists. 'There *was* a Sabine village on
the Quirinal.' Tempting though this deduction was, however,
it soon became less feasible than had at first been thought. Despite
all expectations, no necropolis came to light on the Quirinal, and,
as the anti-traditionalists asked, were three graves enough to
prove that a Sabine village had existed on the hill? Was it not
much more probable, they went on, that a few inhabitants of
Royal Rome had been buried in these graves, bearing in mind that
at this era, the *pomaerium*, the spiritual limit of the city, was distinct from the fortified boundary? After all, the Quirinal was as
close to the Palatine as the Forum, and there was no reason why
the people of Rome should not have used both burial places. The
hypercritics then put the question that made the very postulate of
Boni and the archaeologists of his day seem doubtful: was it
absolutely certain that the incinerators were not of the same race
as the inhumators? In other words, did the necropolis of the
Sacred Way really prove that two distinct races had united to form
the Roman people?

Were there two peoples? The artifacts found in the cremation
graves and the inhumation *fossae* were almost identical; if there
were two peoples, their cultures must have been very closely
related. The slight variations can easily be explained by the fact
that some objects are earlier than others, but the same technique is
apparent in all of them, and there is not the faintest evidence of
a cultural revolution.

It would be entirely wrong to suppose that the first inhabitants
of Rome were marooned on the Palatine. On the contrary, there is
every reason to believe that they were in contact with the neigh-

bouring peoples. Alba is by no means the only region where traces of culture similar to that of the Sacred Way necropolis have been been found. According to tradition, Numa was the first king to insist that his body should not be cremated, but though Numa is considered as a Sabine, it is generally believed that his insistence on burial denoted that he was a disciple of Pythagoras. The burial of the dead, then, was not linked to race, but was bound up with a religious faith. It need hardly be said that the first inhumators knew nothing of Pythagoras, who was born several centuries after their time, but conceivably, the rites and beliefs of other peoples of Central Italy were introduced amongst these seventh-century Romans who finally adopted them. Assuming that this were true, the substitution of one form of burial for another would be the first instance of the infiltration into Rome of foreign religious practices—a phenomenon that was to be repeated again and again until the triumph of Christianity.

Considered by itself, all that could be learnt from the necropolis of the Sacred Way was that from the seventh century B.C. a community was established on the site of the Urbs. Its culture was similar to that of Latium, traces of which have been found throughout the region. The members of this community, originally incinerators of the dead, gradually adopted the practice of inhumation, and this rite had become predominant shortly before the Necropolis was abandoned. Towards the close of the seventh century B.C. it was covered in, and from then on, the domain of the dead became that of the living. The inhumation graves on the Quirinal proved that in the course of the seventh century part of the hill had been occupied by this same people. So much was certain, but at this stage, archaeologists were forced to stop; there was as yet no data that would enable them to go any farther.

THE PALATINE VILLAGE

The opening years of the twentieth century proved extraordinarily fruitful for the history of archaic Rome. In the same year that the graves on the Quirinal had come to light Vaglieri began a series of systematic excavations on the Palatine, which before long yielded results of maximum importance.

From time immemorial the Palatine has been the sacred hill *par excellence*. It was on the Palatine that, according to tradition, Romulus settled his pastoral community, established the first village and founded the Urbs; right up to the close of Antiquity, the Romans pointed out the remains of Romulus's hut on the Cermalus, the western summit of the Palatine overlooking the Tiber. It was on the Cermalus that Vaglieri had elected to dig; the terrain was favourable, for out of reverence for the founder of their city the emperors had not allowed their palaces to encroach on this sacred spot. Right at the outset, Vaglieri uncovered several deposits of sherds similar to those that had been found in the Sacred Way necropolis. He assumed, therefore, that there had been a necropolis on the Palatine, that this necropolis had been violated by a conquering people, possibly the Etruscans—archaeologists are so obsessed by the Etruscans that they come perilously close to seeing them where they never were!—and that the bones from the desecrated graves had been assembled into a vast ossuary.

Vaglieri's hypothesis immediately gave rise to a passionate polemic. It seemed inadmissible that the traditional site of Rome could ever have been occupied by a necropolis. Pigorini, Vaglieri's chief opponent, maintained that the excavations on the Cermalus had disclosed, not a burial place, but a primitive habitat —a domain of the living, and laughed to scorn the blasphemous suggestion that the Etruscans had at one time been overlords of the Sacred Hill. The controversy raged backwards and forwards, and grew acrimonious to a degree, so acrimonious indeed that the excavations were temporarily suspended, leaving the problem unsolved.

A few years later, research on the Palatine was resumed under the direction of Boni, the fortunate discoverer of the Sacred Way necropolis. Boni, thinking it wiser to avoid the Cermalus, where Vaglieri's explorations had led to such high feelings, began excavating on the summit of the opposite slope, the Palatium, where the ruins of the Palace of Domitian can now be seen. Within a short time, he laid bare what were unmistakably the foundations of primitive huts, the date of which he established by the sherds found on the site. Here was a habitat of the First Latial Iron Age, contemporary with the cremation graves of the Sacred Way. Certain artifacts found on both sites were identical, but more significant still, the parallelism also held good in time: the level immediately above the lowest level was contemporary with that of the inhumation graves of the Forum, a fact that demolished the theory that there had been a Sabine village on the Quirinal, and from one level to another the continuity was total. Beyond any doubt, this habitat had slowly evolved and had perpetuated itself from the First to the Second Iron Age. All those theories of a second colonization or of a second wave of immigrants could henceforth be discounted.

Thanks to Boni's excavations and to the numerous elements of comparison furnished by the explorations carried out in every part of Italy from the beginning of the century, S. M. Puglisi was able to resume Vaglieri's researches and carry them considerably further. The results he obtained were proof that Pigorini had been right and Vaglieri wrong; not a single grave came to light on the Cermalus, but many hut foundations were uncovered, the remains of a large habitat contemporary with that on the Palatium. From now on it was impossible to doubt that, from the First Iron Age, the entire Palatine had been occupied by a community whose culture was identical with that of Latium. It was certain that in the seventh century B.C. there had been a Latin Colony on the Palatine which preserved the cultures and skills of Latium until the close of the century, when, due possibly to trade currents from the Greek colonies of southern Italy or to the eastern influences introduced by the Phoenicians, a cultural evolution took place in Latium which led to the dawn of the Second Iron Age. This period came to an end when the necropolis of the Sacred Way was abandoned, and was followed by a third in which the Etruscan influence with its decorative Ionic style was plainly discernible. The first traces of the Etruscans, however, only appeared towards the middle of the sixth century B.C.; long before then, the Latin colonists had left their hill and the Urbs had entered its initial phase.

All that we know about the first inhabitants of the Palatine is that they were in no way different from the other peoples scattered in the many villages of Latium. They may have come from Alba Longa, they may have come from elsewhere—we have no means of telling. But thanks to Puglisi, we can now form some idea of how they lived. Prior to his discoveries, the hut urns had served as models for full-scale reconstructions of the actual huts, but it was difficult to arrive at a true picture from these miniature, stylized clay cabins. The size and dimensions of the real huts, the manner in which they had been grouped together to form a village had remained a mystery until the habitat on the Cermalus was laid bare.

What archaeologists have enabled us to see of the simple, rustic life of the Palatine village might have come straight from the pages of those Roman historians and poets who loved to dwell on the origins of their city. There stood Evander's hut, just as Virgil describes it in Book VIII of the *Aeneid*; there, the cabin of the shepherd Faustulus who found the miraculous twins the Tiber had refused to drown and brought them up as his own sons. There, on the Cermalus, was Romulus's hut, the remains of which could still be seen at the close of Antiquity. The picture of the pastoral community is so faithfully painted by the classic writers that it cannot be the product of sheer fancy; their imaginations must have been stimulated by the sight of vestigial ruins on the Sacred Hill, sustained by the oral tradition handed down from generation to generation (added to, distorted, no doubt, but essentially the same) of the humble beginnings of the city that was destined to become imperial. The discoveries on the Palatine were the justification not so much of the ancient historians but oddly enough of the poets who, less concerned with dates and reigns, have left us so true an image of the remote past.

THE FORMATION OF ROME

Unfortunately, we possess very little precise information on the links which existed between the Palatine and the valley below. As has been said, the first hypotheses were based on the traditional accounts of the origins of Rome, hence it had been taken for granted that the Sacred Way necropolis was the necropolis of the Palatine. But in 1954, doubts arose with the discovery of a grave, contemporary with the earliest of the Sacred Way, in the depression between the Cermalus and the Palatine, and so exterior to both groups of huts. This encouraged the belief that instead of a single village within a common *pomaerium*, there were, in fact, two villages, a conclusion that if correct ended the tradition of a single Palatine Rome. But was such a revolutionary theory justified by the presence of a single grave? Historical laws, unlike those governing natural phenomena, are not absolute, and to draw rigid deductions from them would be unreasonable. Nevertheless, the original hypotheses were badly shaken, and once more uncertainty prevailed.

The idea that there had actually been two villages on the Palatine was greatly strengthened by data that made it seem doubtful

to a degree that the inhabitants of the hill had been the sole occupants of the future site of Rome. Boni himself identified hut
foundations in the Sacred Way necropolis. These huts were identical with the Palatine cabins: the same oval shape, the same framework of wooden posts, the same walls of dried clay and thatch.
Hut foundations are still coming to light in the Forum. Quite
recently, during excavations in the Central zone, the traces of a
similar habitat were uncovered close to the equestrian statue of
Domitian.[8] Other hut foundations were found further to the
south of the Forum in the vicinity of the Temple of Vesta and the
Arch of Augustus. The village near the statue of Domitian seemed
to have been established on virgin soil, while the second had been
built over a covered-in necropolis probably contemporary with
the necropolis of the Sacred Way.

There is every reason to believe that several villages co-existed
at approximately the same time on the future site of Rome. The
Palatine villages may be slightly earlier, but this may be merely an
impression due to the limitations of the later excavations. Certainly they cannot be more than a couple of hundred years earlier,
but it is difficult to arrive at a more exact figure within so narrow a
margin after the lapse of so many centuries when one is dealing
with a civilization that evolved so slowly. What we do know for
certain is that the Sacred Way necropolis, whether it was used
exclusively by the Palatine community or whether it was subsequently used by the inhabitants of the villages that sprang up in
the vicinity, was abandoned and covered in at the close of the
seventh century B.C.; we also know that it was then transformed
into a building-site and occupied by huts which spread out towards the Forum. This stage of development was also a turning-
point; in the level immediately above that of the hut foundations,
archaeologists found traces of stone houses. The city had begun
to take the place of the village.

Here were signs of a considerable departure from the primitive
cabins. We should like to know more about these ancient stone
houses, but unfortunately almost every vestige of them has been
obliterated. We can tell, however, that the transformation pro-
gressed by various stages. At first, the huts were consolidated
with a foundation of stone, but remained otherwise unchanged. A
little later, a further improvement was introduced; mud-bricks,
braced by oak uprights, replaced the clay and thatch of the primitive

walls. Above all, however, it was the plan which changed; rectangular houses whose rooms probably opened on to an inner courtyard took the place of the round and oval huts. At a later date, while the rectangular plan was retained, blocks of tufa were used instead of the mud-bricks, the roofs were tiled, and the interior walls coated with coloured stucco. A long period elapsed, however, before this stage of technical development was reached; the rectangular plan did not make its appearance until the middle of the sixth century B.C., and such refinements as tufa blocks and tiles followed roughly a century later. Towards the middle of the fifth century B.C., it seems that the site ceased to be occupied by private dwellings.

Let us consider the rhythm of the transformation. Only a generation (from the beginning to the middle of the sixth century B.C.) separates the latest of the archaic huts from the huts consolidated with stone. Then, all at once, the rectangular stone house makes its appearance. When we recall that the age of archaic huts lasted for roughly one hundred and fifty years, it becomes clear that the sudden acceleration of this evolution must have been due to some outside influence. Most likely it was that of the Etruscans, traces of whose culture had begun to appear in the corresponding archaeological level on the Palatine.

Towards the middle of the sixth century the Forum was given its first pebble pavement, the habitats were abandoned, and it became a meeting-place. From such evidence as we possess, it would seem that this took place at the time when the first rectangular houses made their appearance and the archaic huts vanished. Once the Forum had been transformed, Rome evolved rapidly, not only in the sphere of architecture but in that of its public life. The Forum was the civic centre, the point of assembly for the inhabitants of the various villages.

Such, then, are the facts established by the excavations on the Palatine and in the Forum. Archaeologists have felt justified in drawing certain provisional conclusions from the data so far available; it may be that in the future, excavations carried out elsewhere will yield results that will cause them to modify the opinions they hold at present.

THE COMITIUM AND ITS MYSTERY

On 15 June, 1899, three years before the discovery of the Sacred Way necropolis, the point of departure for all the research outlined above, a unique group of monuments, amongst them a stele whose inscription proved to be the earliest known in the Latin language, came to light in the north-west section of the Forum. The site was immediately identified as that of the Comitium—the place of coming together, the political centre of the early Republic.[9]

Up to 1899, a medieval road that wound up to the Arch of Septimius Severus separated the Comitium from the Forum. Giacomo Boni, then Director of Archaeological Research for the Forum, decided at the beginning of the year to clear away the vestigial ruins still standing in this area and excavate to the level of the ancient paving. What he expected to find at the depth of a few feet was paving of a kind he had uncovered in previous digs; instead there appeared a black marble paving, thirteen feet long by ten feet wide, surrounded by a white marble balustrade. The dig was immediately suspended, and a few months later a stratigraphical excavation was carried out. This disclosed, beneath the black marble paving, a complex ensemble: a tomb embedded between two moulded pedestals, a transversal platform that seemed to be an altar, and, a short distance away, a conical stele, the top of which was broken off, and on whose faces was an inscription.

The excitement caused by the discovery of the stele can well be imagined. What secrets of the past might its archaic inscription reveal? Alas, the epigraphers who first attempted to decipher it soon had to own themselves beaten.

This in-and-out writing, *boustrophedon,* had appeared in very early Greek inscriptions, but it had never before been seen in those that were in Latin or Etruscan. Now here it was on this stele.

It soon became plain that the ensemble did not go back in its entirety to the same date. The base on which the stele had originally stood must have been cut away to make room for the small sanctuary, since both were of grotta oscura—tufa from the grotta oscura quarries, on the territory of the ancient city of Veii. To make the problem still more complicated, part of a column found by the stele and close to a kind of square-shaped well, was of Monteverde from the quarry of that name also on the right bank of the Tiber, but nearer to Rome.

Even today this complex ensemble remains very difficult to interpret. At the time of its discovery, archaeologists as yet

unaware of the existence of a necropolis beneath the Sacred Way
sought for the key to the enigma in the ancient texts. Festus and
the other writers who mention the *lapis niger* agree that it marked
a burial site, but while, according to some, the tomb was that of
Romulus (a cenotaph, rather, since, after his death, Romulus was
borne off by Jupiter's eagle to dwell eternally with the gods),
others stated that it was that of his foster-father, Faustulus, while
still others claimed that it was that of Hostus, grandfather of King
Tullus Hostilius—all of which does not get us much farther. There
is literary evidence of a tomb of Romulus flanked by two lions
(some texts mention only one lion) in front of the Rostra, the
platform from which political speakers harangued the people, and
which bordered, in fact, on the Comitium. The sanctuary had
clearly contained two statues—probably, the lions in question—
and, on the testimony of the texts, it was plain that there had
existed in the days of Antiquity a tomb linked by popular imagination with the history, or, rather the legend of Romulus. At a
considerably later date, the *lapis niger* had been laid to mark the
spot, and the white marble balustrade erected to ensure that the
feet of passers-by would not profane this sacred ground.

There remained the stele. Would its inscription provide the
clue to the mystery? Unfortunately, the beginning of one line and
the end of the next were alternately missing, and these mutilations,
coupled with the fact that the language was extremely archaic,
made it quite impossible for epigraphers to arrive at an interpretation that could be accepted without reservation. The large
number of interpretations advanced from 1900 onwards are all
open to doubt. The extent of the lacunae cannot be calculated;
furthermore, the words on the inscription are run together, and
have to be broken into groups, necessarily a somewhat arbitrary
process. Finally, there is nothing to prove that the inscription
consists of a single text, indeed, some scholars are of the opinion
that several texts have been inserted between a preface and a
conclusion. Because of the striking variation between the recognizable words and their classic Latin equivalents, the first epigraphers unhesitatingly dated the inscription as early as the
seventh century B.C.[10] Modern epigraphers are more cautious, and
assign it because of its palaeographic characteristics to the middle
of the fifth century B.C. But, as archaeologists have pointed out,
the grotta oscura quarries were only accessible to the Romans

after the fall of Veii at the beginning of the fourth century B.C., and while it is conceivable that a block large enough for the stele might have been imported, it is extremely unlikely that the amount needed for the stele would or could have been brought from what was then enemy territory. The stele may be a copy of an earlier one made in a more friable stone that had rapidly deteriorated. The theory that it is a copy cannot be discounted; the base of the stele is on the same level as the second pavement laid over the Comitium after a major fire, and, as we know, after the conflagration lit by the Gauls in 390 B.C., the Romans restored and rebuilt sacred monuments as closely as possible to their original state. However, this is no more than conjecture formulated to adjust the balance between the respective exigencies of epigraphy and archaeology.

No matter what its actual date may be, we would indeed be happy if we could read the inscription on the stele, but we must resign ourselves to the fact that a complete and satisfactory interpretation is beyond our reach. Several words are comprehensible: RECEI (king); KALATO (*Kalator*, a herald or servant of an augur); IOUXMENTA (in early Latin *iumenta*, beast of burden); SAKROS ESED (Latin: *Sacer erit*, the curse pronounced on any person guilty of profaning the sacred laws, and tantamount to a death sentence.) These words tell us that the inscription refers to some ritual, but this is all we know. The use of the word RECEI—*rex*—does not imply that the stele dates back to Royal Rome. During the Republic, there was a *rex sacrificulus*—sometimes simply called *rex*—who enacted the religious rites that had formerly devolved on the king. It is far more likely that it is to the *rex sacrificulus* that the inscription refers.

Given the few certainties, commentators have allowed their imagination full scope. The latest of the many brilliant hypotheses is that of G. Dumeznil who interprets the inscription as an augural prescription. The key-word is IOUXMENTA. We know that if a beast of burden excreted whilst yoked, it was considered an ill omen, hence, when a religious ceremony was due to take place, the *kalators* made sure that all animals were unyoked. It is quite possible that this precautionary measure is the text of the stele of the Comitium, that most sacred of spots where, before an assembly was held, the augurs were consulted; if the omens were unpropitious, it was suspended forthwith. According to Dumeznil, the word HAUELOD which appears in the inscription is the term for excreta—in classic Latin, *aluus*.

The simplicity, the probability of Dumeznil's interpretation are in its favour, but if it is correct, it is disappointing, for it tells us nothing that we did not already know. Almost invariably, interpretations of mutilated inscriptions leave us exactly where we were before; this is only to be expected, since epigraphers can only fill in the lacunae by drawing on sources with which they are familiar.

The high hopes raised by the discoveries of 1899 were destined to remain unfulfilled. Unlike Royal Rome, the Comitium has kept its secret. Its soil has been so overturned, the vestiges of its ruins so inextricably mixed up that even the most meticulous researches have only led to doubtful, sometimes contradictory, results. The Comitium, the 'Palimpsest of History', as Lugli calls it, still remains, in spite of all the explorations, one of the most mysterious sites of Rome.

THE OLDEST TEMPLES OF ROME: THE CITY OF THE FORUM

After the stratigraphical excavations in the eastern section of the Forum had laid bare the primitive villages, it became apparent that the valley had for a long period of time consisted of two distinct and very different divisions, the first contemporary with the Palatine villages and closely linked with them, the second oriented towards the Capitol. If there existed, as was believed, a fundamental duality in the city, it was precisely in the Forum that its topographic aspect might be brought to light.

It had already been noted that the ancient monuments of the Palatine zone of the Forum were very different in character from those of the Comitium. Shortly after 1870, when the area of the Forum at the foot of the Palatine was being cleared, the remains of the two oldest temples of Rome came to light: the Temple of Vesta and the Regia. The Temple of Vesta is circular and perpetuates the shape of the primitive huts; undoubtedly it was the immediate successor to a centre of the cult of the Second Latial Iron Age. The earlier of two wells discovered in its vicinity contained sherds and votive objects that date back to the seventh century B.C., while the later yielded a variety of artifacts whose date oscillates between the third and second centuries. These finds proved conclusively that far from being new to the region, the cult of Vesta was contemporary with the first huts that sprang up in this zone.

The second temple, the Regia, was built, according to tradition, as a palace for King Numa Pompilius. The Regia, as we can see today, consists of two distinct parts: a trapezoidal enclosure embraces what must have been the main hall, with its vestibule and the porch formed by the projection of the walls. The Regia instantly calls to mind the *megaron* of Mycenaean palaces; while it is utterly unlike the archaic huts, it has an affinity with the rectangular stone houses that replaced them when the Sacred Way necropolis was abandoned. The foundation of cappellacio gives us an idea of its date, and we can safely say that this is as far back in the history of Rome as we can go.

Unlike the Temple of Vesta, whose character was entirely devotional, the Regia was a residence as well as a sanctuary. Yet it was in the Regia that the *ancilia*, the sacred shields, one of which was said to have fallen from heaven, were kept; it was in the Regia that one of the most ancient deities of Rome, the goddess Ops* was worshipped. The Regia owed its dual nature to the fact that it had once housed the King-Sorcerer. From what we know of Royal Rome, it is plain that its people, like other primitive peoples, attributed magic powers to their kings. The sacred rites were performed in their palaces, and they were both the custodians and the owners of the sacred fetishes. Almost certainly the Regia is the concrete evidence of an era when Rome was under the sway of these sorcerer-kings, but, as its architecture proves, this stage in the development of Rome was only reached after the disappearance of the huts. This is confirmed by the fact that the Temple of Vesta alone preserved the primitive shape.

The Regia, as we have said, possesses the characteristic features of the *megaron*;[11] furthermore, the *ancilia*, the large oval shields zealously guarded in the sanctuary, are strongly reminiscent of the deeply indented shields of archaic Greece. This double similarity would not seem to be fortuitous; on the contrary, it suggests that at some given moment, Rome either copied directly the styles of the Creto-Mycenaean civilizations or inherited from Indo-European immigrants the architectural form of the prehistoric house, as well as the shape of the shields. But such a far-reaching hypothesis

* At this time, Ops and Mars were supreme in the Roman Pantheon.

must be firmly based, and all that we know from archaeological data is that the rectangular stone house made its appearance
in the Forum at the time when decorative Etruscan elements were
introduced on the Palatine. It seems extremely unlikely, however,
that the primitive Latin people could have conceived and preserved a plan of which they made no practical use, continuing to
dwell in their mud and thatch, round and oval huts. That
the style was copied from the Creto-Mycenaean civilizations is far more plausible, at any rate to those who are not
prepared to admit that the similarities are due to sheer coincidence.

Whether the above theory is right or wrong, the contrast in
style between the Regia and the Temple of Vesta is proof of the
existence of two successive levels of Roman civilization, two
phases of culture, but it is difficult to define more precisely the
conditions in which they developed, to relate them to a particular
ethnic or cultural influence exerted over them at a given time. The
immensely complex elements of an historical evolution are not so
easily unravelled.

The excavations of the Comitium revealed a third phase of
Roman civilization. The second phase, that of the crude, almost
shapeless architecture of the rectangular stone houses (those of the
Forum, the Regia), was followed by a third, that of the sanctuary
of the two lions in which the Etruscan influence was evident. It
was during this phase that, at the northern extremity of the Forum,
Janus, the strangest divinity in the Roman pantheon, made his
appearance.

The two-faced god rose above one of the city gates: the Porta
Janualis, the Gate of Janus. What is extremely curious is that this
gate of whose existence we have irrefutable evidence, opened not
into the Servian Wall (built round Rome in the sixth century B.C.,
as we shall see later), but directly into the exit from the Forum.
But the Porta Janualis was not unique; everything seems to
suggest that at this time the Forum was a self-contained city to
which various gates gave access: the Porta Janualis on the north,
the Porta Romana (from which a road ascended to the Palatine)
on the south, the Tigillum Sororium (The Beam of the Sisters, a
postern-gate dedicated to Juno) on the east, and finally, the Porta
Pendana (the Gaping Gate) on the south-east. The Porta Pendana,
perched on an inaccessible rock, was always open, hence its name,

but none was allowed to pass through it, for it was under a male-diction.[12]

This 'city of the Forum' to which the gates bear witness, incomprehensible if we adhere to the belief that the Palatine villages progressively absorbed those on the other hills, was dominated by the Capitol, and the Capitol was the political and religious centre of Rome. It was on the Capitol that magistrates who had been elected to office assembled each year to be invested with the *imperium*, the mystic power that passed through them like a magnetic current and made them the representatives of Jupiter Optimus Maximus, who reigned in the Capitolium.[13]

The ancient historians tell us that the great Temple of Jupiter Capitolinus was founded by Tarquinius Priscus, that Tarquinius Superbus continued the work of building it, and that it was only in 509 B.C., the first year of the Republic, that it was completed and dedicated.

In 1919, when part of the Palazzo Caffarelli was demolished, excavations on the site laid bare the sub-foundation of the Temple, built, like that of the Regia, of blocks of cappellaccio. No evidence came to light (as it did in the case of the Mamertine Prison) of anything that conflicted with the traditional date; despite the numerous repairs that the edifice had undergone in the course of the centuries, despite the fact that the almost total reconstruction necessitated by the disastrous fire of 83 B.C. had considerably modified its aspect, archaeologists were able to prove that the major Temple of Rome dominated the Capitol at the close of the sixth century.

The fact that the Temple was already standing at this date is extremely significant. It tells us that by the end of the sixth century Rome possessed a form of government very close to its definitive constitution, and that the concept of a magico-religious power, integral in the political system of Royal Rome, had become autonomous—that is to say, it had become independent of the person of the king and the consuls who ruled Rome after the expulsion of the Tarquins.

The King-Sorcerer was the priest of Mars whom he incarnated during the ceremonies, but at the close of the sixth century Mars ceased to be supreme. Jupiter, the god of the Capitolium, could not have existed in a state where the power did not emanate from him alone. It was Jupiter who invested the magistrates with the *imperium*, Jupiter who was its divine symbol, Jupiter who conferred it on whom he chose, making his will known through the auguries. Undoubtedly it was not due to mere chance that the Capitolium, founded by the Tarquins (the kings of the Etruscan dynasty who had been mainly responsible for the introduction and consolidation of the concept of an abstract power) was dedicated to Jupiter on the very day when the kings, invested for life with the *imperium*, were replaced by consuls who held office for just under a year. The history of this political evolution, glimpsed in the pages of the classic annalists, is written, as archaeology has confirmed, in the soil of Rome.

We see, then, that the City of the Forum, the existence of which must be accepted, marked the emergence of the real Rome. While the Urbs was mainly made up of Latin elements from the large villages which had gradually made their appearance on the hills and in the valley, its political structure was imposed from outside, undoubtedly by the Etruscan conquerors. We have only to examine the archaeological data to perceive that the city was formed by a synthesis of heterogenous elements, and not by the unilinear and harmonious development of a nucleus organizing itself by its own unaided efforts and evolving autonomously.

THE SERVIAN WALL

Livy tells us that when Servius Tullius became king he immediately took steps to protect the city with a complete line of fortifications, a project that had been initiated or perhaps only envisaged by Tarquinius Priscus. Livy is referring to the wall that surrounded Rome in his day, and not to the barricade of an earlier epoch that had enclosed the Forum and its annexes. There is nothing, in fact, to indicate that the Forum ever possessed a system of fortifications; the gates that gave access to it seem to have marked passages through a sacred zone—the zone that became the *pomaerium* of classic Rome. The Servian Wall, on the contrary, was purely military.

According to Livy, the Servian Wall circumscribed not only the Capitol, but also the Palatine, the Caelian, the Aventine, the Quirinal, the Viminal and part of the Esquiline. Archaeologists, far from doubting this account, accepted it so unquestioningly that right up to the late eighteen-hundreds, they continued to imagine they had found traces of the Wall, whose line they de-

ROME Forum Boarium. Sta Maria Egyptiaca, originally a small
Syllarian Temple probably dedicated to Portunus

(*above*) ROME   Vatican. Museo Etrusco Gregoriano. Funerary hut-shaped urns

(*below*) ROME   Palatine Antiquarium. Reconstruction of a Palatine hut

scribed with much fantasy.[14] Shortly after the massive clearance
operation involved in the modernization of Rome had begun,
numerous vestiges of a fortified wall well within the Aurelian Wall
(raised at the close of the third century B.C., and the principal line
of defence right up to the Medieval Age) were disclosed, and were
unhesitatingly pronounced to be the remains of the Servian Wall
that Livy had described; at long last, an authentic trace of Royal
Rome had come to light. But before long, difficulties arose. What
proof was there that the Wall went back to so remote an age? The
evidence of Livy, on whose reliability the hypercritics had already
cast doubts, was not enough. Was it not conceivable that, as had
frequently occurred in the case of other monuments, too early a
date had been ascribed to the Wall? The only way to resolve the
argument was by subjecting the vestiges to a minute analysis.

Almost immediately it became evident that the remains were
not uniform. While square blocks of grotta oscura had mainly been
used, there were also sections in cappellaccio. Now, for reasons
already given, those parts of the Wall for which grotta oscura
had been used could not be earlier than the fourth century B.C.; on
the other hand, the cappellaccio sections might well date back to
Royal Rome. The operative word was 'might'. Some archaeologists, for instance, pointed out that cappellaccio, always available
and quarried locally, might have been used for partial repairs—
indeed, it was apparent that some sections had been patched. In
their view, the presence of the two types of stone did not indicate
that the Wall had been built at two different periods, but merely
evidenced the plan of construction: since cappellaccio was the local,
and therefore the cheaper stone, it had been used for the less exposed sectors, the foundations and the sustaining walls, while the
better-quality grotta oscura had been reserved for the earthworks
and the keypoints of the fortifications. If this hypothesis was
correct, it followed that the entire Servian Wall only went back to
the fourth century B.C. This would explain, its supporters went on,
why Rome fell with such ease to the Gauls, who swept through
Italy in 390 B.C.: at that date, to all intents and purposes, Rome was
an open city.[15]

Livy seems to have realized the implication of his statement that
Rome was entirely ringed with fortifications in the sixth century,
namely that the Romans had made no attempt to defend their city.
He extricated himself neatly from the dilemma by the following

account of the disaster. After the crushing defeat of the Roman armies on the banks of the Allia, most of the survivors fell back on Veii; Rome was thus left almost defenceless, and the panic was such that the gates were not closed. This version of the capture of Rome by the Gauls seemed anything but convincing to those who favoured a later date for the Wall. They pointed out that, according to Livy himself, in times of danger the citizens took up arms and stood shoulder to shoulder with the troops on the Capitol, that it was customary for the entire population to rally to the defence of the city. Surely, they continued, the magistrates who had remained in Rome (when the Gauls rushed in, they sat in their chairs of office outside their residences, stoically awaiting death) would have immediately given the order for the gates to be closed —provided that there were any gates. Obviously, they concluded, the Wall did not exist in 390 B.C., but was built after the Gallic disaster to prevent a similar catastrophe. It only went back, in their view, to the Republic when Rome, grown to be a great power, had called in skilled workmen and engineers from southern Italy and Sicily. This later date also accounted for the use of grotta oscura which did not become available to the Romans until the fall of Veii round about the time of the Gallic invasion.

Clearly, the argument on the date of the Servian Wall was of the highest importance, for if it proved to be no later than the fourth century, an essential part of Livy's history of the first centuries of Rome would have to be discounted. Traditionalists and hypercritics stood opposed on ground which, thanks to archaeology, was to yield up evidence that Livy was right. But before this evidence came to light, the wrangle went on and on. The hypercritics put their case with sweet reasonableness: 'Really, you must admit that it's hardly likely that Rome in barely two centuries, from its foundation in 754 B.C. to the reign of King Servius Tullius towards the close of the sixth century B.C., had occupied all the hills, reached its definite territorial limits. Surely it's more sensible to suppose that at the beginning, and at any rate during the seventh, sixth, and fifth centuries, Rome consisted of isolated villages perched on hills that were natural defences, and that it was not until very much later that they merged together and formed a single city.' Thus the hypercritics gave rise to an idea that has enjoyed considerable support: the idea that for years Rome was merely a federation of villages.

When we take everything into consideration, it seems extremely unlikely that the cappellaccio sections of the Wall are contemporary with those in grotta oscura; for one thing, the former are meticulously constructed, while the latter have obviously been run up hastily and carelessly. Moreover, a recent excavation has revealed that a section of the Wall, in which both types of stone were used, surrounded the Aventine—a discovery that lends weight to Livy's account.[16] The idea that Rome was, if not an open city, no more than partially fortified in the sixth century B.C. and that its unity was only political, is quite inadmissible today.

In the light of archaeological data, the contention that the Servian Wall could not have existed at the time of the Gallic irruption no longer holds good. Let us recapitulate the disaster. All the available forces had been dispatched to the Allia, where they suffered a crushing defeat. The few troops who had been left to defend Rome, even though they had been reinforced by those units which had managed to make their way back to the city, could not hope to hold the entire perimeter of some twelve kilometres. All they could do, therefore, was to make as strong a stand as possible on the Citadel, leaving the rest of Rome open to the enemy. It was a cruel choice dictated by necessity, but the sacrifice was not in vain; the small garrison succeeded in holding the Gauls at bay till a Roman army formed in hot haste fell upon the invaders and routed them utterly. It was not because fortifications were lacking that Rome was taken with such ease, but because even the most formidable walls are useless if there are not enough troops to defend them.

Clearly arguments prefaced by 'is it not more reasonable?' or 'does it not appear more probable?' lead to wishful thinking. Only facts confirmed by the most meticulous archaeological analyses enable us to reach the truth, or at least the near-truth. In the case of the Servian Wall, archaeology has confirmed, even more amply and perfectly than had been hoped, the reliability of traditional evidence. It has proved beyond doubt that the Aventine was included in Royal Rome, yet only some twenty years ago the most ardent defenders of Livy were prepared to yield the Aventine to their adversaries and beat a retreat. Today we know that they had no cause for doubt, that the Aventine did, in fact, form part of the city and was included in its defensive system. We can now take it as almost certain that most of the Esquiline and the Caelian were also circumscribed by the Servian Wall—indeed, there is no other plausible explanation of its line. True, no traces of a cappellaccio wall have yet come to light in these quarters, but this may be simply because excavations are not invariably blessed with luck.

At the conclusion of this long analysis of the archaeological data that has enabled us to form a picture of the origins of the Urbs and its evolution during the first centuries of its existence, we see that the ancient annalists deserve far more credit than they were once given. It would be quite unthinkable today to write off as legendary or imaginary four hundred years of Roman history. We know that on the Palatine, the Quirinal, the Capitol, the primitive villages and the pastoral communities, of whom Propertius loved to sing, really existed. We know that after these humble beginnings, the population rapidly increased as the first links of trade and culture were forged with the rest of the Mediterranean world; we know that when the Forum became the meeting-place of the villagers, the true city was born. It is at this moment that while the most ancient customs and rites persist at the foot of the Palatine, we sense the presence of the Etruscan conquerors on the Capitol, in the Comitium. Rome profited from the lessons these masters taught her, and when she regained her liberty, far from reverting to what she had once been, a village indistinguishable from the other villages of Latium, she accepted the political, social and religious structures they had imposed upon her. From that time forward, she possessed a solid system of defences that protected her against the danger of sudden invasion, the threat of an armed bid to regain power by the exiled kings and the aggressive intents of other Latin cities. In increasing numbers, the rural population sought safety within her walls, little knowing that in the course of time they were to become the Sovereign People. Already, securely ringed by her fortifications, Rome was asserting herself as the Imperial City.

CHAPTER FOUR

Rome and the Archaeologists:
From the Republic to the Empire

THANKS TO THE PATIENT WORK of archaeologists during the last hundred years, the picture of archaic Rome has emerged more clearly, and the ancient historians have come to be regarded with less scepticism. The many discoveries, some spectacular, some comparatively humble and unknown to the general public, have all added to our knowledge of the past; above all, the incessant analysis of archaeological data has led to constant re-thinking and has filled historians with the hope of gradually reaching the truth.

THE REDISCOVERY OF THE FORUM

Less than a century ago, the Palatine was entirely covered by convents and gardens. As for the Forum, it was a stony wilderness of crumbling ruins. The romantic engravings of the day have made us familiar with its mournful landscape, as have the accounts of travellers who visited the Forum to contemplate the vestiges of the grandeur of Ancient Rome. Here is how the Reverend Edward Burton described the sight that met his eyes:

Standing upon the hill of the Capitol and looking down upon the Roman Forum, we contemplate a scene with which we fancy ourselves familiar, and we seem suddenly to have quitted the habitations of living men. Not only is its former grandeur utterly annihilated, but the ground has not been applied to any other purpose. When we descend into it, we find that many of the ancient buildings are buried under irregular heaps of soil; and a warm imagination might fancy that some spell hung over the spot, forbidding it to be profaned by the ordinary occupations of inhabited cities.

What Virgil says of its appearance before the Trojan settlers arrived is singularly true at the present moment:

'. . . and cattle were browsing in the Roman Forum and their lowing was heard in the rich Carinae Quarter.' *The Aeneid*: Book VIII, 360.

Where the Roman people saw temples erected to perpetuate their exploits, and where the Roman nobles vied with each other in the magnificence of their dwellings, we now see a few isolated pillars standing amidst some broken arches; or, if the curiosity of foreigners has investigated what the natives neither think nor care about, we may perhaps see the remnant of a statue or a column extracted from the rubbish. Where the Comitia was held, where Cicero harangued, and where the triumphal processions passed, we have now no animated beings, except strangers attracted by curiosity, the convicts who are employed in excavating as a punishment, and those more harmless animals already alluded to, who find a scanty pasture, and a shelter from the sun under a group of trees. The Roman Forum is now called the *Campo Vaccino*.[1]

In this desert, the few ruins still standing were often inaccurately labelled by guides. For instance, the three columns of the Temple of Castor (attributed by Nibby to the Graecostasis) were pointed out as the remains of the Temple of Jupiter Stator. The learned *ciceroni* knew from their beloved Livy that Romulus, hard-pressed by Tatius and his Sabines, had implored Jupiter's aid, vowing to the god that if he stopped the rout, he would erect a temple to him on that sacred spot; what they did not know, however, was that Romulus had been forced still further back before Jupiter intervened, and that the Temple of Jupiter was situated at a very considerable distance south-east of the Temple of Castor, close to the Arch of Titus.

Today, we are far better informed, and although only one or two excavations have been carried out below the level of the Late Empire, we can identify most of the ruins that have come to light and retrace the broad outlines of the history of the Forum Romanum.

The first event of outstanding importance was the building of the basilicas at the beginning of the second century B.C. The soil of the Forum bears witness to the sudden cultural evolution that took place after the all-conquering Romans had successively defeated Hannibal, Philip V of Macedon, and Antiochus of Syria.

The basilicas were covered porticoes, much the same as modern Bourses; in Rome, as in the Eastern countries, they were used for business and commerce; later, during the Empire, they became the seat of certain tribunals. The erection of these basilicas marks the date when trade relations were established between Rome and the rest of the Mediterranean world. No trace remains of the first of these basilicas which stood between the Comitium and the Mamertine Prison; this was the Basilica Porcia built by Cato the Censor in 184 B.C. To make room for it, Cato 'compulsorily acquired' with State funds a number of private houses and two 'shopping arcades'.² These were pulled down to provide the necessary space; already the city had begun to feel cramped in its archaic Forum.

A few years later, in 179 B.C., the two censors M. Fulvius Nobilior and M. Aemilius Lepidus endowed the Forum with a second basilica, the Basilica Aemilia. During the dictatorship of Sulla, the Tabularium was erected; this huge gloomy building was, as its name implies, the Records Office. None of the texts mention it, but inscriptions tell us for what purpose it was built. (Part of one inscription has been preserved, the other, a copy made during the Renaissance, has vanished.) These inscriptions gave the name of the edifice and the date of its dedication: 78 B.C., during the consulate of Lutatius Catulus. With the Tabularium, the décor of this side of the Forum facing towards the Capitol, was complete.

Up to the middle of the first century B.C., the south side of the Forum was occupied by arcades of shops similar to those that had been pulled down to make room for the Aemilia. These *tabernae* were demolished in turn when Julius Caesar decided to build a third basilica to balance the Aemilia—the basilica that commemorates his name, the Basilica Julia. Caesar's majestic basilica with its seven aisles (the Aemilia had only four) was swept by fire long before it was finished; Augustus continued the work that his adopted father had begun, and increased the size of the structure. Until Constantine's day, the Basilica Julia, completed and dedicated at the close of Augustus's reign, was the largest in Rome. The evolution that had begun four centuries ago had reached its culminating point: the Forum was now an ordered whole, entirely axed on the Capitol, the seat of the throbbing heart of the Empire.

At the time of Caesar's death, the Forum extended eastward as far as the Regia and the Temple of Vesta. Its official limit was the arch raised in 121 B.C. by Quintus Fabius Allobrogicus at the entry of the Sacred Way. Archaeologists have sought in vain for elements of this arch. It was not until quite recently that its foundations were identified.³

When Augustus became Emperor he erected a temple to *divus Julius*, the deified Caesar, between the Regia and the Praetors' Tribunal. This temple was discovered during the course of an excavation in 1872, and disengaged in a later campaign. Only the podium remains, but we know from the design on Trajan's coins what the temple looked like. In the centre of the wall of the podium there is a semicircular recess which originally contained an altar, only the base of which has survived. It must have been on this very altar that the body of the murdered Caesar was cremated.

At some time the recess was closed by a wall. Probably this alteration was made to allow more space on the podium, which served as a second rostra and was adorned with the prows of ships captured at the Battle of Actium. Close to the Temple of Caesar, Augustus erected a triumphal arch, the remains of which have been found. This arch spanned the Sacred Way and marked the entrance to the Forum from which the Temple of Vesta and the Regia were now excluded. Henceforward, they were regarded as annexes of the Palatine.

The Forum of Augustus remained more or less unchanged until the end of the Empire. At its western extremity, between the Temple of Saturn and the Temple of Vesta, a new political platform took the place of the Comitium. The Comitium, too closely associated in the minds of the Romans with the Republic, was re-paved (possibly with the *lapis niger*), and from this time on merely served as the vestibule of the new Curia. But although, as in Republican Rome, the Senate House adjoined the political arena, although the ancient duality of *Senatus Populusque Romanus*, the Senate and the People, continued to all appearances to exist, it was, in fact, the Emperor's voice that predominated in the Senate—his voice that the docile plebs heard in the Forum through the lips of this or that speaker.

The tribunals were still held in the customary places, notably near the Temple of Vesta in the open air. A ring of spectators surrounded the platform on which the judges sat, accused and accusers facing them. No traces of a courthouse in the modern sense of the word have come to light, that is to say, a court of assizes where the *questiones perpetuae* were regularly heard. Justice was dispensed beneath the regard of Jupiter in whose name the principals swore to tell the truth, the whole truth, and nothing but the truth.

As time passed and the population of Rome increased, the assemblies grew so vast that they had to be held in the Campus Martius. The Forum lost its ancient character, but although it ceased to be the centre of public life, crowds flocked there for the games. Before the permanent amphitheatres were built, almost all the gladiatorial combats were staged in the Forum. Crowds of spectators sat squeezed together in a tight-packed mass on the benches, and those who had been unable to get in clambered onto the roofs of the temples and basilicas. The holding of games in the Forum was by no means an innovation, but with the dawn of the Empire lavish entertainments such as wild beast hunts became the rage. Beneath the Augustan paving, excavations revealed the existence of underground corridors and dens seven feet high and five feet wide, similar to those beneath the *cavea* of the Colosseum.

Once the amphitheatres were built the Forum ceased to be a place of entertainment; deserted, desolate, it fell into decay, and was slowly transformed into a kind of graveyard-museum of history where votive objects, statues, columns, inscriptions of every kind recalled the memory of men long dead, events of long ago. Gradually the arena became cluttered up with monuments raised in honour of the various emperors; excavations brought to light the pedestal of an equestrian statue of Domitian close to the spot where, two hundred years later, a similar statue of Constantine was raised. Closer to the Rostra of Augustus were the Anaglyphs of Trajan, whose reliefs commemorated two of the Emperor's good deeds: his institution of a fund to provide for the care and education of orphan children, and his proclamation of a fiscal amnesty which he accompanied by burning the records—a gesture that was greeted with wild enthusiasm by the Roman taxpayers!

Not far away from the Rostra is the monumental triple arch of Septimius Severus; even today it is almost intact. It marked the point at which the Sacred Way joined the road leading to the Capitol. We are now speaking of the year 203 B.C., when the Sacred Way had long been re-routed further north. This re-routing undoubtedly took place during the construction of the vestibule of Nero's Golden House, which had necessitated extensive work in the quarter immediately west of the Forum. The new Sacred Way skirted the Aemilia, and on its verge Antoninus raised a temple to the memory of his wife Faustina who had died in 141 B.C. Antoninus followed the pious example of Titus and Domitian, who had raised a magnificent sanctuary to their father, *divus Vespasian*, at the opposite extremity of the Sacred Way, between the Temple of Saturn and the Temple of Concord. Emperor succeeded emperor, dynasty succeeded dynasty, and each of the great, eager for immortality, erected a temple, a statue, a monument, in the ancient Forum where on appointed days solemn processions wound their way to celebrate the ancient rites of Eternal Rome.

Nearly all these temples, statues, and monuments have disappeared, but even the few that have come to light enable us to picture the hodge-podge the Forum presented at the close of Antiquity. At the end of the seventh century A.D., for instance, when Smaragdus wished to honour Phocas (one of the emperors, incidentally, who contributed largely to the destruction of Ancient Rome), he could think of nothing better than to erect a suitably inscribed column in front of the Rostra of Augustus. A row of similar columns already stood on the south side of the Forum; some have been restored, but as the inscriptions are missing, we have no idea in whose honour they were set up. The columns standing along the Sacred Way of Augustus and Tiberius only record an anonymous glory.

THE DISCOVERY OF THE IMPERIAL FORA

The progressive desertion of the Forum was due to the changes that took place in political life during the first years of the Empire. The drift away from the Forum was, however, speeded up and made complete by the construction, from the time of Caesar to that of Trajan, of more and more fora for the Sovereign People.

The Imperial Fora are frequently mentioned by the classic writers, but for centuries they lay buried beneath the streets of Rome. Only the presence of a few columns and a triple archway (through which formerly ran the modern Via Bonella) revealed the site of the Forum of Augustus. Of Trajan's Forum, only that section laid bare by French archaeologists in 1812 was known; modern buildings concealed the façade of the hemicycles, and a garden had been planted in the earth that overlaid the ancient paving. As to Caesar's Forum, we can only form an idea of what it looked like from the plans made by two architects when it was laid bare in the sixteenth century; unfortunately for us, it was covered in almost at once.

In the space of a mere twenty years—1920-40—a prodigious ensemble was brought to light, occupying an area roughly 630 yards long and as much as 200 yards wide in places, and extending from Trajan's Column to Constantine's Basilica. The vastness of this expanse can be properly evaluated when we recall that the Forum Romanum, even when it had reached its full dimensions, was no more than a bare 100 yards long and 50 yards wide (excluding the depth of the annexes). Equally striking is the fact that while it had taken almost four centuries for the Forum Romanum to assume its definitive shape, the Imperial Fora, the construction of which had been begun by Caesar shortly after 50 B.C., were not completed until A.D. 117, after Trajan's death.

When Caesar decided to endow Rome with a new forum, he certainly did not envisage the new projects to which it would lead. His forum was a mere detail in a vast programme of work, but as it turned out, it was the only item he was able to realize. After the Gallic catastrophe, essential repairs were hurriedly carried out, the monuments that had been damaged restored as near as possible to their original state. There was little change in the aspect of the city, and the centres of its civic life remained as before the Forum and the Campus Martius. The Campus Martius, a vast plain outside the walls of Rome, had originally been used for the massing of troops, but as the *Comitia Centuriata*, the most important of the assemblies, was formed by the *centuria*, the body of citizens enrolled to take up arms in times of war, the Campus Martius had finally become the official venue of all political meetings. The elections were also held there, and every five years, a census of the population was taken on the plain. The number of inhabitants continued to rise and Rome began to feel cramped within her walls. The Campus Martius offered a tempting solution. Was this huge expanse of ground lying at the very foot of the Capitol and within a stone's throw of the Forum to be allowed to remain undeveloped?

The answer was no. A number of private houses were built on the plain; during the civil wars that marked the beginning of the first century B.C., the exchequer was so low that the State was compelled to sell plots of the land. By the time that Caesar had risen to power, so little space remained free in the Campus Martius that it was totally inadequate. The Dictator hit on a radical solution to the problem; he proposed to divert the course of the Tiber to the foot of the Vatican hills. The land thus reclaimed would become a new Campus Martius, Rome would have room to breathe. Taken in conjunction with this vast scheme, the building of a new forum was indeed a mere detail, but as we have said, it was the only item in his programme that Caesar succeeded in carrying out. After the Ides of March and his assassination, the difficulties, let alone the impiety, of diverting the Tiber proved too daunting for his successors, and the project came to nothing. Augustus limited himself to carrying on the work his adopted father had begun; he completed the first of the Imperial Fora on the land that Cicero had been authorized to acquire, in the Dictator's name, for this purpose.

The excavations carried out by Corrado Ricci in 1930-2 have given us a clearer picture of Caesar's plan for his forum. Inspired by Eastern models, he had conceived it as a sacred precinct dependent on a temple dedicated to his divine protectrix, Venus Genetrix, the mother of Aeneas.[4] Probably Caesar formulated this plan after the Battle of Pharsala in 48 B.C., on the eve of which he had vowed to raise a sanctuary to the goddess if she granted him victory. The preliminary work of building the forum had begun, however, in 51 B.C. Even while Caesar may not have visualized the entire layout at this time, his forum is in striking contrast with the Forum Romanum and its miscellaneous collection of temples and basilicas; the unity of the Forum Romanum was only achieved later when the desire arose to create a symmetrical ensemble. Caesar's Forum, on the contrary, was a perfect example of architectural unity. The rectangular area, enclosed on either side by a double portico, was dominated by the high podium of the Temple of Venus Genetrix. Completely different from the Forum Romanum, it bore a resemblance to the forum of Pompeii, constructed in the second century B.C. The conservative character of Roman architecture which extended to secular as well as to sacred buildings, had caused Rome to lag behind the advances made, not only by the Greek cities, but also by those of Southern Italy. With the dawn of the Empire, however, there was a complete transformation; just as the old order had been swept away by the Republic, so the diehard traditions were uprooted for good by the irresistible *elan* of the new régime.

The excavations of Caesar's Forum led to another important revelation: at the time of its construction, the Curia of Tullus Hostilius, where the Senate had met for centuries, had been replaced by a new Curia, the Curia Julia. (It is this Curia, scarcely modified by Diocletian, that we see today.) The Curia Julia, while it opened on one side on the Comitium, as was traditional, also opened on to the vestibule of the Forum, proof that Caesar intended it to be used for the political and judiciary life, such as he conceived it, of the new city. The Dictator designed his Forum, not so much for trading purposes, but principally as a centre for the tribunals. In the serene Forum Julium, irradiated by the presence of the protectrix of the Julian gens, Caesar's magistrates would no longer be exposed to the terrifying violence of the mob which manifested itself with such alarming frequency in the Forum Romanum.

Caesar had originally dreamed of a far larger Forum, but owing to the fact that various owners had obstinately refused to sell their land, his dream remained unfulfilled. Indeed, in order to gain a little more space, it had been necessary to cut away part of the rock from the lower slopes of the Capitol. On this side, the Forum was extended by a steep street, the Clivus Argentarius (the Ascent of the Bankers), which connected it with the Campus Martius. By a stroke of good fortune, when the excavations of Caesar's Forum were resumed at a later date, the ground floors of the buildings that had lined the road in the days of Antiquity were uncovered. At street level were rows of shops, identical with those on the ground floors of the *insulae* (apartment houses), which had come to light during earlier excavations in Ostia; the totally unexpected discovery of the *insulae* of the Clivus Argentarius, hidden so long by parasitic walls, spoke far more eloquently than words of the contrast between Rome and Pompeii. There was all the difference in the world between the agreeable *dolce far niente* pleasure-resort and the industrious capital coping with the problem of housing its ever-increasing population and providing for its needs. While Pompeii drowsed indolently in the sun, Rome was continually on the move, continually changing. The *insulae* of the Clivus Argentarius may only date back to Hadrian (which would make them a couple of hundred years later than the Forum Julium); even so, they were the direct result of Caesar's activities in this quarter. The modernizing of the city that was to begin by endowing it with all that was essential for the fulfilment of its high destiny, was entirely due to the brilliance, the energy, the foresight of a single man: the Dictator, Julius Caesar.

Six years after the Battle of Pharsala, Augustus solemnly vowed to erect a temple to Mars Ultor if the god would grant him victory at Philippi. His decisive defeat of the armies of Brutus and Cassius shattered Republican hopes for ever. The fulfilment of the promise he had made to the god was the origin of Augustus's Forum, which was not completed and dedicated until forty years after the Battle of Philippi.

The centre of the Forum of Augustus, like that of Caesar, was dominated by the temple, which, as we can see from a bas-relief in the Villa Medici, must have been extraordinarily impressive with its eight Corinthian columns and the Flying Victories that surmounted its façade. Nothing remains of it today except its terrace and three fallen columns. At the beginning of the thirteenth century, the Knights of Rhodes established their headquarters on its site, and in 1465, the Priory of the Order was built by Cardinal Marco Bembo. The series of excavations undertaken in 1927 led to the disengagement of all the ancient ruins, but only the loggia of the priory was considered of architectural interest and worthy of preservation.

The Forum of Augustus, planned on the same lines as the Forum Julium, is a document of the highest importance, since it gives us the key to the political thought of the founder of the Empire. While his Forum was dynastic—in the *cella* of the temple, Mars and Venus, the two divinities from whom the Julian gens claimed descent, stood side by side—the assembled statues and busts of the great *duces*, leaders and outstanding intellectuals of Rome, many of them Republican, bore witness to the Emperor's desire to pay equal homage to them all. His Forum was an Aeneid in stone.

Lack of space had compelled Augustus to construct his Forum on the confines of the Suburra, one of the most densely populated quarters of the city, where the squalid huts were jammed so closely together that there was constant danger of fire. To protect the Forum from this threat, a towering stone wall was erected, whose archways allowed free passage to the Suburra and the Esquiline. The portico of Augustus's Forum was enhanced with vast *schola*— apses with a diameter of 45 feet. Certain tribunals were held in these semicircular recesses, but they were mainly used for private or public religious ceremonies. In the *schola* the sons of senators, the young men who were to become the future administrators of the Empire, assumed the *toga virilis*; here, too, governors were invested before their departure to the provinces, and when they returned, it was to the *schola* that they immediately repaired to render account to Mars of what they had achieved during their term of office.

All the mighty leaders of Rome, both real and legendary, from Aeneas down to Caesar, encircled the Forum of Augustus. This endless procession of great Romans, similar to the cortège of heroes that passed before Aeneas and Anchises, symbolized one of the fabled beliefs inherent in the régime: that Rome was a continuous reality, that the *condottieri* of whom Augustus was the *dux*, the latest and greatest, had fought, under the aegis of Mars Ultor, wars, not of conquest, but just wars against the tyrants, traitors, usurpers, and all those men of overweening ambition who dared to threaten the sovereignty of the Roman People. In Augustus's Hall of Fame those who had been implacable enemies during their lifetime were reconciled, linked together with bonds of glory: Marius with Sulla, Q. Fabius Maximus, the *Cunctator* (one who delays) with Scipio Africanus, his bitter political enemy. Had they not, each in his own way, devoted their lives to protecting their mother country and increasing her might?

As was fitting, the priests of Mars had followed their god; the Salians who performed the ancient ritual dance of the *ancilia* had taken up their quarters in the Forum of Augustus. The Salians were noted for their sumptuous banquets, fit, it has been said, for an archbishop; on one occasion, the mouth-watering odours were wafted to the near-by tribunal where Claudius was sitting in judgement, and so whetted his appetite that he adjourned the proceedings and betook himself to the feast!

For the next seventy-five years the emperors who followed Augustus considered that there was ample space for public activities, but throughout this period, the prosperity of the Empire climbed from peak to peak and the population figures had continued to rise. Furthermore, Rome was now the centre of a mighty Empire, and year by year, ever-increasing multitudes streamed in from the provinces under her administration. One effect of this centralization was the multiplication of cases that came up for trial. From Gibraltar to the shores of the Black Sea, from the Sahara to the banks of the Rhine, any litigation of a fairly important nature was liable to be referred to the courts of Rome.

Plainly, the development of the Imperial Fora was not an urban phenomenon; on the contrary, it was the visible manifestation of a political and administrative evolution that was to lead to the complete transformation of the victorious city. To maintain her Empire, Rome had merely to despatch a handful of governors each year to the provinces where they exercised their illimitable powers pretty much as they chose. As we turn the pages of history we see how Rome became the capital of an Empire, we see how determined she was to deal justly with all her subjects and develop the resources of her most far-flung dominions, fully aware that these measures would best guarantee her permanent ascendancy.

In order to maintain the *pax romana*, a corps of officials on whom the Emperor could rely implicitly, had to be organized. The cadre of this corps was formed by senators who, between missions to the provinces, lived in Rome, presided over tribunals and pronounced judgement on colleagues who stood accused of embezzlement or misuse of power.[5] To deal with affairs directly connected with himself, the Emperor had created a new bureaucracy. Its various departments administered by his freedmen were established on the Palatine, within the Imperial Palace, while the tribunals and endless commissions held their sessions in the vicinity of the Curia, in the annexes of the Forum Romanum, and in the Fora of Caesar and Augustus. The space available for civic affairs was clearly insufficient, as Vespasian realized when he became Emperor. Accordingly, he proceeded to construct a new forum round the Temple of Peace that he had begun to build in A.D. 71, the fulfilment of his vow to the goddess who had granted his prayer and given his son Titus resounding victory over the Jews.

Vespasian's Forum, the Temple of Peace, was entirely different from the Fora of Caesar and Augustus. A series of excavations in 1935 and 1936 disclosed it as a vast, almost square peristyle. On three sides were porticoes thirty-eight feet wide; the fourth side opened on to the Argiletum and the Fora of Caesar and Augustus. The centre was laid out as a garden.

The excavations revealed a remarkable innovation, an innovation which proved that the creative powers of Roman architects were of a higher order than has often been supposed. The Temple of Peace, instead of being raised in the centre of a rectangular colonnade, had been integrated into the middle wing of the portico; slightly elevated, it looked more like a chapel installed in an

ROME The interior of the Colosseum

ROME South-east aspect of the Colosseum

ROME The mouth of the Cloaca Maxima

ROME Via Appia. Remains of the Claudian Aqueduct

exedra than a traditional temple. A short flight of steps led up to the sanctuary, on either side of which there was a library: the Greek library and the Latin library. It was these two libraries that gave Vespasian's Forum its true character. The guests whom the Emperor invited to this haven of peace were not men of action but scholars, philosophers, rhaetors—the intelligentsia of Rome who were gradually being driven away from the old fora by the noisy crowds. Vespasian knew their worth to the full; in his judgement their services were indispensable to the State. In addition to the libraries, there was a museum filled with masterpieces of painting and sculpture from countless countries.

The fourth Imperial Forum, that of Domitian, was constructed in the narrow space between the Fora of Caesar and Augustus and the Temple of Peace, and was known in consequence as the Forum Transitorium. It was also called Nerva's Forum, as it was completed by this Emperor, who dedicated it to his predecessor. In that part of his forum which adjoined the east apse of the Forum of Augustus, Domitian raised a temple to his protectrix, Minerva. The sanctuary remained almost intact until the beginning of the seventeenth century, and we possess a number of pictures of it by artists of the day. The Temple of Minerva might well have survived to our own age had not Pope Paul V decided that its columns would serve to adorn the Acqua Paola, the fountain that he was constructing on the Janiculum. The work of demolition was so thorough that recent excavations have disclosed nothing but the foundations of the temple. Of the colonnade of its precinct, only two marble columns are still standing; their shafts are twenty-eight feet high. In medieval times, the quarter surrounding the Temple of Minerva was called, no one quite knows why, by the curious name of Noah's Ark.

It must be admitted that even after the excavations carried out in the last few years we know very little about Nerva's Forum, now almost buried beneath the Via dei Fori Imperiali. Only the south side which forms part of the archaeological zone of the Forum Romanum is exposed, and it can be seen quite clearly that it is in-curving. Since this was unique, the first impression was that this curved plan had arisen from the desire to create a novelty, but a closer examination of the site disclosed the true reason. The Forum Transitorium had to be designed in such a way as to link the Forum Romanum with the Imperial Fora, and its architects found themselves faced with an extremely tricky problem. At the point where the new forum should have adjoined the posterior wall of the Basilica Aemilia (the Aemilia was an integral part of the Forum Romanum and followed its orientation), there stood two ancient and sacrosanct monuments: the Temple and Arch of Janus.[6] Now, the Temple and the Arch were at an angle both to the Aemilia and the Imperial Fora; hence the only solution was to in-curve this side of the Forum Transitorium in order to marry these three different orientations. The plan of Nerva's Forum, far from being preconceived, was an improvisation due to sheer necessity.

With the Forum Transitorium, the first group of fora formed an intercommunicating ensemble. The work begun by Caesar seemed to be complete, but Rome continued to develop, and still more space was needed for civic affairs. Possibly Domitian had attempted to enlarge the Forum of Augustus by cutting away part of the west slopes of the Quirinal, but there is no literary evidence of this, and while the excavations that ultimately led to the disclosure of Trajan's Forum suggested that this had been the case, their results were difficult to interpret. This is by no means the only instance of an archaeological discovery which, far from shedding light on the past, raises problems that are almost insoluble.

One of the most brilliant successes achieved by Italian archaeologists in recent years was the discovery of Trajan's Forum and Market. Excavations of this site had begun in 1812 under French administration, and were carried on intermittently during the course of the nineteenth century. It was not, however, until 1929 and onwards that they led to completely new and unexpected results. Today, Trajan's Forum and Market are amongst the best known of the ancient monuments, yet only a few years ago the existence of the former was only suspected, while that of the latter was undreamt of by all. Thanks to the fact that they were brought to light, we can form a clearer, more accurate picture of everyday life in Imperial Rome.

During the early years of the Republic, before the basilicas were built, there was a daily market in the Forum Romanum. Gradually, however, the stall-holders were edged out by the bankers and money-changers who, by Cicero's day, were in complete occupation. Schoolmasters had long used the Forum as their point of assembly, hence, in addition to being the political, administrative and judiciary centre of Rome, it was also the venue of the intelligentsia. During the Empire, the various activities carried on in the Forum sorted themselves out; the benches of the bankers and money-changers not only filled the Forum but extended to both sides of the Curia, and spread out along the Argiletum and the Clivus Argentarius; the slave-merchants gathered round the Temple of Castor; the jewellers and dealers in precious stones grouped themselves on the Sacred Way, and after the death of Nero, installed themselves in the great portico (still only partially disengaged) that formed the vestibule of his Golden House. From the time of Vespasian, philosophers, rhaetors, grammarians assembled in the serene groves of the Temple of Peace, while the tribunals took over the Basilica Aemilia, the Basilica Julia, and the annexes of both the Forum Julium, and the Forum of Augustus. But year by year, more and more cases came up for trial, business was done on an ever-larger scale, and as the general prosperity continued to rise, more schools and schoolmasters were needed for the children of the flourishing *bourgeoisie*. Rome had expanded beyond all expectations—possibly, this expansion had been foreseen by one man, Julius Caesar, who would have made provision for it had he lived—and once again, at the close of the first century B.C., when the golden age of the Antonine dynasty was about to dawn, the city was faced with the problem of creating more space.

Today, we know how Trajan responded to Rome's requirements. On leaving the Forum of Augustus and after passing through a gigantic arch, citizens found themselves in a huge courtyard, paved with white marble, 155 yards long and ninety-five yards wide, large as the Fora of Caesar and Augustus put together. A large equestrian statue of Trajan rose in the centre of the huge square, whose porticoes, like those of the Forum of Augustus, were enriched by apses. At the back of this immense square rose the Basilica Ulpia, even more impressive than the Basilica Julia; its dimensions were increased still more by an apse in both of its shorter sides. Its double row of columns were in polychrome marble and grey granite whose sober tones brought out the marble's rainbow hues. Beyond the basilica were two libraries similar to those in the Temple of Peace. Trajan's Forum was even more of a breakaway from the conventional Fora of Caesar and Augustus than that of Vespasian. Its portico was not intended to serve as the enclosure of a sacred precinct, but was analogous to that of a Greek *agora* (market place). This innovation, undoubtedly due to Apollodorus of Damascus, was extremely significant; it heralded the coming triumph of Greek forms over those that were traditionally Roman. Never had the Empire been so cosmopolitan; Trajan was a Spaniard, his architect, Apollodorus, a Syrian. From this time onwards, there was an imperial style which contained elements of the styles of every province of the Empire.

One of the two libraries has been completely disengaged. This is the only library that has come to light in the west; no traces have been found of those built by Augustus on the Palatine or those in the Temple of Peace. The library of Trajan's Forum is a rectangular hall surrounded by a two-tiered colonnade whose décor is reminiscent of the Fourth Pompeiian style. There are a series of narrow niches round the walls; these were for the wooden *armaria* in whose compartments the rolls of papyri were stored. At one end of the library is a larger recess which no doubt contained the statue of some god in whose silent presence scholars sat reading and writing, absorbed and undisturbed.

As late as the fourth century A.D. professors and students fore-gathered in the exedras of Trajan's Forum. From two texts, we know that these *schola* were the favourite haunts of Hierius the orator, and Bonifacio the grammarian. Most probably Hierius and Bonifacio were unconsciously perpetuating a tradition; it is almost certain that, from the time when Trajan had built his Forum, intellectuals escaped from the noise and tumult of the crowds to this haven of peace and quiet.

Trajan's Column, towering up between the libraries, has been a landmark for generations. Probably the great esteem in which Trajan was held in medieval times led to its preservation. The story goes that Gregory the Great, after he had gazed at one of the marble groups that commemorate Trajan's virtues in his Forum, lamented that the soul of this great and wise man should be lost, and prayed earnestly for his salvation. An angel appeared to him and said: 'The soul of Trajan will be saved, Gregory, if thou wilt undergo the pains of purgatory for three days or suffer sickness for the rest of thy term on earth.' Gregory answered that he would gladly sacrifice his health for Trajan's redemption, and from that day forward sickness smote him. This incident is most picturesquely described by Dante in Canto 10 of the *Purgatorio*. Even Christian Rome continued to honour Trajan who raised the fortunes of the Empire to the highest peak.

Trajan had decided to exclude commerce from his Forum, hence to satisfy the requirements of trade he built a separate market. This was a complete innovation in the economic life of Rome, furthermore, the plan and architecture of the market were altogether new. To create the necessary space, the west slopes of the Quirinal behind the high retaining wall of the Forum, were deeply hollowed out. The pile of earth and rock removed was as high as Trajan's Column, as we know from the inscription on its base (this inscription had been a puzzle before the excavations brought the market to light)—a height of some ninety-five feet. On the terrain thus acquired, Trajan constructed a highly complex ensemble. Built before the Forum, space was left for the Forum's apse. At street level, opening on to a hemicycle, much like a Georgian crescent, was a row of shops similar to the *tabernae* (stalls) of the *insulae* (apartment houses). On the next floor were more shops, but here, the architectural pattern changed: while the street-level *mercatus* (places of business) were separated by the width of a wall, those above had only a simple pillar between them, hence there were twice as many of them. The novelty of this arrangement can be more clearly assessed if we glance at the three stories of the Colosseum, whose arches are exactly in line, one above the other. Undoubtedly, Trajan's Market, or buildings copied from it, gave the Roman architects of the Renaissance the idea of the broken rhythms which are a feature of the inner court-yards of the palaces of this period.

Above the two-storied façade was a terrace, and behind it, one of the most interesting and busiest markets the world had yet known. A system of interior stairways put its five floors of shops and warehouses into communication. The terrace of the façade opened out into a medieval street, the Via Biberatica—probably *biberatica* is a corruption of *piperatica*—pepper, or, more generic-ally, spice. The Via Biberatica was also lined with shops adorned at mid-height with stone balconies. On the fourth floor of the market, and so above the Via Biberatica, was an immense hall known as Trajan's Basilica, which some archaeologists believe was the Exchange where the current prices were fixed each day. Most probably it was here that the imperial dole of corn, oil and wine was distributed. This dole perpetuated the days when it was the custom for the *patronus* to present his clients with provisions. The warehouses of Trajan's Market were stocked with vast quantities of corn, wine and oil.

THE PALATINE OF THE CAESARS

The excavations that revealed Trajan's Market made a most valuable contribution to the history of Ancient Rome. They dispelled the idea that the Queen of Cities catered solely for the pleasures—and vices—of a corrupt people who fawned on their masters, the emperors, while these same masters trembled before the plebs and flattered them up to the hilt. Thermae, theatres, and amphitheatres were not the only buildings to be erected; the imperial administration saw to it that there was sufficient storage space for the *annona*, the city's food supplies, and tackled all the countless problems involved in keeping the machinery of this city with its population of over a million, running smoothly and efficiently.

Trajan's Market and the Imperial Fora reflect the life of the people, but the imperial palaces mirror that of the Court. Thanks to the archaeological methods of our day, our knowledge of these magnificent residences has grown increasingly exact. The long history of their discovery goes back to the first sporadic explorations on Rome's most sacred hill, the Palatine.

At the close of the tenth century A.D., the Palatine, called at this time the Palazzo Maggiore, had passed into the hands of private owners who cultivated the land, planted vineyards and grazed their flocks in the meadows. For long years, the Palatine preserved this rural aspect, indeed, Marliani had in mind the old, purely, onomatopeic etymology in mind when he wrote: 'The Palatine . . . is entirely covered with vineyards and pastures where horses, as well as cattle and sheep, crop the grass, hence we have every reason to believe that the name Palatine is derived from *belatino*—bleating.'

In Marliani's day, the many towers that had once stood on the Palatine had disappeared. Only one small church, the Church of S. Andrea, was to be seen. The Palatine was an ideal site for excavations, but unfortunately the early explorations were far from scientific; their object was simply to dig up material that could be used for building and to disengage crypts. The crypts were the vast halls of the imperial palaces, half buried in earth, and were particularly prized as they made ideal barns for the storing of hay.

The first important excavations on the Palatine go back to 1536, and were carried out on the order of Pope Paul III, who was anxious that the Via San Gregorio should be levelled and straightened out in time for the forthcoming visit of the Emperor Charles V; the antiquities that came to light were incorporated into the wall erected along the new road. A few years later, Alessandro Ronconi began to explore the family vineyard which was on the slope of the Palatine overlooking the Circus Maximus. It was during the course of these researches that, in the year 1552, Ronconi laid bare the stadium, the oblong garden in the grounds of Domitian's Palace. Pirro Ligorio, who was present, has left us a highly-detailed but somewhat fanciful map of the site, showing the ruins that were uncovered and the objects that were found.

In 1570 the torsos of some eighteen to twenty statues were dug up on this same terrain, and were promptly identified as Amazons. Another statue which resembles the Farnese Hercules also came to light, and was acquired by Cosimo de' Medici, who took it to Florence. Certain nineteenth-century archaeologists advanced a theory regarding the Amazons which has nothing whatever to support it; according to this theory, the torsos—(all traces of which have been lost—they probably vanished into the lime-kilns) —were in actual fact the Danaids that adorned the portico of the Temple of Apollo. True, Augustan poets frequently mention the Danaids of the celebrated portico, but there is absolutely nothing to substantiate the suggestion that the Amazons of Ronconi's vineyard and the Danaids were one and the same. Nevertheless, the hypothesis was generally accepted, hence many of the admirable works that treat of the Palatine contain the statement that the temple raised by Augustus to the Apollo of Actium rose on the southern summit of the hill which overlooks the Circus Maximus. Everything indicates that this was extremely improbable.

On the whole, the accounts we possess of the discoveries made from the sixteenth century to the beginning of the nineteenth, on the site of the Imperial palaces, are very unsatisfactory. Some are disappointingly laconic, others, while they give more details, are so confused that it is difficult to follow them—facts and theories are jumbled up together, and as the identifications of ruins differ from account to account, it is by no means easy to pinpoint the remains to which they refer. Ligorio, for instance, believed he had found the vestiges of the Temple of Vesta in the Ronconi vineyard; presumably, Augustus moved the Temple from the Forum to the Palatine when he became *Pontifex Maximus*. Ligorio assures us that he saw with his own eyes the remains of a circular temple, but we know that all he actually discovered were one or two fragments of rounded cornices whose date is uncertain. On the Palatine, more than on any other site in Rome, scholars gave their imaginations full scope; they scoured the ancient texts, wrung explanations out of them for the slightest find. Furthermore, while these erudite gentlemen argued with one another, they kept quiet about their own discoveries in order that they might be given full credit for them when the time came to publish them—which, alas, it never did!

In spite of all the difficulties, however, the perseverance and zeal of archaeologists led in the end to victory, and the picture we are able to form today of the Imperial Hill, or, rather, of those parts of it which have been systematically explored, is undoubtedly close to the truth.

THE FIRST EXCAVATIONS ON THE PALATINE

We possess a number of quaint accounts of the way in which excavations were carried out in the past, and from one of these we learn of the extraordinary happenings on the site of Domitian's Palace. The land, jointly owned by the Colonnas and the Municipality of Rome until the middle of the sixteenth century, passed into the hands of the Mattei, who built an enormous villa on it; at the end of the seventeenth century, the villa was bought by the Spadas, then, towards 1776, it became the property of a French cleric, the Abbé Rancoureil. At the beginning of the nineteenth century that highly eccentric Scotsman, Charles Mills, acquired the villa, which he transformed into a hideous Gothic castle. Finally, in 1856, the Villa Mills was leased by nuns of the Order of the Visitation, and remained a convent until 1906, when the land it stood on reverted to the State. The entire site then became an archaeological preserve. The terrain had, however, been partially explored by some of the previous owners; of these, none had dug to such purpose as the Abbé Rancoureil. It seems that the enthusiasm of this reverend gentleman did not exactly spring from a thirst for knowledge. What he was after, in fact, was material that could be used for building which he sold on the most advantageous terms; the statues and antiquities he unearthed were an equal source of profit. The story goes that, anxious to keep his lucrative spadework secret, the Abbé refused to allow anyone near the site; at night, he let loose a ferocious dog to keep off unwanted visitors. A certain Benedetto Mori, however, one of Piranesi's young assistants, was determined to make a sketch-map of the ruins the choleric archaeologist had laid bare, and accordingly he crept to the site as soon as it was dark, and threw succulent titbits to the dog. This went on for several weeks, at the end of which time, the animal had grown so tame that it not only wagged its tail when Mori set foot on the site but even assisted him by scratching up the soil.[7]

To the Abbé Rancoureil's explorations, we owe the Apollo Sauroctonus, now in the Vatican Museum. But we are indebted to them for far more than that, since they revealed the existence of a vast palace on the Palatine, situated between the buildings that occupied its summit and the Circus Maximus. The major part of this palace was subsequently covered in, but we know what it was like from Mori's sketches. These sketches, published by Guattani, were extremely useful when excavations on this site were resumed in 1926 by A. Bartoli, who was then Director of Antiquities of the Palatine.

At the end of the sixteenth century the Farnese laid out their famous gardens on the Cermalus. They kept a sharp look-out for antiquities while the land was being dug over, but there is little to tell us what they found. At the beginning of the eighteenth century, the Farnese Gardens passed into the possession of the Dukes of Parma, and in 1722, and again in 1728, Francis I carried out a series of methodical excavations. The Pontifical Authority had shown itself extremely reluctant to grant permission for these researches, and when it did consent it was only on condition that the Duke would pledge himself to share with the Papal Treasury the proceeds of any discovery valued at over 10,000 écus, and solemnly swear not to remove from Rome any life-size statue or any massive marble remains that he might uncover. Francis I refused to agree and stood out so stoutly that finally the Pontifical Authority was forced to surrender unconditionally. Considerable danger was involved in the excavations, and the priest-archaeologist, Monsignor Bianchini, who was in charge of the operations, met with a serious accident when he imprudently inched forward on a crumbling vault which gave way beneath his weight. The unfortunate Bianchini crashed to the ground amidst the ruins, sustaining injuries which largely accounted for his death two years later.

The particular interest that attaches to these excavations lies in the fact that they penetrated far below the Flavian level, and laid bare palaces that had been built long before Domitian's day. From the depths of the hill there emerged stories of these palaces, a labyrinth of corridors and halls which had been buried since the end of Antiquity and which still retained a considerable amount of their original decoration. A number of the plans and sketch-maps made on the site are still extant, but most of the precious marbles, the works of art, in particular the paintings, were removed. Today we can trace the course of the Duke of Parma's excavations; the exploration of the Palatine has been resumed and is still proceeding. Not the least surprise that the Sacred Hill reserves for the visitor who descends below ground is the sudden plunge into the past; the deeper he goes, the further he moves backwards in time.

THE HOUSE OF LIVIA

During the middle of the nineteenth century the Villa Farnese and its gardens were acquired from the King of Naples by Napoleon III. Napoleon, who was passionately interested in archaeology, commissioned Pietro Rosa to carry out a series of excavations. Digging began on 4 November 1861, and Rosa made it his first concern to distinguish as clearly as possible the various levels and to establish the actual terrain occupied by the various buildings. He succeeded in disengaging the upper part of the Flavian Palace, and effected a number of soundings. Good fortune awaited him; in the spring of 1869 Rosa was lucky enough to lay bare a modest-sized house whose decoration, marvellously preserved, suddenly glowed forth from the depths of time. Immediately, a determined effort was made to identify this *domus*, this private house that had come to light almost intact. It was—and still is—the only one of its kind in modern Rome.

Whose house was it? At first, on very debatable grounds, it was called The House of Germanicus. Today, because of the discovery of a fragment of lead piping on which were the letters 'IVLLAE

AVG (ustae)' archaeologists prefer to call it the House of Livia. But to which Empress does this refer? To Livia, the wife of Augustus, or to Livia, the wife of Titus? The second Livia appears to be the more probable of the two. Yet, as the style of the house is quite clearly Augustan, it is almost impossible to believe that it only dates back to the first century A.D. Moreover, other pieces of lead piping found at the same time were inscribed with the name of Domitian and that of a freedman of Pescennius Niger, who, as we know, was contemporary with Cicero. We cannot draw any hard and fast conclusions from these fragments of lead piping, and must therefore turn elsewhere to try and find out why, when the imperial palaces invaded all the land in the immediate vicinity, this modest *domus* was preserved.

The most convincing hypothesis that has been advanced is that it is the *domus Augusti*, described by Suetonius as more like the dwelling of a private citizen than the residence of an emperor, and which was originally the home of the orator Hortensius. The obvious respect with which the house was regarded during the Empire, the fact that it is situated in the midst of the palaces built in the Julio-Claudian era, the technique used in its construction: *opus quasi reticulatum* (built in the pattern of a hut) which dates back to the first half of the first century B.C., i.e. to the day of Hortensius, and finally the style of its decoration, all lend weight to the theory that the house is indeed the *domus Augusti*. In all likelihood, Pietro Rosa's excavations have restored to us the dwelling in which the founder of the Empire spent forty years of his life.

The paintings, marvellously preserved, began to deteriorate rapidly as soon as they were exposed to the air. The surface colouring has lost most of its vividness and the outlines are far from clear, and although the extremely skilful restorations carried out in the last few years have given them back some of their brilliance, we must turn to the archaeological bulletins published at the time of the discovery to form an idea of their original appearance.

The plan of the house is somewhat surprising; it bears only a faint resemblance to that of the classic Pompeiian house, still considered by a few scholars as the Roman house *par excellence*. It must be admitted that even after the excavations carried out some time ago the entire layout is not altogether clear. The house consists of two distinct parts on two levels. A flight of steps leads down to the lower level (it is this part of the house that is shown to visitors) with its four rooms opening on to a small paved inner court, the classic atrium, but this atrium serves a very different purpose from that of a Pompeiian house. It was not, as in the Pompeiian house, an ante-room immediately following the vestibule, but a kind of well that allowed the light to filter through into the windowless apartments where the marvellous paintings were discovered. In the view of archaeologists, the central room is the *tablinum*, those on either side of it, the *alae* or wings, while the fourth room is the *triclinium* (the dining-room furnished with couches). We must not, however, be deceived by these traditional terms. What we have on this level is a private apartment with a suite of salons. We do not know for what purpose each salon was intended, but no doubt the owner of the house used them for this and that as the fancy took him.

The main entrance to the house was on the upper level. Here, too, the rooms are grouped round a rectangular courtyard. From the suites allotted for special services, it would seem that we are now in the public part of the house, but it only bears a rough resemblance to the traditional plan. Originally, there was a passage on this level which ran the whole length of the *domus* and connected the apartments; one of these is decorated with paintings similar to those in the private suite, but unfortunately, they are badly damaged.

The great paintings of the lower story have been so often described, have been the subject of so many commentaries that it will be sufficient for the purposes of this book to touch on their characteristic features. The essential aim of these paintings was to dispel the deadening effect of a blank wall, to create an illusion of space. In the centre of each panel is a *trompe l'oeil* window through which a landscape can be seen. Sometimes, the landscape forms the setting of a mythological episode. In the *tablinum*, for instance, the artist has depicted the deliverance of Io by Hermes. Io (she has tiny horns on her head to remind us that she was metamorphosed into a heifer) is reclining at the foot of a mound surmounted by a column dedicated to her jealous rival, Juno; at Io's side, the hundred-eyed Argus leans on his spear as if it were a shepherd's crook, and beyond the mount, is the winged Hermes, about to spring on and slay the cruel captor of the nymph beloved of Jupiter.

On both sides of these *trompe l'oeil* windows are traces of other paintings, but only one has been preserved. This painting takes us out on to a steeply rising road and leads us to houses on whose terraces women stand gazing at a young female traveller, accompanied by her servant, who has evidently just arrived and is knocking at a door.

Through another 'window', we see an incident from the famous legend of Polyphemus and Galatea. It takes us to the seashore, where the infatuated Cyclops, led by a winged *amorino*, has come to welcome the nereid mounted on her sea-horse, and pour out his love to her.

In the *triclinium* the 'window' opens on to a landscape pure and simple: we look out on to an idyllic garden, a garden with porticoes, and the small, rustic temples that emperors and patricians loved to erect in their parks. But Augustus, faithful to his own policy, Augustus who condemned luxury, had no desire for a sumptuous palace in Rome; he scorned the magnificent residences which the great nobles, grown rich beyond dreams with the spoils of the civil war, had built for themselves, scorned those almost equally magnificent in which his very freedmen resided. No palace, no exquisite grounds; and so Augustus, with his love of nature, the love so deeply rooted in the Roman soul, had compensated himself for the groves, the flowers, the trees he had forgone by giving himself this imaginary painted garden.

Because of its date, the decoration of the House of Livia is of maximum importance. The paintings are an example of the particularly luxurious Second Pompeiian style, earlier by a century than the majority of Pompeiian paintings, which mostly belong to the Third and Fourth style. (Note that these terms do not imply a rigid chronological order.)

THE HOUSE OF THE GRIFFINS

Another house (partially disengaged in the course of the excavations carried out by the Duke of Parma in 1722, but subsequently covered in and disengaged for the second time between 1910–13) affords us an equally precious example of decorations of the Second Pompeiian style. This *domus* is clearly earlier than the House of Livia; its real name is unknown, but because of the lunette of two magnificent griffins on either side of a tuft of acanthus, it is called the House of the Griffins. It lies under the *lararium* (part of the interior of a Roman house in which tutelar Deities were placed) of Domitian's palace, and it is plain that it was severed on more than one occasion by the foundations of imperial residences. The plan of the house is difficult to visualize: we imagine that, as in the House of Livia, there was an atrium round which were grouped several richly decorated apartments. The paintings, like those of the First Pompeiian style, give the illusion of vari-coloured marble walls, but a new motif, one that is not found in the true First style, has been introduced: in the foreground the artist has painted in relief massive columns resting on stylobates with a balustrade running between them. While the surface of the actual wall is not abolished, the projection of the columns creates a spatial illusion: the wall is hollowed out, as it were, and thrown back. If there were an open window in the central panel the decoration would produce exactly the same effect as that in the House of Livia. The omission of a window, however, leads us in a curious way to the realization that the decoration of the House of the Griffins is not Roman painting in the true sense: the purpose of this *trompe l'oeil* painting was merely to imitate in relief the motifs of Hellenic art. It was not until the Second style blossomed out fully (as in the House of Livia) that painting, by unfolding landscapes through *trompe l'oeil* windows, became an autonomous art.

From the technique used in its construction, the House of the Griffins can be ascribed to the close of the second century B.C. Its richness verging on sumptuousness suggests that its owner was a noble Roman of Sulla's day, a supposition to which the descriptions by classic writers of the aristocratic character of the residences on the Palatine at this period lend weight. Cicero, Crassus and most of the notabilities of the age lived on the Sacred Hill; here, although they were only a short distance from the Forum, they were beyond the reach of the importunate plebs.

THE ISIS PAVILION

One more example of Second style decoration emerged from the sub-soil of the Palatine: the Isis Pavilion, discovered beneath the basilica of Domitian. These precious remains were revealed by the excavations of 1722, when several sketches were made of them; from these we can recompose the decoration, which has suffered greatly since it first came to light. In the central panel, as in the House of Livia, there is an open 'window' through which we can see a rustic temple and a group of figures offering up sacrifices. On either side of the window, there are similar scenes which detract from the illusion, for these landscapes are frescoes. The effect, in short, is no longer purely *trompe l'oeil*. Fanciful architectonic elements high up on the wall herald the grotesqueries of the Third and Fourth styles.

This decoration, so precious to the history of Roman art, also furnishes important evidence of the penetration of Eastern religions into the West. Not only is one entire panel devoted to an Egyptianized landscape into which have been introduced the pygmies and water-birds that so often appear in Roman decoration, but scattered here, there, and everywhere are the sacred cult objects, the symbols of Isis. On the basis of this landscape, and on that of the architectural style of the building which is ascribed to approximately the middle of the first century B.C., a hypothesis has been advanced, claiming that the pavilion was part of Caligula's Palace, and was transformed by him into a private sanctuary of Isis. If this is true, the strange scene described by Suetonius was enacted within its walls. While the conspirators, led by Cassius Chaerea, were assassinating Caligula, Claudius, his uncle, hid behind a curtain that hung from the door. One of the imperial guards, about to fall on the murderers, caught sight of his feet and dragged him out. Claudius thought his last moment had come, but the praetorian instantly recognized the brother of Germanicus and hailed him as Emperor. In this totally unexpected manner, Claudius who had never been envisaged as Caligula's successor, became the ruler of Rome.

THE IMPERIAL PALACES

After 1870 systematic excavations were carried out on the Palatine. To free the terrain, almost all the later buildings, amongst them the monstrous Villa Mills, were demolished. The archaeologists who had resumed the explorations of the past made a desperate attempt to create some sort of order out of the almost inextricable confusion which had resulted from the super-imposition of ancient buildings over those of an even earlier date. We possess very little detailed information of the discoveries made in the course of these fruitful researches, as, for one reason or another, many of the reports were never published. However, on the Sacred Hill, we can see for ourselves the main outcome of the excavations; like the Forum Romanum, the Palatine is the scene of continuous archaeological activity, and every year fresh light is thrown on the past.

The Palatine has already yielded up most of its secrets, and we can now follow the broad outlines of its history. The importance of the discovery of hut foundations on the Cermalus has already been stressed in the previous chapter. From this discovery, we gained fresh knowledge of the origins of the Urbs; we came to know of the primitive village that stood close to the site of the *domus Augusti*. We have also come to know of the vestiges of the Servian Wall in this vicinity; they were actually laid bare in 1847, but Visconti and Canina, who were directing the excavations, failed to identify them. A few years later there was a theory that the vestiges uncovered by these two archaeologists were traces of the Palatine city, of the wall raised by Romulus. This theory is quite discounted today.

Occasionally, there is a sentence or two in the account of a discovery from which we see that its importance was not always realized by the discoverer. Monsignor Bianchini, for instance, who explored the *lararium* of Domitian's Palace in 1725, expresses his disappointment that no statue, no fragment of a bas-relief, no inscription came to light, and goes on: 'Nothing was found but a conical stone terminating in a sharp point; it was some three feet high, of a darkish brown colour, and resembled a block of lava. I have no idea what became of it.' Many archaeologists regret the *insouciance* of the learned priest, for they suspect that the mysterious object was none other than the *baetyl* (sacred stone) of Cybele; at the time of Hannibal the Romans dispatched a mission with all due pomp to Pessinus in Phrygia, from whence they brought the *baetyl* to Rome. We must console ourselves with the thought that Monsignor Bianchini's conical stone may not have been the *baetyl* of Cybele. After all, the ruins, accepted for years as the remains of the famous Omphalos of Delphi, turned out to be the remains of a comparatively modern tomb.

The Palace of Tiberius still lies buried beneath what is left of the Farnese Gardens, but of all the ruins that have been disengaged on the Palatine, those of Domitian's Palace appear to us with the greatest clarity. We have already related how they were brought to light. Domitian's Palace occupied the entire summit of the Palatium. On the upper level of the imperial residence were the

ROME   Flavian Palace on the Palatine. View of the garden

ROME   Trajan's Market. Shop sites above street level

official apartments: the great basilica, the imposing State Apartment where huge audiences must have been held, the *lararium*, the Emperor's private chapel, and the immense *triclinium* that could accommodate a vast assembly of guests.

Adjoining Domitian's Palace, there is an impressive pleasure retreat composed of three successive peristyles on the same axis, two on the summit of the hill, the third carved out of its flank and overlooking the Circus Maximus. These peristyles were laid out as gardens. Several pavilions opened on to the lowest peristyle, which must have delighted the eye with its ornate fountains and basins, its statues mirrored in the limpid water, its groves, its great urns filled with flowers, its columns encrusted with polychrome precious marbles. In the second of the three peristyles there had originally been an artificial lake with a tiny island in the centre. On the island, which was reached by means of a bridge, stood a rustic temple very similar to the temples that appear in the Second style paintings in the House of Livia and the Isis Pavilion. Here, on the summit of the Imperial Hill, in the very heart of Rome, a perfect example of one of those parks described by Pliny the Younger, Domitian's contemporary, has come to light. Every detail is exact, down to the stadium, the walled garden where host and guests, reclining on litters borne by slaves, breathed in the fragrant air. This is the same stadium that Ligorio saw, uncovered for the second time.

The Palatine speaks far more clearly than words of the height of splendour and pomp the imperial régime attained. We have only to compare the modest *domus Augusti* with the colossal Palace of Domitian to see what a transformation took place between the era when the Emperor was the First Citizen and that when he became absolute master, the supreme ruler, sacrosanct within the walls of his palace, which was a city in itself. The State Apartments, the throne-room, were besieged by throngs seeking audience, and the divine person of the *Dominus* was surrounded by a protocol, a sumptuousness, a splendour derived from the east and no whit behind the Orient in magnificence.

The very stages of this evolution are discernible in the ruins on the Palatine. The *domus Augusti* was followed by the Palace of Tiberius. We know very little about this palace, apart from its contour which shows us that the space it occupied was only half that taken up by the Flavian Palace. Certain additions to the Palace of Tiberius were made by Caligula; these annexes overlook the Clivus Victoriae, the road leading from the Forum to the Palatine, and an analysis of the technique used in their construction enables us to distinguish them from buildings of a later date. The orientation of Caligula's additions appears in its full significance when we recall that, either as a result of his madness or from some instinctive anticipation of what imperial theology was to become a century later, the young Emperor commanded his subjects to adore him as the living god and linked his palace holy-of-holies to the Temple of Jupiter Capitolinus by throwing a bridge across the Velabrum. To Caligula's claim to godhead, cut short by the swords of his assassins—alas for him, the day when the emperors were openly avowed as divinities had not yet dawned—the stones bear silent witness.

When Nero acceded to power, the Cermalus alone was occupied by palaces. But the bureaucracy that had been created to deal with imperial affairs and which comprised, after the reforms of Claudius, a department that bore most of the responsibility for the administration of the provinces, had vastly increased, and it had become essential to enlarge the prince's palace. The imperial residence housed hundreds of slaves and freedmen; the Emperors relations, with their many attendants, had their own separate quarters with private and public entrances; there were countless guests and their suites, and to accommodate this vast throng more and more space was required. Accordingly, Nero decided to extend the imperial domain by building a new palace, not on the overcrowded Cermalus but on the Palatium. This new palace was the Domus Transitoria; as has already been said, it was devastated by the conflagration of A.D. 64, and its span of life was short.

In Nero's judgement, the damage done to the Domus Transitoria was beyond repair. He turned the loss of this palace to his own advantage, for it enabled him to realize a dream that had long haunted his mind. Every house on the slope of the Caelian had been rendered uninhabitable by the fire, and Nero acquired this land for his new palace. Completely original in style, it was of such magnificence that it fully deserved its name: the Golden House. Utterly unlike the traditional palace, the *Domus Aurea* outraged both the old-fashioned *bourgeoisie* and the conventional aristocracy.

We do not know what happened to the palaces on the Cermalus in the period that elapsed between the building of the Golden

House and Nero's death in June, A.D. 68, but we do know that when Vespasian became Emperor he preserved the *Domus Aurea*. It was only towards the close of the reign of Vespasian's son, Titus, that Nero's dream palace was scheduled for destruction; it was so vast that when it was demolished there was space on the area it had occupied not only for the Colosseum but for the thermae of Titus as well. When Domitian became Emperor, however, he realized the need for a new residence worthy of the imperial might, a residence vast enough to accommodate the ever-increasing number of officials who dealt with imperial affairs, and accordingly he decided to extend his domain by the inclusion of the site of the *Domus Transitoria,* and also a large area of the Palatium. Domitian was undoubtedly inspired by a political motive: the Golden House was associated in the minds of the Romans with the darkest years of Nero's reign, the years of bestiality, tyranny and madness, while the Palatine, on the contrary, was regarded as the symbol of the golden age of Augustus, the founder of the Empire. A return to the Palatine would be greeted with enthusiasm by a large majority whose good opinion was essential to the régime. Domitian foresaw that if this return were to be made, the cadre of the Court would have to be radically transformed. To the double necessity of effecting this reform and winning the goodwill of the people, the site and plan of the Flavian Palace responded perfectly.

THE UNKNOWN QUARTERS OF ROME

The Forum Romanum, the Palatine, and the entire quarter of the Valle delle Camene on the Caelian were included in the archaeological reserve, but the rest of Rome was not so well protected. Nevertheless, the work of modernizing the city which has gone on continuously has led, during the last fifty years, to the disclosure of a number of important monuments. These discoveries shattered theories that appeared to rest on the most solid foundations, and have had far-reaching consequences. The topographers of Rome found themselves faced with new problems, some of which still remain unsolved. Undreamt-of perspectives were opened up to historians, causing them to revise the old interpretations; surprise after surprise awaited them, led them into domains, some of which they had overlooked, some of which were completely fresh to them.

Three instances of these revolutionary discoveries, each of

which has its own particular significance, will serve as illustrations. We shall see what rethinking was necessitated by the revelation of the Sacred Zone in the Campus Martius, the Farnesina Villa, and above all, the temple close to the Porta Maggiore. The greatest change to take place for generations in the study of Roman antiquity was probably brought about by the discovery of this temple which Carcopino significantly calls the Pythagorian Basilica.

THE TEMPLES OF THE LARGO ARGENTINA

The first of these three discoveries was made in the heart of the Campus Martius. In the quarter of the Flavian Circus, there came unexpectedly to light a small but complete section of Republican Rome. As a matter of fact, a few vestiges of the Republican era incorporated into later buildings had already been found in this vicinity, while close to the church of S. Nicola ai Cesarini, the ruins of a small circular temple had been laid bare. In addition, the architect Antonio Sangallo had drawn attention to the presence of another rectangular temple in this same locality. These puzzling remains caused topographers to exercise all their ingenuity, and in the latest works on the subject, the writers agree that the round sanctuary is the Temple of Hercules Custos.

Towards 1914 it was proposed to modernize the entire zone lying between the Capitol and the Via Arenula. Archaeologists protested loudly and asked themselves bitterly what precious vestiges of past glory were doomed to vanish beneath the pick-axes of the demolishers, what traces of that glory might momentarily appear, only to be buried for ever beneath the new foundations.

The proposal to clear the slums was finally adopted, but the archaeologists had not protested entirely in vain. The exquisite medieval church of S. Nicola ai Cesarini whose *cortile* (an internal court surrounded by an arcade) was adorned with ancient tufa columns, was pulled down, but the archaeologist who had acted as spokesman was given authority to oversee and control the demolition work and carry out research in the Largo Argentina, the modern name of the quarter. There ensued a series of discoveries which although not entirely unexpected, exceeded all hopes.

By the end of the year the zone had been cleared and at the beginning of 1927, the bases of the columns of the circular temple were uncovered—proof that the level of the ancient city had been reached. But it was soon apparent to the archaeologists that this level belonged to a fairly late era, and by carrying the excavations deeper five other levels were distinguished, the lowest at roughly twenty-eight feet beneath the soil of the modern city. Great was the excitement when in this level the vestiges of four distinct temples were found. The discovery was of such importance that in 1928 Mussolini declared that it would be sacrilege to cover in these remains and bury them beneath the foundations of modern buildings. The zone was marked off, and further excavations established the dimensions of the temples and the area of the sacred precinct that had been surrounded in the days of Antiquity by a wall, completed towards the east at some stage of the development of the quarter, by the addition of a portico.

The mystery of the Largo Argentina has not yet been solved; needless to say, any number of theories have been advanced, but none of them is wholly satisfactory.

THE FARNESINA VILLA

The fate of the Farnesina Villa was far less happy than that of the Largo Argentina temples. It was discovered in 1879, in the grounds of the Farnesina Palace which were being cleared for the construction of a floodgate that would contain the water of the Tiber. No attempt was made to disengage the entire villa; of the half that had come to light, a large part had to be demolished, the rest was covered in

The engineers who made the discovery were dazzled by the beauty and freshness of the paintings; they felt, they said, as if they had suddenly and unexpectedly found a Roman Pompeii. The decoration of the nine rooms disengaged was almost intact; the ceilings still retained their stuccoed medallions in light relief. The medallions, depicting landscapes and other scenes, were framed with the most delicately executed motifs: candelabra, scrolls, garlands, and beings and beasts from eastern mythology, griffins, Arimaspi, Amazons whose bodies terminated in long volutes, and winged female genii that resembled the Flying Victories.

The decoration of the Farnesina Villa instantly invited comparison with that of the House of Livia, the more so because the paintings bore striking similarities to those of the *domus* on the Palatine. The garlands of leaves, characteristic of Augustan art, appeared in all of them, as did other typical decorative devices of the Augustan era, for example the division of a wall by *trompe l'oeil* columns of a portico beyond which a landscape had been touched in. A stricter analysis, however, revealed notable differences. As in the House of Livia, the surface of the wall was decorated with architectonic motifs simulating openings, but the *trompe l'oeil* intention was less affirmed, the perspective so insouciantly treated that misplaced plinths and columns destroyed the coherence. The artificiality was carried still further; instead of landscapes in relief, the 'windows' framed flatly painted candelabra and figures in hieratic poses. Here already were unmistakable signs of the Third style with its miniatures isolated in the centre of a panel, its brightly coloured seascapes executed at the cost of the architectonic motif that aimed at a spatial illusion. Taking all this into account, archaeologists formed the opinion that the decoration of the Farnesina Villa was quite clearly later than that of the House of Livia, and accordingly they ascribed it to the close of the Augustan era. Their conclusions were only provisional, however, and today, we cannot accept them without reserve.

Quite apart from the question of its date, the decoration of the Farnesina Villa, because of the subjects treated, was a revelation. On one fresco were episodes taken from an unknown story, showing a king dispensing justice, women prostrating themselves before this same king, and prisoners with bound hands being hustled towards the tribunal. Another painting was of Aphrodite seated on a throne, confronted by a youthful Eros. In a series of genre paintings, or rather what appeared at first to be genre paintings, executed in such a way as to give the illusion that they were let into the wall, the artist had depicted a newly-married pair taking their places in the bridal bed, a scene of divination, and others of curious little concerts in which a lyre-player or a young girl with a flute is accompanying a youth, evidently the singer. The stuccoed medallions were devoted to similar subjects: the offering of sacrifices to Priapus or Silenus, or offerings of floral garlands, floral crowns, and wine; a woman with two torches kindling the holocaust on a rustic altar. Not all of these themes were a new departure; several had already appeared in the monochrome frieze of the House of Livia. Moreover, the fantasies of the stuccoed reliefs had evidently been inspired by similar grotesqueries long familiar to the artist, who may have seen them in the

Golden House (the object of researches from the time of Raphael onwards) or in one of the residences discovered beneath Domitian's Palace on the Palatine. Be that as it may, the ornamentation of the Villa Farnesina was the richest, the amplest document ever to come to light. The religious character of the paintings, the preponderance of motifs from the East, particularly from Egypt, gave rise to the theory that the Villa Farnesina was unique in Roman art, and that it had been decorated, possibly built, for Cleopatra, brought to Rome in triumph by her conqueror, Julius Caesar. Here is an example of how even the most sedate and scholarly minds can be carried away on the wings of romance by a great love story!

In reality, the Egyptianizing element in the paintings is not as predominant as it was once taken to be. The deities that appear in them are not Isis and Serapis but Dionysos and Aphrodite; the winged genii, the Flying Victories, that recur again and again, belong to the Greek, as well as to the Eastern repertoire. Finally, in the sacrificial scenes, the sacrifices are made to Dionysos or to the redemptory gods, such as Priapus, or are offered close to tombs and seem to be part of the funeral rites. These paintings diffuse a strong sense of the mystical, the occult that is neither lessened nor contradicted by the genre pictures that lay such stress on the power of love. The themes of the two sets of paintings are actually concurrent: Dionysos and Aphrodite, Bacchus and Venus preside over both life and death, and just as a bough thrusting towards the light between the columns of a tomb is reclothed each year in green, so the soul, led by Eros, perpetuates its life in the sublime act of procreation, triumphing over the mortal clay. Such concepts far from being exceptional in Roman thought occur again and again in the poets of the first century B.C., and had found expression still earlier in certain Epigrams of the Greek Anthology.

The mystical poems of Catullus, the elegy of Tibullus hymning Dionysos-Serapis, and that of Propertius on the redeeming power of love correspond perfectly with the paintings of the Farnesina Villa. The recent hypothesis, founded not on the choice of subjects that appear in the decoration, but purely on architectonic criteria, attributes the Villa to the celebrated Claudia, the Lesbia of Catullus, and the sister of Clodius, the tribune so hated and despised by Cicero. This theory deserves serious consideration, for it is quite possible that this riverside residence was indeed the retreat of a great lady who lived during the last years of the Republic.

Cicero has left us a scathing account of the sister of the man he loathed. He does not spare Claudia—Claudia who surrounded herself with the young dandies of the day and loved to watch them bathe; Claudia who delighted to glide by barge along the Tiber while her joyful company raised their voices in song to the sweet notes of the lyre. No doubt the pleasures in which she and her companions indulged were such as to shock austere moralists, but the paintings, the stuccoed reliefs of the Farnesina Villa make it clear to us that these were not purely sensual orgies. As they let passion have its way, Claudia and her friends were conscious of participating in the universal law of creation, symbolized by Catullus in the union of Ariadne and Dionysos.

THE BASILICA OF THE PORTA MAGGIORE

On 23 April 1917 a monument whose ornamentation possessed certain characteristics in common with the decoration of the Farnesina Villa and led to a better understanding of it came to light by pure chance. The Rome–Naples line was then under construction, and drilling was in progress close to the Porta Maggiore, well within the Aurelian Wall, when the earth suddenly gave way and a great cavity yawned wide. The sounding that was immediately carried out revealed a ventilation shaft, or rather, a well, leading to a subterranean passage. A full-scale excavation was undertaken, and at a depth of about 130 feet, a strange edifice, deeply embedded in the earth, was found.

This curious building consisted of two distinct parts: an atrium some ten feet square led to a kind of rectangular basilica, at the furthest end of which there was an apse, similar to the apse of a Christian church. Two rows, each with three columns, divided the vaulted nave into three aisles. The first impression, that this was indeed a Christian church, was contradicted by the pagan nature of the decoration. Furthermore, as J. Carcopino has rightly pointed out, at the date when it was built 'the Christians who had just begun to rally together in Rome were so pitifully weak that they would have been quite incapable of building an edifice of such dimensions, such opulence.'

Study of the building technique and the style of decoration has shown that in all probability the basilica dates back to the first century of the Empire; its lack of finish, the fact that some of the stucco-work is only roughly touched in, suggest that after a brief period it was abandoned. The hypothesis first advanced by Fornari and developed by Carcopino, seems to fit the case; according to Carcopino, the basilica was the ephemeral creation of the Roman Senator, T. Statilius Taurus who, in A.D. 53, was sentenced to death by Claudius for a number of crimes, amongst them the crime of belief in magic.

Evidence of the belief in magic which incurred the imperial wrath, can be seen on the walls of the basilica: vigorously executed episodes from the legends to which the Pythagorians attached a religious and moral significance. Here, as in the poems of Catullus, are Ariadne and Attis; here, as in the elegies of Propertius, we find Jason and Medea, Paris and Helen, Hercules and Hesione. The symbolic interpretation of these legends will be found in Carcopino's erudite exegesis; this symbolism is complex to a degree, and as it is beyond the scope of this book to follow all its tortuous paths, it is sufficient to say that there is not a single myth that does not contain an inner meaning, which may be mystical, religious or philosophical. One or two details of the decoration of the basilica will illustrate this point.

In the atrium, there are two closely associated themes: the invincible power of love and the dionysiac delirium which is symbolized by a bacchante mounted on a panther. The synchretic basilica of the Porta Maggiore unites two religions, each springing from a different source, but which Eastern philosophy tended to bring together. The cupids playing with butterflies that appear on these walls originate in the Platonic myth that, from the time of the philosopher's *Phaedra*, had taken root in Hellenic thought, and was to be revived by Apuleius in the Cupid and Psyche of his *Metamorphoses*. In the apse of the basilica, there is a strangely compelling scene: Apollo, standing on a rock, is encouraging a maiden, urged forward by a winged cupid, to hurl herself into the sea. The tragic figure is Sappho—Sappho who leapt to death from the Leucadian Rock in order that she might be freed from earthly passion, metamorphosed and united for ever with the universal soul of love.

The basilica, as well as making it plain that mythology continued to be a living reality, that it was not merely considered as a fruitful source of inspiration for painting and poetry, proves that pagan religion was not an empty form, incapable of rousing any response. What might pass for no more than imagery in the poets, what might be taken in the Farnesina Villa as the obscene fancies of an artist catering for degenerates, is undeniably linked in this temple to a religious faith, a religious ritual. Originally, it contained an altar, a table for offerings, and in the basin of the atrium, the remains of these sacrificial offerings were found. These were mainly the bones of sucking-pigs, but there was also the skeleton of a dog, testifying to a sacrifice of consecration offered to the divinities of the sect after the inaugural ceremony.

There can be no doubt that the basilica was a consecrated building, the temple of the faithful who believed that their piety would be rewarded with divine joy in this world, with redemption and rebirth in the next. In the Roman Campagna, Goethe dreamed of the gods of Rome, yet the marble deities he saw in museums were without exception Greek. Nevertheless, because he was a poet, Goethe sensed the might of Roman paganism. The basilica of the Porta Maggiore is proof that this was not mere imagination on his part, that the gods brought to Rome from the East could still inspire hope in Western minds. A few literary texts allow us to glimpse this faith, but it is difficult to assemble them in an order that would demonstrate it more clearly. Of this faith, the basilica in its concrete reality, is an irrefutable witness—a witness we cannot ignore if we wish to break fresh ground and penetrate more deeply into ancient thought.

THE ALTAR OF PEACE

No account of the archaeology of Rome would be complete if it did not include the story of the most extraordinary discovery of all. Even though this discovery was not as important as that of the Pythagorian Basilica in the sense that it did not illuminate the spiritual life of the people, it made possible the reconstruction of one of the great monuments of the Augustan era: the *Ara Pacis*, the Altar of Peace.

We know from the ancient historians that in 13 B.C., after Augustus had brought the wars in Gaul and Spain to a victorious end, the Senate voted unanimously for the erection of an altar to Peace, and that this altar was completed and dedicated on 30 January in the year 9 B.C. The Augustan régime had reached its height, Rome was resplendent, and since she owed her glory to the Julian gens, the Altar of Peace symbolized their apotheosis and her own. But with the passing of the years the Altar of Peace dwindled in importance. After the death of Nero, the Julian dynasty was submerged for ever in the sea of blood of the civil war, and quite naturally, the emperors of other dynasties had no wish to revive the glory of their predecessors. The Altar of Peace was consigned to oblivion and finally vanished from sight; nothing was seen of it until the year 1568, when, quite by chance, remains of it came to light. These remains were exquisite reliefs found by the Perettis, the nephews of Pope Sixtus V, and attributed by them quite erroneously to an arch of Domitian. Some of these reliefs were bought, it seems, by the Grand Duke of Tuscany, who took them to Florence; the others remained in Rome, with the exception of one that travelled as far as the Louvre.

Many years later, on 7 September 1859, when the foundations of the Palazzo Fiano (which stands at the junction of the Via Lucina and the Corso Umberto built over the old Via Lata) were being consolidated, Erzoch, the architect responsible for the work, discovered beneath the palace a huge platform covered with sculptured marble fragments. With great difficulty, some of these were hauled up, and a few years later the mutilated reliefs were deposited in the National Museum of Rome.

That these reliefs were connected with those found by the Perettis some three hundred years earlier escaped notice until 1879, when the German archaeologist, Van Duhn, perceived from an analysis of the style that all these sculptures had come from one monument, and advanced the hypothesis that this monument was none other than the *Ara Pacis*. To Petersen, secretary of the German Archaeological Institute of Rome, belongs the honour of having attempted a reconstruction of the Altar of Peace, a herculean task that took him to every museum in Europe in search of possible fragments. But for his work, a work of immense erudition requiring infinite patience, excavations would not have been possible, would not even have been conceivable. On 22 November 1896, convinced that there were important remains of the *Ara Pacis* beneath the Fiano Palace and the Via Lucina, Petersen wrote to the Minister of Education, urging him to authorize the exploration of this terrain where results of maximum interest could be anticipated.

Permission was duly granted, and in 1903 a trench was opened up in the *cortile* of the Fiano Palace. Fragments of sculpture soon came to light, but before long difficulties arose. All this part of the Campus Martius whose level is scarcely above that of the Tiber, rests on layers of sand and clay permeated by water. The excavators, in order to establish the contour of the monument, were compelled to drive dark, narrow tunnels, and even so, they only succeeded in obtaining a few results before they were forced to a dead stop. The worst-supported part of the Fiano Palace lay directly over the altar, and owing to the soil subsidence, to dig down any further might well cause the entire building to collapse; its balance was already sufficiently precarious. There was no alternative; the exploration had to be abandoned.

In 1937, however, when Rome was making preparations to celebrate with unequalled splendour the second millenary of the birth of Augustus, founder of the Empire, Mussolini ordered the excavations to be resumed. The question was: how were the apparently insuperable difficulties to be overcome? Obviously, heavy pumps could not be used, since they would suck up sand as well as water, and this would endanger the Fiano Palace still more. At length, a highly ingenious solution to the problem was found: this was to refrigerate the site. From a horizontal pipe, a network of pipes ran down vertically, and into these, carbon dioxide was pumped, five tons in all, freezing the ground to a temperature of between minus 30–40 degrees centigrade. By this means, a hard dyke was formed, and the excavators were able to raise the altar.

Once this feat had been achieved, the site was meticulously searched and even the smallest fragments of marble carefully collected. When this work was completed, a plan of the monument, as exact and detailed as possible, was made. But even before all this had been done, archaeologists had been engaged in the National Museum on the reconstruction of the *Ara Pacis*. Directed by G. Moretti, who was then Curator of the Antiquities of Rome, this immense task, involving a year of unceasing effort, was completed by the target date, and the Altar of Peace was one of the principal attractions of the Augustan Exhibition of 1938. Today, the *Ara Pacis*, completely restored, stands quite close to its original site, almost, if not quite the same as it was when Augustus himself dedicated it.

The Altar of Peace with its long frieze on which we can see the procession of priests, the cortège of senators paying homage to Augustus, his family and his dynasty, the Julian gens, has risen, contrary to all expectations, from the depths of time, and with its resurrection, we relive one of the most solemn moments of Ancient Rome: the moment when the achievements of Augustus had begun to bear fruit and spread their benefits throughout the entire Empire. The *Ara Pacis* is the epitome in marble of the long years of united effort that followed the death of Caesar, the effort in which philosophers and poets played their part and which finally secured for Rome new and unshakeable foundations. To historians of art, the Altar of Peace is a document of unequalled amplitude; to historians, it is the concrete evidence of an entire era. Above all, the *Ara Pacis* is a spectacular example of what archaeology can achieve when it is provided with technical equipment commensurate with its value.

CHAPTER FIVE

The Roman Campagna: From Tibur to Ostia

FOR CENTURIES THE ROMAN CAMPAGNA, with its profusion of magnificent villas built during the Empire, its well-kept market-gardens which supplied Rome with fruit and vegetables, was the picture of prosperity. Even before the Urbs was founded, the vast expanse of the Campagna stretching from the sea to the Sabine hills boasted a population sufficiently numerous to carry out notable drainage and sewage schemes and establish flourishing towns. But when Rome's fortunes declined a change came over the Campagna; its inhabitants dwindled in number, the drainage canals were no longer maintained, the land ceased to be cultivated. Everywhere, there were pools of stagnant water, and malaria reigned triumphant over a sparse and wretched population who, in despair, raised countless temples to the goddess of fever.

Barbarian invasions, the brutal destruction of the great villas, the gradual desertion of those that had been left unscathed merely accentuated, if the truth be told, a state of affairs that had begun within the first centuries of the founding of Rome. As the Queen of Cities developed she tended to create a desert around her; not only did she destroy her own metropolis, Alba Longa, transferring its inhabitants to the quarters within her walls, but she also so devitalized cities she spared that they soon lost their importance and reverted to mere villages. By Cicero's day, several had completely disappeared: Gabii, renowned in the era of Royal Rome, was no more than a name, while others, like Lanuvium, were simply the objects of pious pilgrimages. Ever-prudent, Roman religion continued to honour those gods who had obstinately refused to remove themselves to temples within her walls. Gradually, the Roman Campagna became a land of the dead and dying, with its ruined towers, its dilapidated sanctuaries, its scattered monuments exposed to the full violence of wind and rain and the blaze of the sun. Year by year, the changing seasons buried them a little more deeply in a wilderness of sand, earth, and brambles.

THE SUBURBAN VILLAS

For a long period of time, the decay of the Roman Campagna was concealed from sight by the proliferation of magnificent villas. The fantastic wealth of the patricians poured into the countryside, and on the sites of the ancient cities, rose sumptuous palaces where the cream of Roman society enjoyed the sweets of spring and summer amidst parks and groves. The agricultural workers, most of them freedmen, who had formerly cultivated the land, had been long since driven away; armies of slaves now toiled in the fields. But from the beginning of the fifth century the princely villas were gradually abandoned, and the Campagna began to take on that melancholy air that was to enchant the eyes of romantic travellers in the days to come. A number of these palaces were transformed into strongholds; look-out towers were raised on the tombs that bordered the road; the tomb of Caecilia Metella, turned into a keep by the Caetani in the thirteenth century, is a perfect example of these fortified mausoleums.

The history of research in the Roman Campagna has been the subject of several books.[1] It is a history of superficial explorations and innumerable trifling discoveries, for the main aim of archaeologists—for many years these were not archaeologists in the true sense of the term but gifted amateurs who burned with the hope of shedding lustre on their native countryside—was to glorify ruins by associating them with illustrious names. In one of his elegies, Propertius refers to a villa belonging to Cynthia at Tibur, but he does not describe it or provide any clue to its situation. Nevertheless, this did not prevent erudite Tiburtians from asserting that it had occupied the expanse of land between Quintiololo and Ponte dell'Acquoria. The terrain was explored in 1778 and 1819; a few statues, including a muse and two satyrs that had ornamented a fountain, were found, but there was nothing whatever to suggest that this had been the site of Cynthia's Villa. The names attached to many of the innumerable villas discovered throughout the Roman Campagna are equally groundless.

Nevertheless, these explorations were not without value. In the first place, they have helped us to form a better picture of the villas which played such an important part in the lives of the Romans, and in the second, they made a notable contribution to the history of architecture which led to the revision of traditional opinions and a more accurate interpretation of documentary evidence. From these researches, it became apparent that, unlike the *palazzi* of the Renaissance, the villas were far more than magnificent country houses surrounded by parks, were, in fact, infinitely more rich and varied; they formed complex architectural ensembles in which residences and gardens were united in perfect harmony.

On the hills where the little towns of Tivoli, Frascati, and Palestrina now stand architects built up overlapping terraces supported by massive brick substructures. These terraces were laid out as gardens, amidst whose groves rose graceful towers; the grounds were adorned with *nymphae* (grottoes of the nymphs), fountains, and temples; various pavilions served as salons, *triclinia* and resting-places where host and guests might take their ease. The terraces were often bordered with porticoes, and the fortunate residents could stroll from one to another, shielded from the glare of the sun, sheltered from the rain.

The architectural elements of the villas were those of urban Rome (excavations have made us familiar with them), but in the Roman Campagna, they were handled with extreme subtlety, the aim being to ensure that every aspect of a villa commanded panoramic views of the countryside. Architects and landscape gardeners united to make the imaginary perspectives seen through the *trompe l'oeil* windows of the House of Livia a living reality, and created vistas adorned with the deocrative motifs that appeared in paintings and reliefs.

The statues in the villa gardens, instead of standing stiffly in rows as they did beneath urban colonnades, were almost invariably dispersed about the grounds in charming and appropriate groups. Bacchantes, satyrs, Silenus and his ass held their revels round the fountains; Neptune and Amphitrite and their train disported themselves on the banks of the artificial lakes. In the groves and thickets Meleager led the chase, Amazons bestrode their prancing stone steeds. Flora was enthroned in the centre of a rainbow-hued parterre where she had lavished her gifts so freely; wise Minerva presided over the green alley reserved for the master of the residence and his friends—the alley where they strolled up and down, up and down, endlessly discussing some eternal problem.

Inside the villas, the statues were arranged according to the convention that prevailed in town houses, but because they were closer to nature, an awareness of what they stood for filled the minds of men: jovial, licentious Priapus, who warded off the evil eye from the orchards, symbolized the dionysiac spirit of the earth, the hope of survival; the presence of Apollo pervaded those serene

ROME Trajan's Column. Detail of spiral decorations in marble
illustrating Trajan's victories in Dacia

ROME   Nerva's Forum. The Temple of Minerva

evenings when the soul, reconciled with death, experiences a momentary revelation of eternity. In these villas, these terraced gardens, the philosophy of Seneca and Lucretius which in other surroundings might have seemed to be mere words, hollow consolatory sophisms, took on its full significance, its profound truth.

HORACE'S VILLA: THE POET'S LEISURE HOURS

The explorations of the Roman Campagna did at least lead to a few concrete results; today we can identify this or that ruin, associate this or that landscape with a famous figure of the past. Thanks to the determination of archaeologists, the mystery that for so long shrouded the whereabouts of Horace's Villa has been dispelled, an achievement for which we are duly grateful, since we can now contemplate the surroundings of the friend of Maecaenas—the surroundings that were the main source of his inspiration.

The history of the discovery is in itself slightly mysterious, since the honour was claimed by two learned gentlemen, one a Frenchman, the Abbé Bertrand Capmartin de Chaupy, the other, an Italian, the advocate Domenico di Sanctis who lived in Tivoli. Round about 1760, antiquarian societites in Rome and the neighbouring cities had begun to take an ever-increasing interest in the past, and the members of these circles not only held forth on the Etruscans (we shall have more to say about these antiquarian societies in a later chapter) and the finds in the Campagna, but speculated endlessly on the ruins that still lay buried and might be brought to light. Furthermore, the story of a discovery was so often repeated that one of these erudite gentlemen who knew it by heart might easily have wound up by believing that he himself was the discoverer!

Be that as it may, both de Chaupy and di Sanctis affirmed that the somewhat undistinguished ruins in the valley of the Licenza, fourteen miles from Tivoli, and five from Vicoravo, were those of Horace's Sabine Farm. Their identification rested on extracts from Horace's own work; both men had co-ordinated and compared these texts as if they were demonstrating a theorem, interpolating a few *petitio principii* and advancing hypotheses that defied verification, for in archaeology, that science of so many lacunae, an obstinate desire to prove every point merely compromises the whole structure of reasoning. Nevertheless most of the actual arguments brought forward by the Abbé and the Advocate were acceptable. In the first place, the Vicoravo ruins were in the Sabine region; in the second, they were close to a spring that could very well have been the source of a river, and, as we know, Horace refers in one of his Epistles to the spring that gave rise to the Licenza. Furthermore, the mountain outlined against the horizon was undoubtedly Horace's Lucretilus; it is now called Monte Gennaro, but Anastatius mentions that the name Lucretilus was changed.

As there were other ruins in the valley, there was a good deal of scepticism to begin with, but the enthusiasm of the Abbé was so infectious that the gaps in his logic were overlooked, and artists, as well as archaeologists, wound up by agreeing that the particular remains he so stoutly defended were indeed those of the Sabine Farm. Georg Hackert, the engraver, compiled an album of Horatian landscapes imbued with the bucolic charm that was so much in vogue in pre-Romantic days. Hackert's engravings show the slopes of Mount Lucretilus and the green-mantled hills of Vicoravo, on the fringe of whose thickets cattle are peacefully grazing. Like other contemporary artists, Hackert created for Horace an artificial landscape, since but for a few rare exceptions, the eye can only perceive what it is accustomed to seeing.

R. Lanciani, writing of Horace's Villa in 1909, showed little of the enthusiasm displayed by eighteenth-century artists. 'Let it be understood', we read, 'that the excursionist expecting to see great ruins of the Farm and to feel the impression of Horace's presence . . . will be doomed to disappointment. The ruins are insignificant; the Spring of Bandusia runs almost dry, the Lucretilus is bare of its green mantle, and only the general landmarks made familiar to us by the poet can be singled out: the valley, the river, the vine-clad hills, the frowning peaks of the Gennaro massif.' Lanciani goes on to add that it is by no means certain that the ruins are those of the Sabine Farm.[2]

A few years later, in spite of Lanciani's decidedly discouraging opinion, the State decided to explore the site. A series of excavations was carried out by A. Pasqui; after his death, the campaign was resumed by G. Lugli, who published a meticulously detailed report of the results. In 1930 archaeologists of the American Academy undertook further excavations, and succeeded in disengaging still more of the ruins. This enabled the American architect, Thomas D. Price, to construct a graphic and exact—or almost exact—model of the villa that Horace had loved so dearly.[3]

It is indeed fascinating that this dwelling-place should have been brought back to life. It was not, as we can see for ourselves, altogether a farm, neither was it altogether a town house in the country, but rather a blend of the two in which urban elegance was framed in a rural setting. With its immense garden covering some 2,700 square yards, its portico, its overlapping terraces oriented north and south in order to expose the façade to the maximum amount of sunlight, the villa is choice without being luxurious; unlike the vast palaces of this period, it did not require a flock of servants to maintain it, and so managed to preserve something of the ancient simplicity.

Simplicity, in fact, was the keynote of the villa—for example, no precious marbles had been used for its mosaic paving. Its one and only luxury was its garden, in the centre of which a great basin, some twenty-seven yards long and fourteen yards wide, had been hollowed out. In the quiet of the Sabine countryside, the crypto-portico, chequered with light and shade according to the hour, was truly a perfect spot for meditation and peace—indeed, it closely resembles our imaginary picture of the pagan cloisters of the villa where the poet spent almost half of his life. True, fancy has nothing to do with fact, but when an identification cannot be established by scientific means, even an archaeologist has the right to use his imagination.

HADRIAN'S VILLA

Nearer to Tivoli, not far from the road to Rome, is another, far more imposing, but infinitely less touching ruin: the remains of Hadrian's Villa. Neglected, left to decay throughout the Medieval Age, stripped of its marble by limestone-burners, pillaged by countless marauders, only its vastness saved it from total destruction. During the fifteenth century, or possibly even earlier, the Villa became the object of 'interesting researches', and many of the treasures of art that can be seen today in the several galleries of the Vatican museum and in every museum in Europe, are the fruit of these same 'interesting' explorations. Carried out with complete disregard, they caused fearful damage, and it was not until 1724, when the looting had at last come to an end, that Count Joseph Fede acquired part of the land and turned it into the kind of park that was then in vogue. The cypresses he planted are still standing today, and are as much a part of the landscape of the

Villa as the olive-groves of Roccabruna which surround Timon's Tower.

In Count Fede's day, the Villa was shared out amongst several owners; all the land on the south was the property of the Bulgarini, who conceded the right to explore and whose name is for ever associated with the damage inflicted on the Odeon, one of the most interesting monuments that made up the ensemble of the Villa. Gradually, the land held by the various owners passed out of their hands, and shortly after 1870, almost all of it was acquired by the State. Prior to this, however, nineteenth-century antiquarians had become interested in Hadrian's Villa and had made attempts to identify the various buildings. Piranesi produced a large-scale, somewhat fanciful plan, Nibby, Gori, Canina and several other archaeologists added their contributions, but on the whole fiction and fact were so hopelessly jumbled together that little use could be made of their work. We must not judge them too harshly, however, bearing in mind that in their day most of the ruins were inaccessible; the earth that had accumulated over them was a tangle of scrub, and here and there there were even trees which had managed to thrust down their roots between the stones. We owe the partial clearance of the site to the *alumni* of the French Academy who, encouraged by Daumey, undertook the study of the architecture of the various components of Hadrian's Villa.

What a privileged field it must have been for these young architects. Conveniently assembled on the terrain were typical examples of Roman architecture; these had never been overbuilt, and consequently there were none of the difficulties, none of the uncertainties that hamper archaeologists in Rome. In themselves alone the architectonic elements of the Villa, constructed when the Empire had reached its apogee and Roman architects had developed their genius to its fullest, constituted a vast museum of the art of building. Indeed, many elements were seen for the first time, and added greatly to the sum of knowledge; but for the exploration of Hadrian's Villa, we should not have been able to form more than a fragmentary idea of the evolution of one of the most characteristic features of Roman architecture, the vault.

The fact that Hadrian himself designed the Villa and supervised its construction makes it even more precious. Hadrian, who prided himself on his architectural skill, had conceived the idea of surrounding himself with permanent memories of the wonders he had seen in the course of his travels throughout the Empire, and to this end he had brought back not only masterpieces of art but also elements of architecture. Obviously, the evocation of atmosphere had been more important to Hadrian than the assembly of a collection of replicas; had this not been the case, he would assuredly have built facsimiles of the Parthenon, the Ephesian Temple of Diana, and the Mausoleum, monuments universally admired in his day.

Thanks to the ingenuity of the Moderns who succeeded in tracing Hadrian's creations back to their original sources, the components of his Villa were identified, and are now pointed out under their correct names: the Poecile (the Painted Porch of Athens), the Lyceum, the Academy, Timon's Tower, the Canopus of Alexandria (the 'Grand Canal' of the Villa). The Canopus was then the favourite subject of Egyptianized mosaics and paintings, and it was this scene that Hadrian brought to life in his park. Amidst an exotic décor of Egyptian temples and basalt statues, he staged magnificent water-banquets on his Canopus, every whit as sumptuous as those held on the Alexandrian Canopus. Not far from 'Egypt', archeologists, alerted by a passage in the *Life of Hadrian,* discovered an even stranger landscape, an evocation of the underworld. Hadrian, initiated into the Eleusinian Mysteries and familiar with the topography of Hades which held no secrets for the devotees of Demeter, had chosen to extend the scenery of this world with that of the next. But we must not take the inferno of Tivoli too seriously, for the epitaph that Hadrian wrote for himself runs:

Animula vagula blandula hospes comesque corporis quae nunc abibis in loca pallidula rigida nudula nec ut soles dabis iocos:

> Little tender wand'ring soul
> Body's guest and comrade thou,
> To what bourne, all bare and pale,
> Wilt thou be a' faring now.
> All the merry jest and play
> Thou so lovest put away?

This villa-museum, this creation dictated by an emperor's whim, was not, in reality, as extraordinary as it has sometimes been said to be. An 'Academy' and a 'Lyceum' stood in the grounds of Cicero's villa at Tusculum, and we must remember that during this era the art of gardening consisted of blending architecture with nature, of creating a scene reminiscent of some celebrated landscape. This type of gardening invited the imagination to transfigure reality, to transform the mundane frame of routine into a quasi-theatrical décor, thus enabling it to soar to the heights on the wings of legend and poetry. Passionate lovers of the picturesque and exotic, not devoid of a certain wit, these Romans are a far cry from the ignorant, uncouth soldiers of the traditional descriptions, the ravagers and looters who, between one conquest and the next, swaggered about with all the coarseness and insolence of upstarts.

The spirit that pervades Hadrian's Villa gives the lie to this picture. Unfortunately, despite all the efforts that have been made in the past few years to disengage still more of the ensemble, the accumulation of ruins is so great that the material resurrection of the Villa is impossible. The theatres, three in all, have lost most of their seats and the ornaments that decorated their stages; the columns of the Poecile have vanished, and only the immense wall that was its backbone remains; the exquisite peristyle of the Piazza D'Oro has been stripped of its marbles and statues; the cupolas of the thermae have fallen in; the *Cento Cavalli*, the barracks of the praetorians who kept guard over the Emperor, are choked with rubble; the precious mosaics, reliefs, and paintings have either found their way to the museums or lie obliterated beneath the debris. All this destruction makes it difficult to form a true picture of Hadrian's Villa, but although we can only conjure up in imagination its grandeur and magnificence, a new beauty consoles us for its lost splendour. The great basin of the Poecile has been filled with water that mirrors the cypresses planted by Count Fede, the cloudless blue skies of high noon, the rainbow hues of evening when the sun sinks to rest behind the olive-trees of Roccabruna. These reflected landscapes, more romantic perhaps than those seen by Hadrian, imbue with a strangely poetic intimacy the memories of the past.

OSTIA

Tinged with poetry and imagery at Tivoli, archaeology regained the full might of its truth on the banks of the Tiber, only a few miles away from Hadrian's Villa. The resurrection of Ostia is worthy to rank with that of Pompeii and Herculaneum, and with that of Ancient Rome between the Capitol and the Colosseum. With the discovery of Ostia there came to light one of the most important cities of the Empire, one of the lungs of its capital, the port which assured its food supplies for several centuries, a city whose evolution from 325 B.C., the date of its foundation, up to the dawn of the fifth century A.D., kept pace with that of Rome.[4]

Yet by A.D. 537, when Vitiges and his hordes threatened the capital, Ostia had already become a desert. Sand washed down by the Tiber had silted up the harbour, and ships could no longer put in. The sparse and wretched population was ravaged by malaria and defenceless against the savagery of raiders from the sea. Before long Ostia suffered the fate of all the ancient cities that were not protected, as were Pompeii, Herculaneum, and Stabiae, by a thick shroud of ashes: it was transformed into a marble quarry. The domes of Florence, Pisa, and Orvieto were partly constructed with the marble shipped by the Florentines and Genoese from Ostia. The ruins still visible above the sand which accumulated year by year, were stripped and demolished, and their materials were either fed into the lime-kilns or utilized for the construction of some tower or fortress on the territory of the abandoned port.

At the close of the eighteenth century Ostia became the object of the usual interesting researches, the usual treasure-hunts for works of art. To Pope Pius VII belongs the honour of having initiated the first systematic excavations; the digging was done by convicts from the Civitavecchia prison. But it was not until the middle of the nineteenth century when Pius IX occupied the Papal Throne that the ancient city really began to return to light. At long last, the ruins that were disengaged were carefully protected, and wherever possible, objects were left on the site of the discovery; those that had to be removed were meticulously classified before being transported to the Vatican museum.

After 1870 Ostia was scheduled by the State as one of the most important sites of permanent excavations—excavations that were directed by such eminent archaeologists as Pietro Rosa, R. Lanciani, Borsari, Gatti, Dante Vaglieri, R. Paribeni, and Guido Calza. Calza, who only retired a few years ago, achieved brilliant results, and his name will always be associated with the resurrection of Ostia. Today we can see almost the whole of the city as it was at the height of the Empire, but the ambition of archaeologists went much further; as well as endeavouring to arrive at a picture, as exact and detailed as possible, of the imperial city, they wrestled with the teasing problem of Ostia's origins, and made every effort to trace its history step by step.

The classic historians unanimously attribute the foundation of Ostia to King Ancus Martius, in which case, Ostia would have been the first fortified outpost to be established at the mouth of the Tiber. The Moderns were more circumspect, and were inclined to believe that the original settlement did not go back beyond the middle of the fourth century B.C.; in their view, the establishment of the outpost was the direct result of the decisive defeat of the Etruscans. In the hope of elucidating the problem and cutting short the argument that had arisen between traditionalists and hypercritics, Calza carried out stratigraphical excavations which revealed below the levels of Republican and Imperial Ostia vestiges of the original city, the *castrum*, which had been surrounded by a massive wall. Calza formed the opinion that Roman occupation of the territory did not date back beyond the fourth century B.C., and thus it became clear that the ancient historians whose evidence with regard to early Rome had proved so accurate had been utterly at fault in regard to Ostia. Hence we see that the problems raised by the past cannot be lumped together and solved by the same means; each must be tackled separately in the light of particular facts.

Ostia, which had been occupied without a break and had evolved throughout six centuries, was a far more difficult proposition for archaeologists than Pompeii, Herculaneum, and Stabiae, where life had come to a full stop in A.D. 79. They were faced with the question of how much of the top level, the imperial level it would be necessary to sacrifice in order to bring to light the earlier epochs. Fortunately, they hit on happy expedients, and the informed visitor can now easily follow Ostia's evolution and can see beneath the roads of the second century A.D. the vestiges of an Augustan house replaced at a later date by some other edifice. The walls have been consolidated, and each fragment of masonry fitted into place, although, as Calza has pointed out, archaeologists did not go to the length of rebuilding an entire section in order to restore a few remains to their original position. The plan of the imperial city is visible, and some of the houses have been reconstructed, giving Ostia an extraordinary sense of reality and life. Their reconstruction, it should be said, was essential, for the rooms were not on one level as they were in the majority of Pompeiian houses, but were grouped on different floors. The balconies and alternating windows of these tall houses were characteristic features of Ostia's architectural style.

Three-quarters of Ostia are now uncovered, and we can follow the history of a Roman city from the fourth century B.C. to the era of barbarian invasions. Nowhere else in Italy is so lengthy a history, written with such clarity, to be found, a history, moreover, that illuminates the development, even the formation of the architectural style of Imperial Rome and brings out the capital's ever-increasing economic might. At Ostia, each stage of the conquest of the sea can be traced, a conquest imposed on the Latins, who accepted it, and finally realized that the life of the Empire depended upon it. At the same time we can see the changes this conquest brought about in the structure of society, in the daily lives of the people. As Ostia became a flourishing port, there emerged a middle class which, as time passed, grew more and more independent of the ancient aristocracy.

As we have said, the original Ostia was only a fortified outpost. Hemmed in by solid walls, it occupied a narrow strip roughly 217 yards long by 135 yards wide, on the left bank of the Tiber, parallel to its course, and probably some 200 yards distant from the sea. (Because of alluvial deposits, the sea has greatly receded since the days of Antiquity.) The plan of the *castrum* (fort) was rudimentary. Two straight roads, the *decumanus*, oriented east–west, and the *cardo*, oriented north–south, led to the four gates, the classic plan of the Roman camp. The wall, like the later sections of the Servian Wall, was constructed with tufa blocks, and could thus be conveniently dated. The vestiges of buildings found in the *castrum* could not, unfortunately, be identified, but a few architectonic terracotta fragments suggested that the original Ostia had had at least one extremely archaic temple of the Etruscan style. Sherds of red-figured Greek ceramic and fragments of vases from other countries were proof of the currents of trade that had flowed across the peninsula from Magna Graecia to Campania, to Etruria, and finally to Latium itself. At this period, Ostia was an advance post of Rome, and the Republic's only outlet to the sea.

Up to the fourth century, however, no use had been made of

Ostia. For hundreds of years Antium had been the only port of Latium; its prolonged struggle against Rome ended in its crushing defeat in 338 B.C. From this time on, Ostia, while it by no means claimed to have replaced its fallen rival, inherited part of its trade. In the next two centuries, as its prosperity increased, an agglomeration of new buildings spread beyond the limits of the *castrum*; traces of a few houses of the Pompeiian type have been found, at least one of which goes back to the second century B.C. Undoubtedly, merchants had already settled in the city which afforded such a convenient anchorage for ships from southern Italy and Sicily. At the beginning of the first century B.C. Sulla, who had realized Ostia's strategic value during his campaign against Marius, took steps to ensure that it was adequately fortified, and encouraged its development. Ostia was thus included in the great Syllanian plan of urbanization which led to the reorganization of Italian cities and their modernization on the lines of the great Greek capitals.

The new wall with which Sulla endowed Ostia took in a vast area of land, so vast, indeed, that even when the city had reached its apogee, it only extended beyond it at a few points. Meticulously constructed, the wall circumscribed sixty-nine hectares, an expanse thirty times as great as that occupied by the original *castrum* and far exceeding the limits of the existing city. By allowing so much space, Sulla was pursuing the policy which had been adopted in Pompeii, and in Rome at the time the Servian Wall was erected; the amplitude of the enclosure was a provision for the future, and opened up vast new possibilities for the development of Ostia.

Once the city was secure from attack, building proceeded apace, and before long, the roads running from the centre, the original *castrum*, to the periphery, were lined with houses. In the centre itself, temples multiplied, and sacred precincts were established in the quarters adjacent to the walls. Ostia's growing prosperity was reflected in the luxurious residences with their atria and peristyles that sprang up here, there and everywhere. There was plenty of space for these great homes of wealthy merchants and equally wealthy landowners who preferred to reside in the city with their retinues of attendants whilst armies of slaves cultivated their vast estates in the near-by countryside. In the new streets rows of *tabernae* displayed their wares under colonnades which protected customers from the vagaries of the weather. The aspect of the city was that of Ciceronian Rome, an aspect which cannot be seen in the capital because of the superposing of later levels, but which can be distinguished with relative ease at Ostia.

Cities aged rapidly in the first century B.C., and Sulla's 'modernized' Ostia was out of date at the end of a mere three-quarters of a century. With the advent of the Augustan era, the pattern of its urbanization, like that of Rome, was almost completely changed. During the closing years of the Republic most of the maritime trade flowed into the ports of southern Italy and Sicily. Pozzuoli was the gateway to the east, but in the not so distant future Claudius was to construct a harbour at Ostia with two long jetties and a lighthouse, and this was to cost Pozzuoli its title.

In the transformed Claudian Ostia, warehouse after warehouse was erected to store the huge amount of corn destined for the provisioning of Rome, and at last, the slow, interminable transportation of supplies by lumbering wagon between the Campagna and the capital came to an end. In one sense, the work of Claudius had only put the seal on Ostia's development, which was well under way during the reign of Tiberius. The public buildings erected in the old *castrum* date back to his day, and we know from their magnitude that by this time the population of the city had greatly increased. On the site of the old port situated on the south a temple was raised and dedicated to Rome and *Divus Augustus*. Between this temple and the Capitolium, the Temple of Jupiter, which had been in existence for a hundred years, a vast rectangular forum, calculated to please the eye, was laid out. Ostia was determined that foreign navigators when they set foot on Italian soul would not form the impression that they had landed in a barbarous country whose inhabitants were ignorant of even the elementary rules of urbanization and architecture.

Before the dawn of Christianity, in the last few years of Pagan Rome, Ostia could boast of a theatre. Like Pompey's theatre (built in 55 B.C.), it had a vast promenade, over 170 yards long by 86½ yards wide, behind it; this huge peristyle was probably laid out as a garden, but it was typical of Ostia that the promenade combined business with pleasure. On the four sides of the peristyle were offices, workshops, and *tabernae*. Already, the broad outlines of what was to become under the Antonines, the Piazza delle Corporazioni, could be seen.

At this period, too, in Ostia, as in Rome, the first public thermae made their appearance. The most notable sign of progress, however, was evinced by the *horrea*, the warehouses in which the corn for the dole was stored. The multi-storied *horrea*, erected round the four sides of a rectangular courtyard, were a characteristic feature of Ostia's architecture. The walls that faced the street were usually lined with *tabernae*; for years, shops had been put up along the walls of the basilicas and even along those of the *domus*.

While the afflux of population did not in itself constitute a problem, since there was plenty of space available, there was an urgent need for more houses, and as most of the new-comers only had modest means quite insufficient for the purchase and upkeep of a *domus*, homes of a less costly type had to be provided. The housing question was brilliantly solved by means of the *insulae*, apartment houses with medium-sized rooms; these were erected in blocks either on the four sides of an inner courtyard or along the streets.

The *insulae* of Rome are a century earlier than those in Ostia, but it was in the latter city that archaeologists saw them for the first time. We do not know from what source the idea of the *insula* was derived; some archaeologists are of the view that it was taken from Syrian models, while others believe that it was an adaptation of the tenement house of Ancient Egypt, the common lodging-house of the slaves who, 2,000 years before the birth of Christ, toiled in blood and sweat to build the pyramids.[5] Probably, the *insula* did not originate in any one source, but was the composite outcome of various converging tendencies—tendencies that may even be traced to Minoan Crete, as is suggested by the models in the museum of Heraklion of multi-storied houses whose windows open, not on to the inner courtyard, but on to the street. Now this is precisely the principal innovation of the *insulae* which differed from the *domus* not so much on account of their height (a *domus* often had several stories—the top floors were frequently let by the owners), but because of what we might call their extrovert character. The space between the blocks merely defined the four roads that constituted them, and access to the apartments was gained by flights of steps from the street.

The large-scale development of *insulae* and the almost total elimination of *domus* with *atria* and peristyles bear witness to a social and economic evolution of the utmost importance in the formation of a modern city. The *domus*, the quasi-collective home of a *familia*, with additional quarters for the freedmen and slaves, gave way to the apartment just large enough for a married couple and their children. Each set of apartments in the *insulae* built in Trajan's day consisted of three rooms: a bedroom, a lounge, and a kitchen with an adjoining latrine. Here we have already the modest flat of the urban *bourgeoisie* which after long centuries made its reappearance in our own day. This does not mean, however, that with the close of Antiquity, the *insulae* vanished from the scene. Many Italian cities, from Genoa to Calabria, remained faithful to them, and for long years, continued to build similar blocks.

The apartments of the first *insulae* contained none of the creature comforts that would allow them to qualify as homes; they merely provided shelter for the citizens during those hours of the day and night when they were not abroad on business or pleasure. At least, when they had finished working, when they left the *thermae* or the theatres, they could be certain of a roof over their heads. It is remarkable how the *insulae* multiplied in Ostia' as the number of thermae (the first of which were built during the reign of Trajan) increased. The thermae were a must for the middle classes. They were less essential to the wealthy Ostians, since each *domus* had its private baths, and, equally important, its peristyle laid out as a garden where the *familia* spent the leisure hours. The *bourgeoisie*, on the contrary, possessed no such amenities, and depended on the thermae, their 'clubs'. At the end of the day's work they would forgather in the luxurious setting of the thermae to while away the time in agreeable conversation until the dinner hour. The excavations of Ostia have fully illuminated this aspect of social life which can only be glimpsed in the urbanization of Ancient Rome and inferred from texts. In Ostia, far more clearly than in any other city, we can follow the gradual upgrading of the classes that had been underprivileged for so long; we can see how, little by little, they attained some degree of comfort, how finally they became well-to-do. These changes in the structure of society, changes that can only be deduced from the pages of the classic writers, are the warp and woof of life, the tapestry of history.

Pompeii only evokes in our minds a small Campanian pleasure-resort. Herculaneum, for many years far less known (its resurrection, of which more will be said later, only dates back to the opening years of the twentieth century), completes the picture of life in the days of Antiquity, but the history of both these cities came to an end in A.D. 79. The life of Ostia, however, continued beyond this date, and the city reached its apogee at the time of the revolutionary social and economic changes brought about under the Antonine dynasty, changes that could bring no benefit to Pompeii and Herculaneum in their winding-sheets of lava. Ostia, on the contrary, situated so close to Rome, kept pace with the capital in every stage of the evolution, hence the resurrection of this city has placed the history of Rome in a truer perspective, added depth to it, and allowed us to see it three-dimensionally.

During the second century B.C., the urban development of Ostia greatly increased. In addition to new and handsome public buildings, new blocks of *insulae* were built, and these testified to the growing desire to provide better standards of living. A real garden city was created; the apartments looked out on to an immense garden filled with flowers and trees and ornamental fountains, a solution to the problem of communal living which bears a striking similarity to the schemes of our own day. The apartments were arranged as in the old *insulae*, but they had been made far more attractive. It seems that for the first time, the planners had concentrated on providing the citizens with real homes. Undoubtedly those who benefited most from the amenities were the women who spent most of their lives indoors, unlike their menfolk who strolled for hours on end beneath the colonnades and paid daily visits to the thermae.

The graphic reconstructions in Ostia have made us familiar with these charming *insulae* with their balconies gay with flowers, their shutters painted in vivid colours, their gardens framed in lattice-work. These reconstructions may possibly lay too much stress on the modernity of ancient Roman urbanization; be that as it may, the *insulae* whose family apartments bridged the gap between the magnificent *domus* and the squalid hovels of the slaves, the dark dens at the back of the *taberna* that served as living-quarters for the owner, his wife and children, were one of the most fruitful and characteristic creations of a civilization that believed wholeheartedly in human justice.

The architectural style of Trajan's Market, unique at the time it was built, reappears in Ostia. Here we see the same rhythm of solids and voids; the vertical façades are relieved, not with the addition of elaborate stone ornaments, but with arches and arcades supported on brick pillars. This essentially utilitarian architecture with its uncluttered, almost austere lines, its massiveness, its harmonious proportions, has its own special kind of beauty—a beauty that would be marred and disguised by artificial embellishment. Only in a few of the public buildings were precious marbles used; Ostia was a glowing city of rose-red brick, that enchanting rose-red that we see in Bologna and in the French cities of the Garonne.

PRAENESTE

At the other extremity of Latium, on the hill where Palestrina, the ancient Praeneste, stands, there came to light a few years ago a monumental ensemble that had nothing whatever in common with modern industrious Ostia. Between January and June 1944 bombs dropped in a series of air-raids flattened the centre of the small medieval and baroque city, and the clearance of the wreckage revealed the ancient Roman Temple to the Goddess of Fortune. The presence of this temple was known, but exploratory digs had only disclosed a few unrelated fragments; these had been analysed in great detail by a number of writers, notably by Delbrück, whose book was published in 1909. Archaeologists had taken a particular interest in the two great mosaics that enhanced two of the annexes of the temple; one depicted a submarine landscape with fishes of every hue, the other, a huge composition, partly anecdotal, partly geographical, portrayed the entire valley of the Nile from the mouth of the river to the cataracts. These mosaics had been discovered early in the seventeenth century; the fomer was left *in situ,* but the latter was detached from the ground in 1630, and taken to Rome to be restored. It was finally brought back to Palestrina, and is now one of the treasures of the Barberini Museum. Until 1944, however, modern buildings masked the entire upper part of the temple and the three magnificent terraces of the ramp with their monumental flights of steps.

The bombing had completly devastated that quarter of Palestrina lying between the Cathedral and the Barberini Museum, but the debris had protected the ancient buildings, the presence of which had long been suspected. The archaeological authorities immediately decided to clear away the worst of the wreckage in order to ascertain the condition of the site; little by little, vestiges of the past were disclosed, and once it became clear that the terrain would furnish material for a complete study of Praeneste, the exploration became of the utmost importance. The campaign was long and arduous, extending over a period of ten years; more than 50,000 cubic yards of earth had to be removed as well as 10,000 cubic yards of rubble, the aftermath of the raids. This operation alone raised extremely tricky problems; to make matters worse, the fragmentation of the bombs had loosened the soil round the foundations of the shattered houses, and every precaution had to be taken to avoid dislodging avalanches of earth. Progress was painfully slow, as all the debris had to be carefully sifted for minute architectonic fragments that would otherwise have been lost. But year by year, the physiognomy of the temple appeared with greater precision: flights of steps, hemicycles cut into the hill, porticoes were uncovered, as well as the final stepped hemicycle which dominated the ensemble. Partial restorations had to be effected on the spot, otherwise the violent rainstorms that occur in Italy would have caused irreparable damage. These restorations gave the temple that was slowly coming to light something of its ancient aspect. It finally became certain that the sanctuary occupied a comparatively small expanse, and that it did not extend, as had been maintained, over the whole area on which Palestrina stands, hence it was possible to disengage it in all its antique splendour.

Although all the historical and geographical problems to which the temple has given rise have not yet been solved, we can follow, thanks to the excavations, the broad outlines of its evolution. Here on Latin soil is an example of an architectural style clearly inspired by Greek models, yet genuinely inventive and adapted to a cultural and religious centre that was undoubtedly Roman. The Temple of Fortuna Primigenia (according to the priests, the goddess was the first-born of Jupiter) was originally a grotto where the lots were cast. The *Antro delle Sorti* still exists, and it was here that the submarine mosaic was found. In the days of Antiquity, the water trickling from the rocky walls rippled over it making the fishes appear extraordinarily lifelike. Adjacent to the cave was a sacred precinct (the Cathedral of Palestrina stands over this site), and facing it, an archaic temple, only a few vestiges of which were found. Parallel with the cave, at the eastern extremity of the precinct, a huge, rectangular hall was uncovered. The wall nearest to the hill terminated in an apse; the floor had originally been covered with the nilotic mosaic. This hall was the lowest level of the temple. Above it, on the hill, two converging flights of steps led

ROME   Arch of Titus. Bas relief of the spoils of Jerusalem

ROME   Museo Ludovisi Boncampagni alle Terme. Sarcophagus with sculptures depicting a battle between Roman soldiers and barbarians

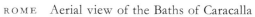

ROME   Aerial view of the Baths of Caracalla

to the three magnificent ramps: the Terrace of the Hemicycles, the Terrace of Arches with Half-Columns and the so-called Cortina Terrace, and so to the great esplanade surrounded by a portico whose immense central exedra was surmounted by a *tholos* which crowned the whole complex structure. This huge cupola dominated the southern plain and transformed the hill into a gigantic backcloth, visible for miles to travellers coming from Rome.

The disengagement of the Temple of Fortuna Primigenia is one of the most valuable contributions to our knowledge of the past made by Italian archaeologists in the last few years. In this temple, we see, as it were, the birth of Italian monumental architecture, the aim of which was to create a décor; unlike the classical temple of Greece which was a pure volume, the Roman temple formed the façade of a city square. The richness of the Syllanian Temple of Praeneste surpassed all the limits of ancient architecture, and its importance was grasped by artists of the sixteenth century; in 1546, Palladio was able to study it in its entirety, for its super-structure was not yet masked by the parasitic buildings of a later day. It is extremely probable that Ligorio was inspired by the Temple of Fortune when he designed the gardens of the Villa D'Este at Tivoli, with their tiered terraces and central loggia; here, too, the hill was treated as a 'backcloth'. Thus we can see that baroque, the style of architecture that is more profoundly Italian than any other, was originally inspired by the Syllanian Temple of Praeneste.

CITIES AND VILLAS OF THE ROMAN CAMPAGNA

Not all the enigmas of Latium, the Roman Campagna and the *castelli* that dominate it, have been solved, but the patience of archaeologists has elucidated a large number of them. Today, we have a far clearer picture of Tusculum (the modern Frascati) where Cicero built his villa. For instance, an inscription has come to light from which we learn that the inhabitants observed a strict rota when drawing water from the brook for their gardens—a humble document, yet one which brings Tusculum to life and reminds us that the custom exists to this day in the villages of Provence. It is this continuance of ancient customs that lends such a familiar aspect to the resurrected past.

By means of inscriptions, tombs and mile-posts, the highways that linked Ancient Rome to the neighbouring cities and the distant provinces have all been traced, the secondary roads linked up and the network of the great arteries radiating from the capital is now plain. The course of the aqueducts that supplied Rome with water has also been plotted—a tricky task, this, involving endless time and patience, for the channels appeared to be hopelessly confused. However, by raising the levels, by a minute examination of each channel, archaeologists and engineers finally succeeded in untangling the skein. This pioneer work shed light on a technique, that of hydraulic engineering, of which the Romans were masters. The classic writers have little to say on this subject, but in our own time a page has been added to the history of techniques, a page that is essential, for without it, the entire history of civilization would be incomplete.[6]

Researches in the extremely difficult domain of Roman building techniques were undertaken at the beginning of this century. For long years, the Romans were invariably referred to as masters of building, by those who had in mind the Cloaca Maxima, the aqueducts of the Roman Campagna and the Pont du Gard. A number of archaeologists have inventoried as completely as possible the Roman techniques of wall building, from that of putting together unequal blocks for massive walls (at one time, these blocks were called Cyclopian, too early a date having been ascribed to them) down to the different methods of facing brick walls that were employed during the Empire.[7] A comparison of these systems with those used in the construction of edifices whose date had been established enabled each stage of the evolution to be definitely fixed, and we are now in possession of means that permit us to ascribe a date to monuments whose chronology is unknown to us. Archaeologists are no longer in danger of committing gross blunders, of attributing to the fourth century B.C. a monument built in the first century B.C., of ascribing to the Augustan era an edifice erected during the reign of Constantine.

Now that we have arrived at a more exact idea of the chronology of the various monuments scattered throughout the Roman Campagna between the *castelli* and the coast, from Ostia to the Pontine Marshes, we can follow, not only the fluctuation in styles, but also the changes in customs and usages. We have seen how the country villas, few in number at the end of the second century B.C., multiplied during the first half of the following century when an ever-increasing importance was attached to intellectual pursuits, and to a leisured atmosphere conducive to study. Two centuries later, under the Antonines, as well as having become innumerable, the villas were far larger, far more complex. In the great days of the Empire the country houses of wealthy patricians were staffed by an army of servants; each villa, in fact, housed a retinue of attendants numerous enough to populate an entire village. An example of these vast residences, one that recalls Hadrian's Villa at Tivoli, is the Villa of Herod Atticus at the very gates of Rome. Palatial dwellings of this type were no longer mere summer retreats; they were focal points round which the peasants established themselves, and in the provinces, they played an important part in the stabilization of the rural population.

It was only when the might of Rome became unshakeable that the Campagna became covered with villas. In the past, many cities had flourished in Latium, but as the Republic drew to a close, they had reapidly decayed. These cities, almost forgotten at the time of the Empire, have not escaped the watchful eyes of archaeologists. Some lie buried beneath the foundations of parasitic buildings and the disengagement of their ruins gives rise to the problems encountered in Rome. A number of these sites are almost unencumbered, others are deserted and vestiges of the ancient walls are still standing on the hills—those Cyclopian walls which antiquarians of a former day loved to study. Many of these lost cities have never been explored, and this is understandable, since other researches have undoubtedly been more urgent. Nevertheless, a little more knowledge of Latin urbanization during the golden age of the Republic would be a precious asset; how much we might learn from even a few vestiges of all that vanished for ever during the bloody civil war when city after city was captured and recaptured by Sulla and Marius, who left behind them a trail of desolation and destruction.

NORBA

While the exploration of these sites is a task for the future, aerial photography has already contributed to the resurrection of the remote past. An extremely interesting aerial survey was made of the city of Norba, situated on the western slopes of the Lepini Mountains.[8] Preliminary digs had prepared the ground; sections of the wall, in particular the gates, had been disengaged, a few of the principal monuments had been identified, and those whose date had been fixed by the sherds of pottery found, were pin-pointed as landmarks. As a result of the aerial survey, we can now see in broad outlines the city of Norba as it was between the third and fourth centuries B.C.

The aerial photographs showed that Norba's wall, shaped like an irregular pentagon, enclosed a plateau bounded on the south and west by unscalable crags, sloping gently down towards the north-east. Norba possessed two distinct acropoles. On the smaller acropolis which occupied the south-west angle of the city, were two temples (not identified), the larger of which marked the ter-mination of a broad road, the *decumanus*, oriented from south-east to north-west, traversing the entire city. Both acropoles were linked to the city by a series of terraces with intercommunicating flights of steps; undoubtedly, houses had been built on these terraces. The larger acropolis dominated Norba on the north, and it was on this hill that the advance party of archaeologists had identified the remains of the Temple of Diana. South of the *decu-manus* was a zone divided into long rectangles by a series of roads parallel to each other and at right-angles to the *decumanus*. It was in this zone that the preliminary dig had uncovered the Temple of Juno Lucina which apparently formed the centre of a sacred precinct. From the aerial photographs it could be seen that a huge, oval-shaped reservoir marked the geometric centre of Norba, but none of them threw any light on the site of the forum which remains unknown.

The data is admittedly meagre, and it is impossible to follow in any kind of detail the history of the city. What remains of it cannot be earlier than the fourth century B.C., although, according to tradition, Norba was founded by the Romans in 497 B.C. in order to hold back the Volscians, who had abandoned their mountain fastnesses and were streaming down to the shores of the Tyrrhe-nian Sea. Possibly during the Samnite Wars, Norba was enlarged; possibly it then took on its definitive form and was surrounded by the wall whose vestiges have been found. Whether this was so or not, we note with interest that even at this early date care had been lavished, not only on the city's defences, but on the creation of monumental zones and perspectives that recall those of Greek cities. We can form a clear picture of Norba, with its dead straight, sharply rising roads, intersected here and there, as are the streets of medieval Italian towns, with flights of stone steps, its terraces lined with houses. An austere city, a massive stronghold that had withstood many a siege, a city that retained the imprint of its military origins—this was Norba. After the Second Punic War, the Carthaginians were interned within its walls, and it does not surprise us that, unaccustomed to such grimness, such rigours, they implored the Romans to ameliorate their lot. Their prayer was granted, and they were allowed to install themselves in the valley.

During the civil war, Norba was caputed by Sulla, and from then on, practically ceased to exist. From a few restorations that date back to the Empire, we know that the city still had a small population at this epoch, but to all intents and purposes, it was dead. Hence, we see Norba as it was in the days of its splendour, the mute witness of an age when Rome had not yet become mistress of the world, when her population had not yet massed themselves in the valley, that promised land supplied with corn, wine and oil from richer countries.

The aerial survey has shown traces of habitations on the mountains surrounding Norba, vestiges of sustaining walls that prove the existence of terraces contemporary with the first years of the city. These frowning heights were the cradle of Virgil's hardy Italian breed, dauntless warriors who formed the backbone of the legions and who quitted the ungrateful soil of their native province to become citizens of Rome, the mighty capital where life was truly sweet.

CHAPTER SIX

The Search for Herculaneum, Pompeii and Stabiae

IN THE YEAR A.D. 79, DURING the reign of Titus, Vesuvius erupted and buried three cities of Campania. The thick layer of cinders, *lapilli* and mud that covered the valley of the Sarno between the volcano and the coast, was the winding-sheet of industrious Herculaneum, situated close to Naples, of indolent Pompeii at the mouth of the Sarno, and Stabiae whose villas stretched along the seashore as far south as the peninsula of Sorrento. The commission of senators dispatched by Titus to the scene of the catastrophe, recommended that the three cities should be rebuilt. A start was even made to raise funds for this purpose, but in the end nothing was done. The devastation was on too vast a scale, and plainly the meagre results that were all that could be hoped for did not warrant a salvage operation of such colossal proportions. When the news first broke, when the heart-rending plight of the survivors became known, hurried plans to rebuild as many as possible of the shattered houses had undoubtedly been made, but later, in the stark light of the appalling facts, these schemes were abandoned. After the first shock of horror, the Empire shrugged its shoulders; after all, it had only lost a few villas, a small fishing town and a luxury pleasure resort. Some fifteen years earlier, the régime had coped with the gigantic task of rebuilding Lyons, almost wiped out by fire; no wonder that it decided unanimously: 'Never again'.

Fifteen centuries later nothing was to be seen in the stricken area but a few poor villages: Resina and Portici on the site of Herculaneum; Torre Annunziata on the site of Pompeii; Castellamare di Stabia on the site of Stabiae. Yet the ancient cities whose lives had come to a stop in the distant past, were not entirely forgotten. There was a locality near Pompeii, for instance, known as La Civita. This was a name often given to regions where vestiges of antiquities were found in abundance, but the name of *the* city, the name of Pompeii was forgotten. So thick was the layer of volcanic ash that the ploughshares and hoes never penetrated it;

even the heavy implements used in construction work were not massive enough to break through it and reveal the ruins below. At the end of the sixteenth century a channel was dug to divert the water of the Sarno in the direction of Torre Annunziata, but this barely disturbed the level of the ancient soil. The workmen turned up a few inscriptions, but these did not arouse the slightest interest.

THE FIRST EXPLORATIONS OF HERCULANEUM

We owe the discovery of Herculaneum, Pompeii, and Stabiae, not to a lucky chance, but to the antiquaries who had become convinced as they pored over the classic texts that beneath the Neapolitan soil lay ancient cities which, they told themselves with a mixture of bitterness and hope, would yield endless treasures if only anyone knew where to dig. At this time Naples was under Austrian domination, and hatred of the foreign rule, filled every mind with nostalgic thoughts of the grandeur of the past. At length, an Austrian general with the resounding name of the Prince D'Elboeuf, who had listened attentively to the erudite scholars, decided to explore the region of Portici, where fragments of antiquities were frequently found, and where, if literary evidence was to be trusted, Herculaneum had once stood. Accordingly, quite at random this military gentleman bored a number of vertical wells in the hope of bringing to light rare and precious objects. Today, the very thought of D'Elbouef's treasure hunt makes us shudder; his squad of labourers broke up every obstacle their picks and spades encountered, battered down the remains of walls, overturned the various levels and smashed to pieces any small finds that had no particular artistic or monetary worth. Fortunately, all this damage had only a limited effect, as Herculaneum was more deeply buried than either Pompeii or Stabiae. It seems that a river of mud had flowed over the city, and had eventually hardened into a stone winding-sheet which at some points was seventy–eighty feet thick.[1] Even today this shroud makes explorations extremely difficult; it was not until the twentieth century that systematic excavations became possible, and even with modern equipment, progress is painfully slow.

The Prince of D'Elboeuf bored his wells in 1719, but his activities were soon interrupted. Within a few years the Hapsburgs were ousted by the Bourbons, and in 1738 King Carlos III decided to explore the archaeological riches of his kingdom on his own account. As director, he appointed Rocco Gioacchino Alcubierre, a colonel in the Engineers. Would not the operations involve the construction of a system of underground galleries and tunnels? Very well, then, was not a colonel in the Engineers the very man for the job? Winckelmann, who watched Alcubierre at work, did not share the monarch's opinion; Alcubierre, he wrote, 'knows as much about archaeology as a shrimp about the moon!'

Alcubierre ordered deep shafts to be sunk, and by sheer luck they led to discoveries which greatly enriched the Naples Museum. His explorations disclosed the Theatre, the Villa of the Papyri and the Palaestra, traditionally called the basilica, and which Alcubierre insouciantly referred to as the Temple of Theseus or the Temple of Jupiter, as the fancy took him. The colonel's diggers were convicts (we have already spoken of the convict labour employed at Ostia), and the sole aim of his researches was to bring to light as many valuables as possible; indeed, when the Swiss engineer, Carl Weber, pointed out to him that detailed maps should be made of the ruins laid bare, Alcubierre pooh-poohed the idea, remarking that he could see no sense in such a procedure!

Nevertheless, despite all the blunders, Alcubierre's explorations aroused keen interest, and ten years after the start of his campaign, there appeared a number of monographs of varying merit on the discoveries at Herculaneum. In 1755, the newly founded Academy of Herculaneum, amongst whose members were many scholars of note, undertook the publication of a series of volumes on the antiquities of the city. These eight in-folio volumes, edited by Monsignor Bayardi, a man of remarkable erudition, are still the main work of reference for archaeologists who are attempting to put in order the accounts of the first excavations, which are in an appalling state of confusion.

The publication of these volumes aroused enormous interest in France, and did much to revive the taste for antiquities.[2] Unfortunately, this important work, valuable as it is, leaves much to be desired; it rarely gives the provenance of discoveries, and even when it does, the descriptions of the site are so vague that it is almost useless. Furthermore, the reproductions of the paintings are so poor that much of their character is lost; indeed, in some cases, it is impossible to make out what they represent; worse still, they contain many inaccuracies. The scholarly Monsignor Bayardi was

wedded to his study, and was not prepared to leave his comfort-
able chair to go crawling along the tortuous and perilous galleries
constructed by Alcubierre's convicts. In the Campagna, archaeology took its first steps blindfold.

THE FIRST EXCAVATIONS OF POMPEII

For all his blunders, at least this much goes to Alcubierre's credit:
he was responsible for the first excavations carried out at Pompeii.
The following extract from a letter he addressed to the King on
23 March 1748 tells its own story:

A few days ago, while I was inspecting the canal which carries the water
of the Polviere to the aqueduct of *La Anunciada*, I learnt from the
superintendent, Don Juan Bernardo Boschi, of a locality some two
miles from the aqueduct known as *La Civita* where several statues have
been found, as well as other vestiges of the ancient city of Estabia—
[*sic*]—and accordingly, I decided to reconnoitre this region and gather
further information. This I did, and subsequently formed the opinion
that ruins and antiquities could be brought to light far more easily than
on the present site— [i.e. Portici]. As for some time past, the exploration of these ancient ruins has disclosed nothing of importance, I am
wishful of suspending the present operations, and am extremely eager
to proceed with my men to *La Civita* in order to carry out an exploratory dig. I am equally anxious to extend the search to Gragnano,
another region in the locality.

Thus Alcubierre 'gave birth' to the excavation of Pompeii. The
colonel, however, had no idea that it was this city he and his convicts were about to disengage, in fact, the ruins were only identified for certain in 1763, fifteen years after the explorations had
begun. In this year, there came to light the inscription of T.
Suedius Clemens, the military tribune who had been charged by
Vespasian to restore to the municipality of Pompeii certain lands
that had been wrongfully acquired by private owners. As soon as
the words REI PVBLICAE POMPEIANOVM were seen, the truth was
known: Alcubierre, who had never doubted for a moment during
all these years that he was exploring Stabiae, had, in fact, been
exploring Pompeii!

But let us go back. Alcubierre was authorized by the King to
proceed to *La Civita*, and on 30 March 1748 the colonel initiated
his campaign. In April he submitted his first report:

The first object we found in the vicinity of the tower of *La Anunciada*
was a painting eleven palms wide by four and a half palms high—

[roughly nine feet by four feet] depicting great festoons of fruit and flowers, a man's head (of great size and excellently executed), a helmet, owls, other birds, and a miscellany of objects . . .

On 19 April a skeleton, that of a male, was uncovered; lying beside it were 'eighteen bronze coins and one silver coin'. Alcubierre had brought to light the first of the countless pitiful victims, overtaken by death as they fled in panic, swathed in a common winding-sheet of molten lava.

All objects found on the site, including paintings that were torn from the walls, were immediately transported to the palace, and no sooner had the booty been borne off than the trenches were filled in. Here is Winckelman's description of the procedure:

It is such that barely an inch of soil is left unturned. The main trench is pushed forward in a straight line, and as the diggers advance, the soil on either side of the trench is marked out into minute squares of six palms—[a little over five feet]—and thoroughly overturned; when a square on one side of the trench has been gone over, the soil from the square on the other side immediately opposite to it is used to fill it up; this second square is then minutely investigated, and the procedure is continued along the length of the trench. This method is used, not because it is less costly than others, but because it prevents the upper layer of earth from caving in.

One would have expected Winckelmann to protest vehemently at what was less of an archaeological research than a methodical system of pillage, but not at all—far from registering disapproval, he actually supported Alcubierre in his decision not to attempt to disengage the city, observing that 'where would be the gain, since all that would come to light of the houses crushed between huge masses of lava, would be the shattered walls? It would be foolish indeed, to undertake such an operation merely to satisfy the idle curiosity of a few . . .' Such was the verdict of the Father of Archaeology![3]

Winckelmann's indignation knew no bounds, however, when he learnt that some discovery had been irreparably ruined by Alcubierre's carelessness. One instance is that of the bronze quadriga of the Theatre of Herculaneum which suffered disaster after disaster until all that remained of it was just sufficient to re-cast a single horse. This unfortunate animal was so badly moulded that after the first shower of rain it became dropsical! The energetic colonel also tore out, one by one, from the wall into which they had been sealed, the bronze letters of a vast inscription. The letters were flung haphazardly into a basket, and dispatched to Naples—possibly Alcubierre had decided to test the I.Q. of the erudite members of the Academy of Herculaneum!

The first excavations of Pompeii were on the north, close to the Nola Gate, but Alcubierre soon undertook others at the east and west extremities of the city, in the Amphitheatre (from the year 1748 onwards, accounts of this exploration appear in the diary of the excavations)—and in the Street of the Tombs outside the Porta Ercolanese, where, in 1749, the first intact inscription was found, a 'poster' indicating the way to 'the Baths of M. Crassus Frugi. Sea-water and freshwater baths. Freedman, Januarius.[4] So, without the slightest method, the exploration of Pompeii proceeded, indeed, very often we do not know to what buildings, even to what quarters Alcubierre is referring in his reports. With the passing of time, results from the colonel's point of view grew less and less satisfactory, and his final report dated 26 September 1750 reads:

I have judged it advisable to dismiss some of the men who have been working under me at the *Anunciada*, since, for a considerable period, nothing of value has been found.

Accordingly, Alcubierre and his convicts returned to the site of Herculaneum. Pompeii had not made a sufficiently generous contribution to the royal exchequer!

THE VILLA OF THE PAPYRI

From 1750 Alcubierre worked in conjunction with Carl Weber on the site of Herculaneum, where a marvel soon came to light. A peasant digging a well near the Augustine convent uncovered an ancient paving, and hastened to tell the archaeologists of his find. This was in June 1750. The well was carried down to a depth of 950 feet and at this level the excavators penetrated into the garden of a villa which proved to be unbelievably rich in treasures.[5] Here were found the great bronzes which are the glory of the Naples Museum: the Sleeping Satyr, Hermes Resting, the Drunken Faun, but these were only a foretaste of what was to come. In the apartments of the villa were an incredible number of busts representing scholars and philosophers in the guise of Hermes. Clearly, this sumptuous villa had been the home of an intellectual; the particularly happy choice of classical sculpture (for instance, the monumental 'Female Dancers' whose Doric peplums fall in such cadenced folds, the 'Head of an Ephebe', copied from a model of the fifth century, and next to it, the 'Head of an Athlete', a very early piece of work) and its predominance over sculpture of a later date (mostly inspired by Greek art, though there were a few examples of the Lysippic style) pointed to the fact that Alcubierre and Weber had discovered a true Sanctuary of the Muses.

In November 1753 the villa revealed an even more amazing secret. A trench pushed through the square peristyle disclosed a modest hall containing a far richer treasure than sculpture, yet one that was initially a bitter disappointment to the discoverers, who expressed their feelings in much the same way as the two bald men in Aesop's Fables when they found a comb: 'The gods have been good to us, but fate is not so kind, and we've found a lump of coal, as the saying is, instead of hidden treasure!'

The hall was the library of the villa, and the wooden shelves that still lined its walls, the *armarium*, accessible on all sides, in the centre, held countless rolls of papyri. But as soon as hands were laid on them, the spindles crumbled away—time had transformed them into briquettes of coal. Most of the papyri, however, had survived the depredations of the centuries, and we can imagine what high hopes they raised; if the owner of the villa had selected his books with the same exquisite taste that he had shown in choosing his sculptures, what masterpieces of literature might not be deciphered on these miraculously discovered papyri. How to unroll them—that was the problem. After a number of disastrous attempts had been made, the Jesuit priest, Padre Biaggio, a native of Genoa, was called in. Padre Biaggio was the Latin Scribe and the curator of miniatures in the Vatican Library; he possessed a remarkable gift for copying, down to the least detail, unusual types of writing, even if the language was one with which he was unfamiliar. The King of Naples paid him thirty ducats a month (roughly £10) for his services. Padre Biaggio constructed a highly ingenious piece of apparatus: a kind of wooden cradle or frame across which threads had been stretched to form a support for the papyrus, the blank side of which was given a thin film of paste to prevent it from curling back. With infinite precautions, the slow process of unwinding it then began, and as each fraction of a millimetre came away, it was coated with goldbeater's skin lined with silk to give it more body. When a sufficient length of the *volumen* had been unwound, it was re-wound on layers of cotton. The patience and care needed for this most delicate operation can be assessed when we are told that it took at least four or five hours to unroll a finger's length.

In all, 1,800 papyri were found in the library. Many crumbled to dust when attempts were made to unroll them, many remain unrolled, but thanks to the Academy of Herculaneum, the texts of those that were unwound and deciphered were published in two series. The first series of ten volumes, *Collectio Prior*, appeared between 1793 and 1850, the second, consisting of eleven volumes, *Collectio Altera*, between 1862 and 1876.[6]

The first batch of papyri to be deciphered was a crushing disappointment, for instead of a decade missing from Livy, a lost book of Tacitus, an unknown tragedy from the pen of Theopompus, an equally unknown comedy from that of Ephorus, or Menander or Alexis, all that the gods had restored after so many centuries was the highly specialized library of an epicurean philosopher. Three-quarters of the deciphered papyri turned out to be treatises by Philodemus of Gadara, a contemporary of Cicero's, who had previously only been known as the author of a few *vers galants* and who would doubtless have been forgotten if he had not had as his patron Julius Caesar's father-in-law, L. Calpurnius Piso. There were treatises on rhetoric, music, the nature of the gods, the vices and virtues, death. On scraps of some of the papyri were extracts from Epicurus's Treatise on Nature, and passages from Metrodorus; an excerpt from a work by Chrysippus, a Stoic who had somehow strayed into the enemy's camp, was deciphered on one fragment. All these rolls were in Greek, but a number were in Latin. Unfortunately, these were in a very poor state of preservation, nevertheless, a few stanzas of an epic poem on the victorious campaign of Octavius in Egypt were deciphered, proof that the library had remained 'alive' after the death of Philodemus and that fresh *volumen* had been continually added to its shelves.

Once more, it was Winckelmann who expressed the general disappointment at the irony of fate which had restored after all these centuries works devoid of the slightest interest:

Even supposing other rolls in the Greek language were to be deciphered, as far as they can be deciphered, for they are mutilated and worn, what profit would be gained? Do we not already possess many treatises on rhetoric, and is not Aristotle's Treatise on Rhetoric more than sufficient? Do we not also possess many treatises on morality, and is not Aristotle's Treatise on the Vices and Virtues worth more to us than all the rest put together?[7]

The unrolling of still more treatises by Philodemus seemed as profitless to the Father of Archaeology as the disengaging of the crumbling walls of Pompeii, proof of how blind the most brilliant scholar can be when he deals with a subject outside his own particular sphere.

The historians of ancient philosophy, the philologers of a later day did not share Winckelmann's opinion. They pored laboriously over the mutilated papyri, and their patient endeavours bore fruit. Not only did the passages from Epicurus lead to a better understanding of Lucretius's *De Rerum Natura*, but when this poem was read in conjunction with the treatises written by Philodemus at the same date, it appeared in a new light. By comparing the work of the poet with that of the philosopher, we appreciate more fully the profundity, the originality of Lucretius; we realize the effort he must have made to free himself from the academic preoccupations and doctrinal subtleties of Greek Epicureanism which obscured its true metaphysic. Contrasted with the hair-splitting niceties of Greek Epicureans, the Roman genius shines out with striking brilliance. But this was not all that the study of the papyri yielded. Another treatise by Philodemus deciphered long after the day of Winckelmann and his contemporaries, contained fairly long excerpts from a treatise on the Poetic Art by the philosopher Neoptolemus of Parion, excerpts that make us almost certain that this treatise was the source of Horace's celebrated Epistle to the Piso Family, more generally called his *Ars Poetica*, a work that was a model for philosophical writers for generations to come, up to, and even after, Boileau. Even the smallest scrap of the past, useless though it may seem at the first glance, has its value; sooner or later, it will be fitted into place in the vast, the endless fresco on which archaeologists, philologers and historians are working incessantly in the closest possible collaboration.

THE EPICUREAN CIRCLE OF THE CAMPAGNA: THE SHADE OF VIRGIL

The discovery of the Villa of the Papyri, undoubtedly one of the most luxurious villas of an age of luxury, immediately raised the question: who was its owner? The preponderance of treatises by Philodemus suggested to Winckelmann and others that it was probably the philosopher himself. This, however, is very unlikely; a Greek philosopher, a dependent of Piso, would not have been in a position to surround himself with such a galaxy of treasures. Only a patrician of enormous wealth could have assembled so fabulous a collection, and the hypothesis favoured by the majority is that he was none other than Piso himself. While it must be borne in mind that countless rich Romans practised Epicureanism, the papyri lend weight to the theory; the names of Virgil, Plotius Tucca, L. Varius Rufus, Quintilius Varus and Horace have been deciphered on them, names that evoke the Epicurean circle formed round Philodemus and his fellow philosopher, Siron. Maecenas was the patron of this circle, and Virgil was amongst its members at the period when he lived in Naples.

We can imagine the long, fruitful conversations that went on in the garden of the villa and in the shady groves of Pausillipus where Siron lived. At this period, 30 B.C., Piso the Consul (he had become consul in 58 B.C.), Cicero's adversary, had been dead for some thirty years. Piso, if we are to believe Cicero, was anything but an aesthete; his taste was for sensual pleasures, and night after night, he held high carousal with the little Greeks, tippling the wine bought by the barrelful from the near-by tavern, from dusk till dawn when the crowing of the cocks convinced him that the soul of his grandfather, a Gaul—*Gallus*, a cock—from Piacenza, had returned to the land of the living. It is extremely hard to picture this Piso surrounding himself at Herculaneum with such exquisitely chosen treasures, but assuming that he had been the owner of the villa, it would have passed on his death to his sons. Ninety years later, when the Epicurean circle of the Campagna had been broken up (Virgil died in A.D. 19 and Horace seems to have detached himself from the group shortly after A.D. 30), Vesuvius erupted and engulfed the villa in a sea of molten lava. Philodemus must have been the link between the two generations: that of Piso the Consul and Cicero and that of Virgil and Piso's sons. The memory of all these great men must have been deeply reverenced by the people of Herculaneum and the surrounding country; the scene of their reunions must indeed have been a hallowed spot, and it was precisely here that Alcubierre, Weber and their team of convicts had forced their way in without so much as a by your leave.

Admittedly, fancy plays a larger part than fact in this picture, but to reconstruct the past in this way, provided we remember that the construction is only provisional, subject to revision—is a stimulating exercise, and to use one's imagination is no crime.

THE EXCAVATIONS OF POMPEII: THE HEROIC AGE

In 1754 a treasure found by chance at Torre Annunziata led to a renewal of interest in the site, and excavations were resumed at three different points: on the south of *La Citta*, in the Amphitheatre, and in the so-called Villa of Cicero outside the Porta Ercolano. Nine years later, as we have said, the ruins were identified as those of Pompeii. From this time forward, the explorations went on without a break. The houses disengaged were no longer covered in, and gradually, entire streets and quarters were laid bare.

For many years, the exploration of Pompeii proceeded in a somewhat haphazard manner under the remote control of the Academy of Herculaneum (which, at a later date, was to become the *Accademia delle Scienzi e delle Belle Arti* of Naples). The political upheavals in the Kingdom of Naples slowed or accelerated the work. When the French were in power, it was given fresh impetus by Joseph Buonaparte and Murat who were passionately interested in Pompeii; in Murat's day, the squads were greatly reinforced, and at one time, as many as seven hundred sappers were employed on the immense site. The diary of the excavations frequently mentions a visit by the King or the Queen; on some occasions, they were merely interested spectators, on others, they would issue directions. At the time of the Parthenopian Republic, General Championnet immediately took steps to ensure that the director of the explorations, La Vega, who had been appointed to this post after the death of Alcubierre in 1780, should remain in charge. As a mark of gratitide to the general, a villa disengaged close to the basilica in 1799 was called the Villa Championnet.

Throughout this period, efforts were mainly concentrated on disengaging the Forum, a task that was completed in 1813. Concurrently, research had been carried on at several other points— the Street of the Tombs, the Amphitheatre, etc. From the diary, we learn the number of men employed on the different sites; this

ROME The Via Appia

THE ROMAN CAMPAGNA   Horace's villa

TIVOLI   Hadrian's villa

figure varied according to the amount of work to be done, and at times there was a labour force of over six hundred, and as many as twenty wagons were used to cart away the rubble.

At the beginning of the summer of 1815 the French crisis brought work to a complete standstill, and reading between the lines of the diary, we can appreciate with what difficulties the engineers in charge of the site were faced. So great was the risk of pillage that at one moment an urgent SOS was sent to war veterans, asking them to volunteer as guards. When the excavations were resumed in August, it was with a greatly reduced labour force; it numbered no more than forty, and instead of twenty wagons, there were three at most. This explains why it took so long to disengage the Forum. While this work was still going on, however, a new method of research was introduced, one in keeping with the advances made by archaeology. The man responsible for it realized that the disengagement of a villa here, a monument there was useless, that the true aim of the excavations was to reveal the city in its entirety, trace its roads, gain all possible knowledge of the conditions that had governed it, learn what had been the daily life of its inhabitants—in short, to reveal to the world a human panorama.

FIORELLI AT POMPEII

Many years were to elapse before the new system was perfected. In 1860 the Kingdom of Naples was incorporated into United Italy, and shortly afterwards, Giuseppe Fiorelli was appointed Director of the Pompeiian excavations. Fiorelli immediately asked for maps, only to find that the only maps that existed dated back to the last century and after a hundred years of exploration, were naturally quite useless. A large number of villas dotted about here and there had been disengaged, as had the Forum, the Theatre, and the Temple of Isis, but these were only a few separate islands. Fiorelli racked his brains, and finally worked out a system for the methodical disengagement of the city. He roundly denounced the errors of the past, trounced his predecessors for their inability to carry the exploration to its logical conclusion, and pointed out that the chaos was such that it was impossible to identify with any certainty the sites where discoveries were made. He then laid down three cardinal rules for the disengagement of a city:

1. First and foremost, the line of the walls must be traced, and the gates identified;
2. The work must be carried out systematically. One site must be completely cleared before proceeding to the next; and
3. At the same time as the roads are being cleared, the water-conduits and drainage canals must also be cleared and cleaned up.

How many pictures had been irretrievably ruined by the heavy spring and autumn rains in Campania; how many hours had been wasted by dumping rubble into temporarily abandoned trenches, and by clearing it out when work on them was resumed. Above all, how wise Fiorelli had been when he laid down that it was essential to determine the topography of a site and establish fixed landmarks. For—and this was the great technical lesson archaeologists learnt from Pompeii—an exploration may at the start be clearly visualized, 'possessed', as it were, by a man who is on the site hour after hour, but after a few weeks, details become blurred, mistakes creep in, and recourse must be made to the day-to-day diary of the excavation which must be meticulously kept: the depth at which each find was made, the exact position of the find in relation to fixed landmarks, etc. After a few years, one archaeologist is replaced by another; the records alone are permanent, and when the vast site of a city is being explored failure to keep these records scrupulously will inevitably lead to chaos. The diary of the excavations carried out by Fiorelli's predecessors were deplorable, and he undertook the vast task of editing it; the lacunae in the two precious volumes he produced are proof of the difficulties he had to overcome.

Fiorelli devised a coherent plan of action for the future excavations. Once he had determined the circumference of the walls and identified the gates where the main roads terminated, he numbered each gate and divided the city into nine regions to follow the lines of the main roads. Each region was subdivided into numbered blocks, each block into numbered buildings. (At a later date, a similar plan was adopted for the excavation of Ostia.) At this time, only the western sector of Pompeii had been fairly well cleared; Regions VI, VII, and VIII were in this sector and conformed with certainty to the line of the main roads. On the other hand, Regions I, II, and III, as well as Region IV and Region IX on the east and in the centre of the city, had to be modified later. These modifications were comparatively slight, however, and Fiorelli's topography is still the basis of works of reference and guide-books.

The names given to villas and streets before Fiorelli's day have become traditional. Most of them are purely fanciful—the Street of the Tombs, for example. One of the most beautiful of the villas owes its name to an error; exactly opposite it, there came to light the tomb of a certain M. Arrius Diomedes, a freedman, and although this same freedman had absolutely no connexion with the exquisite house, it was nevertheless called the Villa of Diomedes.[8]

In another quarter of Pompeii stands the House of the Surgeon where a complete set of surgical instruments was discovered (they are now thought to be those of a veterinary surgeon). The House of Sallust derives its name from the electioneering 'poster' on its façade which asks citizens to vote for Gaius Sallustius, and has no link whatsoever with the historian. Some villas were named after the sculptures that adorned them: the House of the Faun, the House of the Little Bronze Bull; or after some striking architural feature: the House of the Coloured Capitals. Others were given the names of celebrities who had visited the site: the House of Joseph II (the royal visit took place in 1769); still others were given names that commemorated events that had occurred at the time of their disengagement: the House of the Silver Wedding, commemorating the twenty-fifth wedding anniversary of the King and Queen of Italy, celebrated in 1893; the House of the Centenary which marks the eighteenth centenary of the eruption of Vesuvius.

In the early days of the excavations when conditions were chaotic, it was extremely difficult to fix the identity of the isolated houses that were disengaged, hence archaeologists had hit on the expedient of giving them fanciful names. One or two of these were descriptive: the House of the Crypto-porticus, the House of Homer, so called because of its celebrated paintings of scenes from the Odyssey. With the passing of time, however, such appellations became rarer and rarer, and for the past fifty years at least villas have been given names that are authentic. We owe this great step forward to the work of Matteo della Corte, one of the greatest Pompeiian epigraphers, whose erudition and patience led to the identification of the owners of many of the villas.

LIFE IN POMPEII: THE FIRST GLIMPSES

To whom did the exquisite houses belong? This was one of the trickiest problems raised by the city, and prior to the work of Della Corte it had remained almost insoluble; amongst the crumbling walls, the skeletons of the inhabitants overtaken by death heaped up everywhere, how was it possible to find an answer to the question? In the early days it was not considered to be of any importance; as Winckelmann might have remarked, even if it *were* possible to answer it, what useful purpose would it serve?

Nevertheless, the problem was in the nature of a challenge, and before long archaeologists realized that even though it might appear to be sheer idle curiosity, mere waste of time, it was well worth taking up. This opinion was first voiced by Fiorelli; the discovery of rings engraved with names in a number of villas had brought him round to this view. Two of these rings used for sealing letters and legal documents, engraved with the names Aulus Vettius Restitutus and Aulus Vettius Conviva, identified the owners of one of the loveliest villas, disengaged between 1894–5, and restored down to the last detail. The celebrated House of the Vettii is the pride of Pompeiian guides and the source of endless amazement to visitors.

True, we do not know who the Vettii were, but the signet ring tells us that Conviva was an *Augustalis*, a member of the confraternity that upheld the cult of the Emperor. Now, the *Augustales* were mainly recruited amongst the freedmen, and we have no reason to believe that Conviva was an exception. In fact, the names of Conviva and Restitutus are most likely those of slaves who, when freed, retained them as surnames. Be that as it may, the Vettii were undoubtedly extremely wealthy, highly respected citizens; amongst the surviving archives of the banker Caecilius is a contract signed by Conviva on his behalf, proof that he was one of the notables of the city and qualified to act as guarantor. Various indications led Della Corte to believe that the Vettii derived their fortune from the wine and oil trade, the mainstay of the economic life of Campania. These two freedmen freed in turn a number of slaves whose names appear in various documents. In many respects, the Vettii resemble Petronius's Trimalchio, the freedman who, grown fabulously rich, became the owner of a sumptuous villa and a vast estate. The identification of Conviva and Restitutus has afforded us valuable evidence of the social and economic life of Pompeii in A.D. 79.

As only a few signet rings came to light, some other means of identification had to be found, and Della Corte conceived the brilliant idea that the solution to the problem was contained in the electioneering posters. We know that when the municipal elections were approaching (Pompeii was administered by two *aediles* and two *duumvirs*) the entire population caught the election fever, and each citizen did his utmost to persuade his neighbour that the candidate he favoured was the best man for the post. The names of the distinguished supporters of each nominee were painted on the façades of houses, a favourite vote-catching device. Della Corte proved that these 'posters' were not stuck up haphazardly. The electoral agent only called at houses where he knew he would find backing for his man, and it was on the façades of these houses alone that he painted his cunning affiche which made it appear that the owners were canvassing actively for him. Thus if we read:

C. GAVIVM RVFVM II VIR9um) O(ro) V(os) F(aviatis) VTILEM R(ei) PVBLI(cae) VESIONIVS PRIMVS ROSGAT.

which, translated, means that 'Vesonius Primus asks the electors to elect C. Gavius to the post of *duumvir*' and assures them that 'he will serve the city well', we know that Vesonius Primus was the owner of the villa.[9]

Thanks to Della Corte's ingenious discovery, a large number of villas were correctly named. Moreover, through advertisements, it became possible to ascertain to what use various buildings had been put. For example, if we see on a façade the words *Muliones rogant* (the muleteers ask you . . .), we know we are standing in front of a muleteers' 'rank'. Of course, the advertisement may equally well have been painted on the façade of the house where the president of the muleteers' corporation resided, but a simple examination of the building will clear up this little problem.

As the identifications increased in number, the inhabitants of the city took on life and substance. Let us take a look at them. There are the *pomarii*, the fruit-sellers, who met at the house of Helvidius Vestalis; there are the *aliarii* (also spelt *alearii*), the dice-throwers, who foregathered in this tavern—their bets scratched on the walls are still legible; over yonder is the 'Gold-smiths' College' whose members held their assemblies in the tavern adjoining the House of the Two Coelii. We know a little of the history of the Two Coeili. They were related to the Roman general of that name who, in 99 B.C., covered himself with glory in Spain when he captured Clunia. Now the emblem of Clunia was a boar, and this boar, which appears on the coins minted by the victorious general, is also to be seen in the House of the Two Coelii. In the adjoining apartment there is a mosaic of a fortified city; no doubt Clunia, with its gates and towers. Plainly, the Two Coelii had been proud of their distinguished ancestor and had kept his memory green. Many other owners of villas had honoured their forebears, perpetuated their family traditions or expressed their personal foibles in various mosaics, and this did not escape the notice of the ever-alert epigraphers.

Before Della Corte's day, however, countless inscriptions painted on the façades, innumerable *graffiti* scratched hurriedly on the walls, were effaced for ever. In 1871, after one hundred and twenty-three years of research, Pompeiian epigraphy could only boast 3,329 inscriptions. Thirty years later, thanks to Fiorelli and his successors, Michele Ruggiero (who directed the excavations from 1875 to 1893), Giulio de Petra and Sogliano, the number had more than doubled. Since then, a further 3,000 inscriptions have come to light, for in modern explorations nothing escapes the watchful eye of archaeologists. Nowadays, an expert epigrapher is permanently on the site, ready to take 'squeezes' of even the smallest inscriptions that are found; to photograph and transcribe them. Thus, even should the façades on which they are written crumble to dust, even should the rains wash them away, we would still have permanent records of them and the loss would not be total.

THE AGE OF RESTORATIONS

The aim of Fiorelli's systematic excavations was to arrive as soon as possible at a general view of the city, but the amount of work involved could not be completed in his lifetime, and even today, about two-fifths of Pompeii are still buried. In 1872 Fiorelli reckoned that it would not take more than sixty years to clear the whole site; the present director, Professor Amadeo Maiuri, how-ever, calculates that another century is needed. If the pace of the explorations has slowed down, this is not because less interest is shown in them but because research is carried out far more meticulously than in the past, and naturally this acts as a brake. The care lavished on inscriptions, the pains taken to protect each new find, however small, the precautions that must be observed to avoid damage—all these measures are given precedence over speed.

From the time of Fiorelli, a new spirit prevailed in Pompeii. The excavations were no longer carried on in the hope of enriching the museum of Naples with statues, statuettes, paintings, furniture, utensils, objects calculated to arouse the enthusiasm of antiquaries and provoke endless dissertations amongst the erudite. Soon, Pompeii ceased to resemble a sacked city, for the principal aim of M. Ruggiero and G. de Petra was to restore its ancient aspect. The buildings were re-roofed, the walls consolidated, columns re-erected; paintings were no longer detached from the walls, furniture was repaired and put back exactly where it had been found. When we enter one of these restored villas we get the eerie impression that the centuries have rolled away, that the life of the city has only just come to a stop. The feeling is so strong that we wonder at times whether the restorers did not go too far and create a false image. When we visit the House of the Vettii, for example, so crammed with statuettes, fountains and knick-knacks that it puts us in mind of a late nineteenth-century drawing-room, we cannot help remembering a little uneasily that it was precisely at this period—between 1894 and 1895—that it was disengaged and restored.

There is eternal war between archaeologists and architects, for while the aim of the former is to preserve objects *in situ*, that of the latter is to restore a building to its original shape, and accordingly they regard the objects treasured by archaeologists as part of the debris. All the more credit is due, therefore, to De Ruggiero, de Petra's mentor, for though he was himself an architect, he invariably showed moderation and good sense. Both were in evidence when he restored the House of the Silver Wedding in 1892; after setting up the framework with absolute exactitude, he proceeded to give a practical demonstration of the difficulties involved in the construction of a large *tetrastyle atrium* (in this case it was fifty-seven feet by thirty-eight feet) which opens into the roof and is supported by four columns, one at each corner. (There were three styles of atria: (*a*) those supported on beams, known as the Tuscan atrium; (*b*) the Tetrastyle atrium supported on four columns; (*c*) the Corinthian atrium supported on six columns. They had an opening in the roof to let in the light and a system of gutters to carry off the rainwater into the central ornamental pool.) De Ruggiero's successful reconstruction brought out a detail of everyday life in Pompeii for which we would seek in vain in erudite books: plainly the interior colonnades of the houses had been furnished with curtains, for without their protection, the inhabitants would have found the heat and glare intolerable.

Inspired by Ruggiero, de Petra reconstructed the atria and peristyles of the House of the Vettii and the House of Lucretius Fronto. Subsequently, a number of other villas were brilliantly restored, amongst them the exquisite House of the Golden Cupids, to which the finishing touches were put in 1902.

We owe to de Petra a particularly happy idea that has done much to bring Pompeii back to life. Behind the apartments centred round the atria there were almost invariably peristyles laid out as gardens. If, said de Petra, it were possible to find out what flowers, shrubs and trees once grew in these gardens, they could be brought back to life. Accordingly, horizontal trenches were dug, and instead of removing all the earth at once, each layer was carefully inspected, every detail was noted down: the presence of carbonized roots, the consistence and colour of the soil, the traces left by garden ornaments, fountains, statues, reliefs, masks, etc. The vegetable tissues were subjected to a chemical analysis which revealed to what plants they had belonged, and after this long, slow work had been completed, the search went on until the marks of trellis-posts, pergolas and the thin wooden supports for the climbing plants that arched over into a green arbour, were located. Finally, after a minute study of the gardens appearing in frescoes whose date was roughly A.D. 79, the gardens of Pompeii, faithful in every detail, were re-created with all their pristine beauty.[10]

This side of de Petra's work was not the subject of regular reports, but we can see the results for ourselves. Peristyles such as that of the House of the Golden Cupids and the House of the Vettii, as well as the immense garden of the House of Loreius Tiburtinus (disengaged at a much later date and now in process of being restored) give an exact idea of the setting in which the inhabitants of Pompeii spent their daily lives.

THE GREEKS IN POMPEII

For years, dazzled by the marvel of the city they had brought to light after so many centuries, archaeologists seem to have given no thought to the history of Pompeii, a history that had covered many pages before it came to a tragic end in A.D. 79. They studied the Pompeiian house, they studied Pompeiian décor and Pompeiian life, but it does not appear to have occurred to them that this was not enough. All that they were searching for, in fact, was more light on the Last Days of Pompeii. It was not until the end of the nineteenth century that they were infused with a new spirit; they perceived at last that Pompeii, brutally wiped out in a few hours, had had a past, a character which distinguished it from other cities—from Rome, Naples, Lyons.

The realization slowly dawned—only dimly, it must be admitted—that what was true of Pompeii could not have been true in any other province or at any other time. The Pompeiian house, so long accepted as the perfect example of the classic house, could not, in fact, have resembled the majority of Roman houses, since the characteristic features of its architecture and ornamentation derived from local traditions. It had long been common knowledge that Andalusian houses were quite unlike Castilian houses, even though Andalusia and Castile were both provinces in Spain; why, then, had it been assumed that the 'Latin house' and the 'Pompeiian house' were identical? Only ignorance can account for it—it must be remembered that this was before the disengagement of Ostia.

Today, thanks to the discoveries in Rome, and above all, to those in Ostia, we are far better informed. Fifty years ago, however, Italian archaeology was scarcely out of its infancy, and it was impossible to foresee its magnificent development, the successes it was to achieve. We know now that the multiplication of terms of comparison is no substitute for the study of a site, and the study of the site of Pompeii had not been inspired by the desire to go back beyond the days of the Flavian dynasty when the city was in full flower.

The idea that the history of Pompeii could and should be traced back to its beginnings was obviously suggested by the advance made by archaeology in Greece and the East where it had afforded many celebrated instances of the fact that a site cannot be said to have been 'read' unless it has been excavated at depth. In 1899, a few soundings into the subsoil of Pompeii were carried out in the Triangular Forum, on the site of one of the city's earliest monuments, a temple in the Doric style, by the German archaeologist von Duhn and the architect Jacobi; the following year, the excavations were resumed by A. Sogliano. But the results obtained by the new method were slender, and the mystery of the origins of the city remained as baffling as ever.

Nevertheless, one important fact emerged. Decorative elements similar to those from the Greek colony of Cumae had been found round the temple, proof that at one stage in its pre-Roman history, Pompeii had come under Greek influence. The temple with its flattened capitals, its columns set closer together than those of the classic Doric style, indicated that this Greek phase had occurred in the sixth century B.C.

For several years, the work of restoration was given priority at Pompeii, and only a few stratigraphical excavations were carried out in the hope of solving two problems that had led to great controversy in the archaeological world: how had the scene changes been operated in the Great Theatre, had or had not the basilica of the Forum been roofed in? No decisive results were obtained, and the arguments went on.

In 1907 and 1911 trenches pushed beyond the walls uncovered two pre-Roman necropoles. The Samnite graves were virtually the first irrefutable proof of a long chapter in the history of Pompeii, a chapter that had begun at the close of the fifth century B.C., when the Samnites swooped down from the Apennines and captured the city, and which had not ended until 80 B.C., when a Roman colony was installed there after the Social War.

Just as the broad outlines of Pompeii's history had begun to appear, an unexpected problem suddenly arose: in a modest house in Region VI there came to light a column which plainly bore the imprint of the Etruscans, and instantly war broke out. Pro-Etruscan archaeologists felt quite justified in claiming that their favourite people had exercised a decisive influence on Pompeii, and on the strength of this one column, highly ingenious theories were advanced in the attempt to demonstrate that the rectangular grid plan, visible almost throughout Pompeii, had been imposed from without by the Etruscans; to support these theories, they cited the ancient Etruscan city of Marzabotto, near Bologna, also built on the rectangular grid. In addition, they drew attention to the testimony of the classic historians; Pliny the Elder, for instance, writing of the peoples who had conquered the Campagna before it was finally conquered by the Campanians themselves, mentions the Oscans, the Greeks, the Umbrians and the Etruscans.[11] The debate was of major importance; the question that had to be answered was: had the Greek influence discernible in Pompeii (the Doric Temple in the Triangular Forum) emanated directly from the Greek colonies which, beginning with Cumae, had been established all along the Campanian coast, or had it made itself felt indirectly through the Etruscans who had brought to Italy the forms of culture and art that they had acquired from Eastern Hellenism? The entire concept of the cultural relations that had existed between the peoples of pre-Roman history depended upon the answer.

In 1926, in the hope of contributing some material argument to the controversy which, for the most part, consisted of opposing theory to theory, Professor Maiuri, who, since 1924, has been director of the Pompeiian researches, undertook a series of excavations into the subsoil of the northern sector of the city, aimed in the first place at disengaging that sector of the wall between the Porta Ercolano and the Porta Vesuvio. Before long, it became apparent that this wall, on which the whole of Region VI is oriented, was beyond all doubt a Greek fortification, and could not have been erected prior to the Greek re-conquest of the Etruscans who had occupied Pompeii round about 530 B.C. and 474 B.C.

The origins of Pompeii, then, did not go back to a Greek colony but to an Italic community founded in the dawn of history by peoples of the Oscan race. But during the first half of the sixth century B.C., the Greek traders of Cumae had been quick to grasp the value of the site as a centre of commerce, had promptly taken possession of it, and assured for themselves full control of the Sarno, a natural trade route and the principal outlet to the sea. Undoubtedly it was these Greeks who built the Doric Temple of the Triangular Forum and the Temple of Apollo adjacent to the zone that was to become the Forum of the Roman city. We do not know to which deity the Doric Temple was dedicated, but a few indications suggest that it may have been Athene whose cult was spread by Greek navigators right along the coast. Professor Maiuri's excavations further proved that in its original form, the Temple of Apollo was contemporary with the Doric Temple. It certainly existed at the time of the Etruscan hegemony, as we know from the fragments of black-figured ceramic and sherds of Italic pottery with Etruscan inscriptions found in a *fossa* at the foot of the temple. The date of the deposit oscillates between 550 and 470 B.C., and the vases with Etruscan inscriptions must have been votive objects directly connected with the temple. While it is conceivable that the cult of Apollo may have been introduced into Pompeii by the Etruscans—Apollo, one of their greatest deities, reigned at Veii—it is far more likely that it was inaugurated by the Cumaeans, who had already established it in Pozzuoli, Naples, and Ischia, and that the Greek divinity was accepted without demur by the Etruscans when they conquered the city. At this era Pompeii was not yet surrounded by a wall; it comprised of little more than the nucleus of the old city (i.e. Regions VII and VIII), whose irregular roads radiated from the Forum and came to an end on the sheer cliff that in those days practically overhung the sea. The Etruscan conquerors did not apparently alter the city in any way; their tenure came to an end in 474 B.C., when they were decisively defeated by the Cumaeans and their allies, the Greeks of Syracuse, at the naval battle of Cumae. The Hellenes regained control of the entire Campanian coast, and from then on, Pompeii began to prosper and expand.

This was the era when Greek urbanization was at its height, when it was synonymous with the name of Hippodamus of Miletus, who popularized the rectangular grid plan. New quarters rose up round the nucleus of Pompeii, and a fortified wall was erected round the city to protect it from the danger of attacks by peoples of the hinterland. The area enclosed was out of all proportion to the actual agglomeration, since the wall followed the same line as the Roman wall that ultimately replaced it; this line, however, like that of the fortifications round Rome, was dictated by the shape of the terrain.

The new Pompeii had plenty of space. Its quarters were laid out in the rectangles bounded by the main roads, the *decumani* and *cardines* that crossed the city from gate to gate.[12] There were a few irregularities due to the fact that the various orientations of the ancient Oscan nucleus had to be fitted in, but as we can see today, the imposition of the grid plan is unmistakable.

The Greek colonists who erected the wall round Pompeii simultaneously introduced the Hippodamic plan. Long before the Romans installed themselves in the Campagna, the city boasted an urban plan thought by archaeologists to be traditionally Roman (we have seen the same plan at Norba, but Norba was created a century later than Greek Pompeii) and ascribed to the Romans for years. It has been suggested that the geometric plan sprang from the augural science of the Etruscans, but in the case of Pompeii, its source was undoubtedly Greek.

Pompeii no longer appears to us as a phenomenon, a city divorced from time and history. The tireless work of archaeologists has replaced it (or perhaps we had better say partially replaced it, for there are still many uncertainties) in its proper perspective. As we have seen, in order to reach this point new methods of research had to be continually thought out; above all, the exploration of Pompeii had to be directed towards its true objective, an objective whose scope was far wider than the search for buried treasures. The aim of this immense task that has already taken two centuries is not the accumulation of rich booty, but a quest for knowledge that will lead to a more exact, a deeper understanding of the past.

THE SCIENTIFIC EXPLORATION OF HERCULANEUM

Pompeii has long outshone her two rivals, Herculaneum and Stabiae. As we have seen, the exploration of Herculaneum was a far more difficult proposition, and after the disengagement of the Villa of the Papyri, it had to be abandoned, since the poisonous fumes of sulphuric gases had made it increasingly dangerous. Finally, in 1763, the galleries and shafts were closed.

Sixty years later, in 1825, another attempt was made to explore Herculaneum; as sapping had proved disastrous, it was decided to proceed by the open-trench system employed at Pompeii. The laborious digging led to the partial disengagement of a single villa, the House of Argus, so-called because of an exquisite painting of the legend of Io. The political crisis of 1855 brought the work to an end, and the site was left idle until 1869, when excavations were resumed at the express desire of the new King of Naples. In the next six years, despite intensive activity, only the façades of two blocks and that of the Thermae were disengaged, and in 1875 Herculaneum was once more abandoned. The technical difficulties, the seemingly disappointing results (no magnificent sculptures and paintings, no new library, nothing in fact that would flatter national and regional pride had come to light), the danger of undermining the little town of Resina if the excavations were pursued seemed sound reasons for closing the site for good.

In 1927, however, thanks to the policy and initiative of the new Government, the situation changed. Herculaneum was included in Mussolini's archaeological programme, and it was decided to pursue the exploration at no matter what cost. From this time forward, Herculaneum has slowly come to light, and the characteristic features which differentiate it from other cities of the Campagna are gradually being revealed. The vast mass of solidified mud which makes conditions so difficult moulded itself round the ruins; as well as saving them from brutal destruction by fire, it excluded the air, hence even the smallest objects are in a far better state of preservation in Herculaneum than in Pompeii.

Materials, foodstuffs, pieces of wood were almost intact. In Pompeii, due either to the conflagration caused by the fiery rain of red-hot cinders or to the slow process of oxidization, all the wood has been carbonized and only traces of it remain. In Herculaneum, on the contrary, even the fibre of the wood has been preserved thanks to a kind of fossilization; the disengaged houses still retain their staircases, and each detail of the home-life of their occupants has survived. Here are the cupboards they used, here are the portable partitions they used to close off their private apartments, here are their tables and chests. Visitors can use the stairs to reach the upper levels; their treads are covered with plate-glass, but the framework is perfectly sound.

Even the plaited rushes used for the walls and roofs of the poorer houses are still intact despite their fragility.[13] In Pompeii scarcely a villa had retained its roof; the roofs have been very cleverly restored, but in some cases, their likeness to the originals is doubtful. In Herculaneum it was not so much a question of restoration as of substitution, of replacing with new wood a piece that was crumbling away, but whose shape, dimensions and position could be determined with absolute precision. When one of the streets of Herculaneum is being explored, the scaffolding, the struts and ladders give the impression that it is a building site where a new city is in the course of erection.

Thanks to the sketches made by Weber and La Vega during the first campaign and to the results obtained since 1927, we can now form a general picture of Herculaneum. The five *cardine* and the two *decumani* have been traced. Herculaneum is also laid out on the rectangular grid, but the irregularities are fewer than at Pompeii, suggesting that there was no old quarter that had to be fitted in. At the present stage of the excavations this is only a surmise, and if they are continued in the region of the Forum—this will entail the evacuation of an entire quarter of Resina and the rehousing of the inhabitants—they may disclose traces of an Italic pre-colonization on the site where the Cumaean Greeks founded classic Herculaneum.

Owing to the various eruptions of Vesuvius, particularly those of 79 B.C. and 161 B.C., the shape of the promontory on which Herculaneum stood was greatly changed after the city's foundation. Originally, Herculaneum was much closer to the sea, and was undoubtedly a strategic point, an advanced trading post for the Greeks of Naples and a port of call for the Greeks of Cumae. During the course of the fifth century B.C. all this commercial activity brought prosperity to Herculaneum. Its inhabitants were mostly humble fishermen who cast their nets in the Bay of Naples, but after the annexation of the city by Rome in the first century B.C., wealthy patricians and merchants built themselves villas by the sea. During the period of independence Herculaneum was surrounded by fortifications, but these gradually crumbled away, and up to now no traces of them have been found. Between the probable line of these fortifications and the shore was a suburb once believed to have been occupied exclusively by fishermen and sailors, but which, as we know today, was an entirely *bourgeois* sub-topia.

Unlike Pompeii with its countless dead who had succumbed in the streets or in the shelters in which they had vainly sought refuge, Herculaneum has only yielded a handful of skeletons. The city was closer to Vesuvius than Pompeii, and when the volcano erupted the inhabitants must have realized that to delay would be fatal. No more than ten of them appear to have perished in the disaster, though it is possible that the skeletons of more victims may come to light.

According to the traditional version of the catastrophe, almost the entire population of Herculaneum had betaken itself to the theatre on that particular evening. We can imagine the panic that ensued when suddenly Vesuvius began to spew forth a rain of fire. Fortunately, the port was not far away, and it was only a short crossing to Naples. In Pompeii, situated farther from Vesuvius, the danger was not so immediate, and the people could not make up their minds to leave the city. When they realized that flight was inevitable it was too late; the cockleshell boats could not weather the mountainous seas. Pliny the Elder was in command of the Imperial Fleet at Misenum, but as soon as he saw the great cloud of dust and ashes he set sail for Stabiae. Here he put in, but when he had lain at anchor for a day and a night, he realized the significance of the great pall of darkness shot with fiery streaks —Vesuvius had erupted. Fascinated by the spectacle, Pliny delayed his departure, and the great naturalist paid for his scientific curiosity with his life. Many inhabitants of Pompeii wasted precious hours in packing up their most treasured possessions, preparatory to leaving and the delay proved fatal. They perished with those who had been unable to tear themselves away from their homes, with the servants and slaves who had been left behind to guard the villas of their masters.

The inhabitants of Herculaneum were no less attached to their homes, their possessions, but they had had no choice; to hesitate meant certain death, and abandoning their worldly goods, they had taken instantly to the boats, and escaped with their lives. In the houses of Herculaneum, where each object stands in its customary place, we have the eerie sensation that only a few seconds have elapsed since their panic-stricken occupants quitted them for ever.

Pompeii was a provincial city with its own traditions, its own history; its *bourgeoisie* was solidly entrenched, its political life intensely active, its economy, founded on agriculture and the produce of the fertile countryside, stable. Herculaneum, however, was scarcely more than a suburb of Naples which was only some four miles away, and many of its houses were built to accommodate the overspill of the population from the larger city. Adjoining the immense villas and the more modest *domus* of the 'Pompeiian' type, were *insulae* similar to those of Ostia. We can imagine the diversity of this region of the Campagna where each city had its

OSTIA ANTICA View of the street leading to the Porta Laurentina

PALESTRINA Detail of the Nile Mosaic

own particular features; the history of the different aspects it presented is written in its stones. During the Republic, Pozzuoli, on the other side of Naples, was the centre of a maritime trade. It was a Greek city and enjoyed a large measure of autonomy; its cultural influence was exerted over the entire region. Gradually, however, the princely residence of the Roman patricians spread right along the coast; some were built at the very gates of Naples. These villas not only lined the shore in the direction of Pausillipus and Cape Micenus, they also extended beyond Pompeii and Stabiae to the vicinity of Sorrento. In this huge and luxurious seaside resort, Herculaneum played only a menial part, catering, as did other villages, for the needs of the wealthy holiday-makers. The fishermen and artisans of Herculaneum lived on what they could make out of the indolent pleasure-seekers.

STABIAE

Beyond Pompeii, also on the coast, stood Stabiae. Shortly after Alcubierre had begun to explore Pompeii, he carried out a few excavations in the vicinity of Gragnano, one of the two comparatively modern villages built on the site of the buried city. These random researches, pursued without a clue, yielded a not unpleasing crop of paintings and mosaics.[14] Exploration was resumed at Gragnano in 1775, but in 1782 work came to a stop and the site was abandoned. It was not until 1950 that it once more became a scene of activity; the results that have been obtained up to date in this new campaign have been most promising. An immense ensemble has been disengaged, probably a villa, though this is by no means certain. There are two peristyles on different levels with a communicating flight of steps, and grouped round the peristyles are a number of apartments, one of which was used for thermal baths.

In the last few years, exquisite paintings have been discovered; unfortunately, these were in a deplorable state and had to be reconstructed from small scraps. The individual style of these paintings leads us to believe that Stabiae had its own school; they are boldly and vigorously executed, and the artists were not daunted by the difficulties of foreshortening or of those involved in the creation of huge compositions on ceilings. Up to now Stabiae itself has not come to light. During the Social War, the city was razed to the ground by Sulla, and its homeless inhabitants found refuge in the neighbouring farms, but even though its population was dispersed, vestiges of Stabiae's walls must still exist, and within them traces of the original nucleus. The mystery of the strip of coast between Naples and Sorrento is far from being dispelled. Perhaps the archaeologists of the future, armed with better equipment than we possess today, will discover Stabiae; perhaps, better informed than ourselves, they will have cause to be thankful that we did not succeed in finding the city. After all, did not we in our turn rejoice with good reason at the fact that so many of the treasures of Pompeii had been overlooked by Alcubierre and his convicts?

CHAPTER SEVEN

The Discovery of the Etruscans

ANCIENT ROME NEVER ENTIRELY ceased to exist; she lived on in the minds of men and in the concrete reality of her monuments. Confused memories of the burned Campanian cities lingered on through the ages, and when Pompeii and Herculaneum finally came to light, much that was discovered was only the confirmation of what had previously been known of their civilization. But the revelation of the Etruscans burst forth with the suddenness of a lightning flash in the eighteenth century, playing havoc with all preconceived ideas, making it seem as though the sum of knowledge so hardly won was as nothing in an immense sea of ignorance. For, by the time that Rome had become an imperial city, the Etruscan world was no more and all its splendours had been forgotten. In Cicero's day, this world which had played so large a part in the foundation of the Urbs and contributed so much to its constitution, its language, arts, customs, and religious practices, was merely a subject of curiosity for a few erudite scholars.

Amongst the last of the Romans to devote attention to the Etruscans was the Emperor Claudius. Claudius was a passionate historian and since, like his ancestors, he was of a cautious disposition, he steered clear of the burning questions of the day and immersed himself in the remote past of a people that was slowly dying out and whose language was only spoken by a handful of octogenarians. Obviously, Claudius regarded the Etruscans, once the masters of those who were allowing them gradually to disappear, as less inflammable material for an historical study than the civil wars and the eventful era of Augustus. Unfortunately, his book has not survived, and we can measure the loss when we recall the passages about the Etruscans in the Emperor's famous Discourse of Lyons, recorded on a bronze tablet. Clearly, Claudius had not been taken in by the fictitious accounts of Roman annalists, had not shrunk from the truth, humiliating as it was to national pride. But after Claudius, silence fell once more and the glory of the Etruscans was sealed in the darkness of their inviolate tombs.

(163)

From the time of Claudius, little more was known of the Etruscans than their name; the brief accounts by classic historians of the vanished people were more often than not contradictory. Their knowledge was limited to the fact that the Etruscans had been bound up with the early days of the Urbs and with the constitution of the Republic; Livy tells us that one of their kings, Lars Porsena, had striven to re-establish the royal régime after the expulsion of the Tarquins, and adds that the Tarquins themselves had close family ties with the Etruscans.

Furthermore, the execrated King Mezenius symbolizes the might of the Etruscan tyrants, just as Turnus, King of Ardea, symbolizes the petty Italic rulers who held sway before the coming of Aeneas and his Trojans, and Evander the earliest of the Greek colonists who settled in Southern Italy. But in Virgil's epic pages, what is fiction, what is fact? From Cicero, Varrus and a few other writers, we learn that the Etruscans were versed in the occult sciences, that they had religious beliefs and practices peculiar to themselves, which were often a source of inspiration for the priests and diviners of Rome. But from these few meagre facts, who could have dreamt of the splendour of a civilization which at a given moment in history dominated the emergent Urbs, who could have dreamt of the might of an empire that imposed on a vast area of the peninsula the political structure that led to the formation of classic Rome?

The oblivion to which the Etruscans were consigned was partly due to human agency, to a kind of conspiracy of silence, but nature was also to blame. The silence that blanketed Tuscany was that of a countryside stricken by malaria, the scourge that had ravaged Italy ever since the day when the patient cultivators of the land had ceased from their labours; with pools of stagnant water everywhere, the contagion spread from village to village, city to city. The disease that had decimated the population of Ostia did not spare the inhabitants of Tuscany; from the mouth of the Tiber to that of the Arno, the scene was one of utter desolation. Nor was this all. During the fourth and third centuries, the Romans, fearful that the vanquished might one day attempt to rise, forced the Etruscans to leave their cities. The displaced inhabitants raised new homesteads elsewhere, but the glorious cities, abandoned for ever, had soon begun to decay, a process that was all the more rapid because the buildings were constructed in brick, wood, and other perishable material. Within the crumbling walls, earth accumulated over the ruins, grass and trees took root and, at the end of a few centuries, nothing could be seen but woodland glades and meadows.

THE TREASURE HUNT

This combination of circumstances explains why so little was known for years about the Etruscan cities—cities that only today are beginning to seem a little less mysterious. For centuries, knowledge of the Etruscan world did not extend beyond its tombs. Deeply buried in the earth, these massive, vaulted chamber tombs resisted the ravages of time; occasionally a ploughshare driven into the soil with more force than usual struck against a tomb and split it open, and the peasants, conquering their fear, crept inside, sure that their daring would be richly rewarded. At times, however, terror proved stronger than the hope of gain, and they would hurriedly block up the mouth of the hell in which they had glimpsed malevolently grinning demons.

In the course of the years, however, the looting of tombs in Etruria developed into a flourishing industry. When Pope Innocent VIII learnt that golden ornaments had been found in a tomb in Tarquinii (the modern Corneto), he dispatched emissaries to acquire them on his behalf, but by the time they reached the city, the ornaments had taken the same road as the other treasures discovered in Etruria: they had either vanished into some private collection or had been melted down for the price of the metal.

It was not until the middle of the sixteenth century that some idea of the significance of these discoveries was formed. The light began to break in when two statues, the Chimaera and the Minerva, were found at Arretium (Arezzo.) While it was apparent at once that these two bronzes had been inspired by Greek sculpture, it was equally apparent that they were informed by a spirit which made them very different from Hellenic bronzes. Benvenuto Cellini was commissioned to restore the Chimaera, and we can imagine what his feelings must have been as he scrutinized with his craftsman's eye this marvellous statue, so technically perfect and yet so barbaric in its conception. From the depths of Italian soil there had emerged a work entirely alien to the classic Greek spirit of serenity. Three years later, in 1556, a third statue, the Orator, came to light on the shore of Lake Trasimene, and this third find made it abundantly plain that during the golden age of Rome there had existed a school of sculptors who had succeeded in infusing a truly national spirit into their work.

These exquisite statues, deprived of their past and their history, were the isolated witnesses of a lost world. It was not until the eighteenth century that an essential step in the right direction was taken, that of assembling such evidence as there was in order to arrive at an understanding of the Etruscan civilization.

ETRUSCOLOGY: THE FIRST PHASE

The credit for pioneering the way to the study of Etruria belongs to Sir Thomas Dempster. This erudite and eccentric Scots baronet had graduated in law in Paris when he was only seventeen. After obtaining his degree, he travelled extensively in Italy, and from 1616–17 lectured on jurisprudence at the University of Pisa. It was during this period that, on behalf of Cosimo de' Medici, he set to work on a book designed to give a picture of royal Etruria prior to the Roman conquest.

To be truthful, *De Etruria Regali libri septem* would not have been epoch-making, would have been no more, in fact, than the compilation of an extremely erudite humanist with an amazing knowledge of the texts relating to the Etruscans had not its author had the idea of illustrating his seven volumes with engravings of all the Etruscan monuments that had come to light. Shortly after he had completed this work, Dempster's restless spirit drove him from the University of Pisa to that of Bologna, where he dismissed the Etruscans from his mind.

A century later, in 1723, his work which had remained in manuscript form was published in Florence, thanks to Thomas Coke. The senator Filippo Buonarotti, one of the Florentine scholars who had become deeply interested in the Etruscan world contributed a remarkable commentary on the ninety-three plates in which he sought to prove that the language and culture of Etruria were at the very heart of Italian history. He advanced many daring hypotheses on the Etruscan civilization, but in the sphere of linguistics he was less happy. This is a domain in which scholars invariably trip up. Dempster, for instance, stated that the language of the Engubine Tablets was Etruscan, whereas, as we now know, it is Umbrian; most of our knowledge of the language and religion of non-Etruscan central Italy comes, in fact, from the

Tablets. The linguistic hypotheses of Buonarotti were not, on the whole, any better founded. Buonarotti's errors, however, did not detract from the value of the plates which familiarized a large public with the Etruscan monuments. In Dempster's book, which Bloch calls 'the first modest corpus of the monuments of Etruria', there appeared the first reproduction of an Etruscan tomb painting; this was from the Tartaglia tomb discovered in Corneto in 1699 by the advocate Targaglia.

The publication by Coke of Dempster's book and Buonarotti's commentary marked the beginning of what might be called funerary etruscology, since at this era, its principal object was the study of Etruscan tombs. Scholars had gradually come to realize what treasures were buried in the soil of Etruria. Throughout the eighteenth century the Etruscans continued to exercise their spell over Italian archaeologists who remained absorbed in their researches even though in the fifties new vistas had been opened up by the discovery of Pompeii and Herculaneum. Undoubtedly the explorations of these cities were infinitely more alluring because of the priceless treasures they yielded, but princely fortunes were needed to finance operations on such a scale. It was far simpler, far less costly to explore a grotto or two in the solitudes of Corneto or Vulci. Moreover, the labour involved was almost certain to prove profitable, for in addition to the strange paintings that covered the walls, almost all the tombs contained a great abundance of decorated vases, ornaments and artifacts of every kind.

Unfortunately, as was too often the case during this period, many of the treasures of the Etruscan tombs were lost or irretrievably damaged as archaeologists, scholars, collectors, and dealers in antiquities failed to take the necessary precautions. Frequently, no inventory was made, and 'interesting' objects were removed and dispersed at random. The wall-paintings which had remained intact while the tomb was air-tight and there were no variations of temperature, deteriorated with extreme rapidity once the underground chambers were opened, and as archaeologists often failed to make sketches of them, they have been lost to us for ever.

Descriptions of the discoveries fared little better; many languished unpublished for years and finally disappeared. One case in point is that of the manuscript of Padre Gian Nicola Forlivesi, a monk and a native of Tarquinii, which is mentioned by scholars of this period, but which has vanished without trace. These happy-go-lucky individual explorations were presided over by pure chance, and as the lone archaeologist's notes on his discoveries were apt to go astray, it was likely that the outcome of his researches would never be known. From time to time, artists, amongst them the English painter, James Byres, made sketches of the Etruscan tombs; an album of sketches was ultimately published, and it is thanks to these that the history of certain important discoveries has survived to our own day.

ETRUSCOMANIA

During the eighteenth century academies and learned societies were very much in vogue. It comes as no surprise, then, to learn that etruscologists founded the Etruscan Academy in Cortona in 1726. In order to give it a true Etruscan flavour, they addressed their president as *Lucumon*—the Etruscan word for king or for the headman of an Etrurian city. Almost immediately, shoals of erudite monographs appeared, and in addition, the archaeologist A. F. Gori undertook the task of enlarging and bringing up to date the work of Dempster and Buonarotti. The first three volumes of Gori's *Museum Etruscum* came out between 1737 and 1743; they contained a large number of illustrations, but it must be said that these were not always accurate. In spite of errors, however, the passion for all things Etruscan persisted, and the continuous study bore fruit: when an artifact came to light, archaeologists knew at a glance whether or not it was Etruscan. In 1738, for example, when the celebrated Ficorini *cestus* was discovered at Praeneste, they agreed without hesitation that the figures engraved on it were the work of an Etruscan craftsman.

Had the great discoveries of Pompeii and Herculaneum been made at an earlier date, the archaeology of the Campagna might very well have eclipsed that of Etruria, but fate had decreed otherwise, and long before attention was drawn to the buried cities, the Etruscans had become the rage. Moreover, other reasons that had little to do with the spirit of pure research but were nevertheless exceedingly powerful, helped to keep etruscology very much alive. At the outset of the excavations in the Campagna it seemed that a new chapter in the history of Greek art was about to open, but actually it was new only in one sense since behind it lay a vast accumulation of traditional evidence. The Etruscan world, on the other hand, was so little known, so bizarre that it fascinated archaeologists with its strangeness. They had the impression that they were adventuring into untrodden realms of history, an exhilarating sensation during an age when Western thought, weary of conformity, was seeking for new worlds to conquer.

It was, however, a patriotic motive that kept etruscology in the foreground at this particular time. Pre-Risorgimento Italy was making a desperate effort to assert her national pride, and believed she could do so through the Etruscans. These people rekindled all the hopes of a country which had been forced to resign itself to the· thought that the civilization of Rome had been no more than a dim replica of Hellenism. Italy had become convinced that the Etruscans would furnish the proof that far from being an accident, a 'flash in the pan' in a long night of decadence, the civilization of Rome had been truly national. This renascent faith was based on decidedly shaky foundations. For example, at the time when he was writing his commentary for Dempster's book, Buonarotti had advanced the theory that the Etruscans were descended from the Egyptians, that they had escaped the tyranny of Greek culture, and that therefore Italian civilization was not the daughter of Hellenic civilization, but its sister, or, better still, its cousin. It must be remembered that in Buonarotti's day, scholars readily subscribed to the belief that the Greeks were heavily indebted to the Egyptians, that omniscient people, in whose doctrines Plato himself had sought the light.

In their enthusiasm, the early etruscologists attributed every find to the genius of the Etruscans. For instance, they labelled as Etruscan all the vases discovered in the tombs whereas, as we know today, the majority of them were Greek. Gori, who was amongst the first to publish descriptions and illustrations of these ceramics, stated categorically that they were Italic. The fact was that Gori and other Tuscan archaeologists were subconsciously influenced by regional pride, hence it was left to the unbiased Winckelmann to point out that many of the vases came from the Kingdom of Naples and could not possibly be Etruscan:

They are classed as Etruscan simply because archaeologists have been content to follow in the footsteps of Gori and Buonarotti, who discovered them in the tombs; as both these antiquaries were of Tuscan birth, the natural desire to add to the glories of Tuscany caused them to attribute these exquisite ceramics to the Etruscans.

Winckelmann played his ace when he drew attention to the fact that the inscriptions on many of these vases were Greek. He boldly went on to aver that the Etruscans, far from being a people in their own right, were, in fact, an offshoot of the Greeks—that they were none other than the Pelasgians, immigrants, as both Plutarch and Thucydides testify, from Attica and Arcadia. Three hundred years before Herodotus, Winckelmann continued, the Pelasgians, the first Greek settlers in Italy, were joined by a second wave of Hellenic immigrants who colonized Magna Graecia, and it was these colonists who 'civilized' Etruria. Thus, in the most elegant manner, Winckelmann disposed of a problem that had given rise to an awkward little query as to the absolute supremacy of Greek art.

Winckelmann found little difficulty in maintaining his position, partly because facts were few and far between, partly because the etruscologists of his day were so given to exaggeration that they made themselves ridiculous. The learned academicians of Cortona solemnly holding their sessions under their *lucumons* were un-doubtedly subject for laughter, as were their affirmations that the world was indebted to the Etruscans for this or that valuable invention. Guarnacci, the founder of the Etruscan Museum of Volterra, laid himself open to ridicule when he claimed in his *Memorie Storiche Etrusche sul piu antico Regnio d'Italia* (published in Lucca between 1767 and 1772) that the Etruscans were supreme over all the races of Italy, and in some respects, over the Greeks. But in spite of the absurdities of Guarnacci and his fellow etrusco-logists, the lively imagination of these scholars produced the de-sired effect, and, in consequence the glory of the Etruscan city of Florence, the modern capital of Tuscany, was greatly enhanced. Indeed, a hundred years later Florence was the centre of the young Kingdom of Italy, the legitimate heir to that other long-lost kingdom whose historical reality Guarnacci had sought to establish.

Despite all their extravagances, however, the rabid etruscolo-gists were defending a just cause; naïvely, clumsily, yet instinc-tively aware that they were right, they did battle against another school of thought whose adherents were given to equal excesses and could fairly be classed as Graecomanes. The *casus belli* was, in fact, badly defined; both sides agreed that beauty was an absolute and could be attained once and once only, but whereas the pro-

Hellenists maintained that this absolute beauty had been attained by the Greek sculptors of the fifth and fourth centuries, the pro-Etruscans claimed that their favourite people had discovered the secret of the Absolute for themselves with no help whatsoever from the Greeks. Thus the Etruscan question became linked to the great anti-classic movement of liberation which was not without political implications.

The Etruscans, looked upon as revolutionaries, commanded the sympathy of the Moderns. In a few years' time, with the dawn of the Romantic Age, the Etruscans were to figure as the *carbonari* of history. Perhaps the picturesqueness of their tombs, the ghostly presence of death that the very word Etruscan evoked, the solitude of the Maremma, where archaeologists sought for traces of the lost civilization and where the silence was only broken by the bleating of sheep tended by shepherds in flowing cloaks, contributed to the spell. Added to this, the marvel of the discoveries, the grandeur, the terrifying character of the wall-paintings in the *hypogaea* (burial chambers), inevitably captured imaginations already attuned to the vibrant keynote of romanticism.

MARIETTE VERSUS PIRANESI

It does not surprise us that Piranesi should have been one of the most ardent supporters of the Etruscans. Piranesi, brimming with zeal and faith, but with very little scientific knowledge, was convinced that in the marvellous tombs he had found a bizarre and magnificent world—the Rome of the Tarquins. This world formed the subject of his book: *Della magnificenza ed architettura dei Romani* published in 1761, a book he had profusely illustrated with reconstructions of the most impressive character whose purpose was to prove that the Romans of the classic era had no need to resort to Greek architects, since the Etruscans had already invented every architectural form and device.

To tell the truth, Piranesi's Q.E.D. was hardly convincing, and one wonders how he could have persuaded himself that he had said the last word. Apart from the funerary paintings, the art of the Etruscans was unknown at this period, and Piranesi's remarks on this subject are the product of sheer imagination. The least debatable pages of his book are those devoted to the Cloaca Maxima, whose remains justly invited comparison with the Etruscan tombs. Elsewhere, Piranesi, who paid no attention to chronology, attributed to the Rome of the Tarquins (by which he meant the Rome conquered by the Etruscans) innumerable ruins which, in reality, only date back to the Empire. When he had recourse to Latin texts, he frequently allowed his fancy full play; for instance, he seized on Vitruvius's description of a Tuscan temple, and produced a reconstruction of such a temple, complete down to the last detail of its ornamentation—and this at a time when the terracottas of Conca, the statues of Veii, the whole of sixth century Etruscan art were unknown. Had Piranesi been correct, we should have been compelled to admit that by the might of Italian genius alone, Royal Rome had surpassed in its architectural and romantic splendour, not only Athens, but a hundred Corinths.

While Piranesi's talent was greatly admired, few supported his contention, which was, in fact, promptly attacked by a Frenchman, a well-known amateur of the arts and a brilliant classical scholar, Jean-Pierre Mariette. A lengthy open letter in which he claimed for the Greeks the honour of having taught the Romans everything they knew about architecture appeared on 4 November 1764 in the *Gazette Litteraire de l'Europe*.

Signor Piranesi maintains [Mariette wrote], that when the first Romans wished to erect massive buildings, the solidity of which astonishes us, they were obliged to enlist the assistance of Etruscan architects who were their neighbours. One might as well say 'the assistance of the Greeks', for the Etruscans, who were Greek by origin, were ignorant of the arts, and practised only those which had been taught to their fathers in the land of their origin.[1]

Mariette's voice is that of Winckelmann. He expressed his viewpoint clearly and forcibly, but his arguments lacked substance, and instead of attacking Piranesi for the glaring errors he had made, his complete disregard of chronology, the unconcern with which he had taken elements from here, there and everywhere for his reconstructions, he merely assailed his romantic opponent with a string of dogmatic but highly debatable assertions. Mariette, in fact, was wrestling with the problem of the Greeks versus the Etruscans in its entirety, a problem so complex that even today it remains unsolved. True, the ancient historians, notably Herodotus, tell us that the Etruscans came from the East and that they were of Lydian origin, but it by no means follows that these Lydians were Greek even though they may have been Hellenized, or that these emigrants who left the Orient towards the eleventh century B.C. had been initiated into the architectural techniques that came triumphantly into their own in the classic Greece of the fifth century.

In this exchange between Mariette and Piranesi which typifies so admirably the attitude of the two schools of thought, the antagonists oppose each other with such vague concepts that we feel we are watching a duel between shadows. Like other scholars of the day, they had made the mistake—even in our times, this mistake occasionally occurs—of oversimplification; in other words, they had joined issue over Greece versus Rome, Rome versus Greece without taking into account all the complexities this question involved. That the Etruscans were Hellenized is undeniable. The proof is to be found in their alphabet alone which is directly derived from an archaic Greek alphabet, adapted more or less awkwardly, to the exigencies of a different system of phonetics. But this same Greek alphabet was itself derived from a Semitic alphabet. Are we to take it, then, that Greek belongs to the same linguistic group as Arabic and Hebrew? Undoubtedly, the Etruscans 'borrowed' in the widest sense of the word the Greek myths and legends that form the subject of their funerary paintings, but if this makes them Greek, then we must perforce admit that Racine was Greek, and deprive the Golden Age of French literature of all its originality and genius.

Fortunately, an erroneous interpretation has never constituted an insuperable barrier to the progress of knowledge; for a time, the way may seem to be hopelessly barred, scholars may waver, but as the sum of data is increased, a thousand cracks appear in the barricade and finally it is breached. Despite all the polemics, the enthusiasm for etruscology, the romantic ardour and regional pride of etruscologists were soon to bear fruit.

In the early days progress had been slow and laborious, and many etruscologists had spent their entire lives in patient research. Amongst them were such men as the Abbé Matio Guarnacci, who retired to the ancient city of Volterra in 1757, where he founded the museum that bears his name. Guarnacci directed a number of explorations, principally on the site of the necropolis outside the walls of Volterra. From these excavations, he assembled a very large collection of terracotta and alabaster funerary urns decorated

in relief with genre scenes or episodes from mythology. Guarnacci's collection was the irrefutable proof of a civilization that had
existed in the remote past; in the light of his discoveries, dogmatic
assertions were of little weight.

Inspired by their founder, the Abbé Onofrio Baldelli, the
academicians of Cortona also set up a museum (the present
museum of Cortona), and brought out nine profusely illustrated
volumes of *Dissertazioni* to which numerous scholars from many
European countries had contributed.

Even if scientific etruscology owed nothing else to the first
toilers in the field, it would be impossible to overlook these men
who, as Justi, Winckelmann's biographer, wrote, 'unhesitatingly
considered it to be their duty to devote their whole lives to the
study of a people who remained to them a closed book sealed with
seven seals, to the search for inscriptions, not a single line of which
they could read'. Justi described them as 'poor devils' and with
contempt dismissed their pitiful gropings. Yet, but for these same
'poor devils', etruscology would never have been born, its fundamental facts would never have been known, and one of the most
brilliant and fascinating pages in the history of Ancient Rome—
fascinating because of its very mystery—would never have been
written.

SCIENTIFIC ETRUSCOLOGY

Most archaeologists agree that scientific etruscology stems from
the work of the Abbé Luigi Lanzi, a Florentine who dedicated his
whole life to the study of the antiquities of his native Tuscany.
Lanzi, enthralled, like so many other scholars both before and
after him, by the enigma of the Etruscan language, produced a
book *Saggio di lingua etrusca e di altri lingui antiche d'Italia* in which,
with great ingenuity, he sought to prove that Etruscan was
related to the ancient Italic group of languages. Naturally, he
failed to do anything of the kind, and Lanzi would not occupy
such an honoured position in the annals of etruscology had he not
undertaken what he no doubt regarded as his secondary work: the
classification and arrangement of the Duke of Tuscany's Etruscan
collection. Paradoxically enough, this proved far more fruitful
than the ambitious *Saggio*, for not only did it lay the foundations
of the present archaeological museum of Florence, but it gave
the scholars of the day a far better understanding, a far deeper

appreciation of the originality, the vital significance of the Etruscan civilization. Furthermore, Lanzi proved conclusively that, as Winckelmann had maintained a century before, certain vases that had been labelled Etruscan were, in fact, Greek. He thus dissipated once and for all a cloud of confusion extremely detrimental to etruscology.

Despite Lanzi's valuable work, his endeavour to define the Etruscan phenomenon in its true limits, scientific etruscology owed its beginnings not to Italian archaeologists but to those of the recently founded German Institute in Rome. The first meeting of the *Istituto di Correspondenza Archeologica*, held on the Capitol on 21 April 1829, the anniversary of the foundation of the Urbs, was an event of maximum importance for every branch of Italian archaeology. The aim of the *Istituto* was the co-ordination of work in the sphere of archaeology and the promotion of a spirit of international co-operation. Its programme (a programme whose broad outlines the academicians of Cortona had envisaged) was of unprecedented amplitude. The *Istituto* had come into being through the efforts of a young German archaeologist, Edward Gerhard, who had won the support of a number of savants and who had been fortunate enough to find such patrons as Prince Frederick of Prussia and the Duc de Luynes.

Etruscology was one of the first branches of archaeology to benefit from the newly-formed *Istituto*. Several recent discoveries of great interest had once more focused attention on Etruria; in 1827, there had come to light in Corneto, one after the other, four Etruscan tombs with marvellous wall-paintings. Two of these tombs, the Stackelberg and the Bigi, went back to archaic times. With the financial aid of the *Istituto*, the explorations were continued, not only in Corneto, but also in Bomarzo, Chiusi and Vulci. When a tomb was explored, reproductions of the wall-paintings promptly appeared in the *Istituto's* publication *Monumenti*. In addition to innumerable vases, archaeologists had the good fortune to find inscriptions considerably longer than the epitaphs that had previously come to light. True, these inscriptions could not be deciphered (even today, they remain largely undecipherable), but their discoverers found satisfaction in the thought that an accumulation of these documents would lead at some future date to a solution of the Etruscan mystery.

In 1836, at Cervetri, the Archpriest Regolini and General

Galazzi opened up the celebrated tomb that bears their name. This discovery was nothing short of a revelation to etruscologists. The abundance of the funeral furnishings in the central chamber (the tombs on the periphery of the tumulus had been ransacked centuries earlier), the orientalizing character of the tomb shed a sudden and unexpected light on the political and economic might of Cervetri during the seventh century B.C., approximately one hundred years later than the traditional date of the foundation of Rome.

The discovery of the Regolini-Galazzi tomb ranks in importance with that of the Mycenaean tombs made by Schliemann eight years later in 1874. It proved that at the time when Rome was only just beginning to emerge from her humble beginnings, her Etruscan neighbours had attained architectural standards that could compete with those of the great cities of the East. True, the full significance escaped the archaeologists of the day, indeed it could not be grasped till the Cyprus excavations brought to light eighth-century Anatolian artifacts which were obviously related to the earliest of those found in the tomb and so permitted it to be dated.

On the evidence of literary texts alone, the opinion was formed at the time that the Regolini-Galazzi tomb was a vestige of the Homeric civilization. Thus, before Schliemann's discoveries at Mycenae, Italian archaeologists advanced the hypothesis, which we now know was correct, that at the height of the heroic age, before the miracle of classic Greece had taken place, a civilization had existed whose marvellous techniques and refinements put seventh and sixth century Athens in the shade. Romantic poets and critics, however, continued to cling to the fallacious notion of an artless Homer singing of the beginnings of mankind—we know how many years it takes for archaeological evidence to impose its truth on literature! Nevertheless, the germ of the idea that was destined to revolutionize the concept of the Homeric world during the latter half of the eighteenth century came into being at Cervetri.

Sponsored by the *Istituto di Corrispondenza Archeologica*, several works by scholars specializing in etruscology were published; one was devoted to Etruscan mirrors, another to Etruscan funerary urns. The aim of the *Istituto* was to bring out a complete set of books on each subject; for the purposes of reference and scientific

POMPEII   The Temple of Apollo

POMPEII   The House of the Faun

POMPEII   The Colonnade surrounding the Forum

comparison, such sets were indispensable. Thanks to the *Istituto*, we now have a corpus of Etruscan mirrors and another of Etruscan funerary urns; both were completed by G. Korte who added the fifth and final volume to the former as early as 1897, and the last volume to the latter in 1916. Long before the full sets were available, however, etruscologists attempted syntheses. In 1828, K. O. Muller's *Die Etrusker* was published; it leant too heavily on texts, however, and so lost much of its originality and value. A new edition of *Die Etrusker* came out in 1877; this edition, edited and drastically revised by Deecke, is still useful.

Muller and Deecke wrote from the historian's point of view, but their contemporary, George Dennis, a British consul who spent many years in Italy, described Etruria through a traveller's eye. His *The Cities and Cemeteries of Etruria* appeared in 1848; it went into many editions—the latest, greatly enlarged, was published in 1878. Dennis was more interested in writing graphic accounts of the sites, the moment of discovery, the conditions under which it was made than in advancing a coherent theory of the history and civilization of the Etruscans. Nevertheless, all the fundamental facts of etruscology figure in the pages of his extremely entertaining and picturesquely written book, which is a most delightful guide.

Throughout the nineteenth-century articles and illustrations in *Monumenti* and the publication of works sponsored by the *Istituto* kept etruscology very much to the fore. Major discoveries added red-letter days to its annals, discoveries that either upset all preconceived theories or imposed a completely new approach. It would take far too long to follow the explorations step by step; there is only space in this book to recall a few of the most outstanding which shed fresh light on Etruria. The list is headed by the disengagement of the Francois Tomb which, like the Regolini-Galazzi Tomb, marked an epoch in the history of etruscology. Alessandro Francois, the archaeologist whose name it immortalizes, one of the most illustrious discoverers of tombs during the mid-nineteenth century, has left us many moving and thrilling accounts of his explorations. His knowledge of the soil of Etruria was supreme, and when other archaeologists believed that a site was exhausted, Francois knew instinctively that it had not yet given up all its treasures. Moreover, he unhesitatingly set himself to disengage tombs so massive that success seemed impossible.

Francois's energy was inexhaustible, but he also possessed the infinite patience required to reconstitute some precious ceramic from minute fragments. It was Francois, for instance, who restored the wonderful vase found at Chiusi.[2] The crater which commemorates his name is one of the major examples of the ceramic art of Attica.

Francois was equally fortunate in the sphere of etruscology. Sponsored by the French historian, A. Noel des Vergers, he carried out researches at Vulci which led to the discovery of the famous tomb that was to shed one more ray of light on the most obscure period of Royal Rome. Its disengagement was fraught with difficulties, and in a letter to des Vergers, Francois describes a dramatic and highly critical moment:

One evening, I was on my way to the site where we had already laid bare the *cippus* from which we knew that we had found the approach to the *hypogeum*, when my overseer hurried up to me in great agitation. He told me that the operation had gone very badly, that in his opinion, the tomb had caved in, the chamber was now inaccessible, and that we should have to give up the work which had been carried on with such toil and sweat for fifteen days. I was stunned, for I had placed high hopes on this *hypogeum*. 'Let's take a look,' I said, and when we reached the site, I saw a huge mass of debris that made me think that all was lost. By this time, it was almost dark, so I returned to the chateau of Musignano. I was in such a state, however, that I was unable to close my eyes, and two hours before daybreak, I was back at Ponte Rotto. As soon as my overseer and the workmen arrived, I ordered a hole to be dug in the centre of the debris, and when this had been done, I lay flat on the ground, and wriggled into the aperture. At a distance of ten or twelve palms, I managed to raise myself into a sitting position; I lit the torch I had brought with me, and to my intense joy, the first object I saw was a fragment of black nenfron. Now this could not have been dislodged from the vault, which was in travertine; its presence in this spot was therefore due to human agency, and this told me that what I had feared, namely the destruction of the *hypogeum*, had not taken place. I looked around me more attentively, and at a distance of some twenty palms away, I caught sight of an opening. I crawled towards it and let myself down, and almost immediately found myself in a vast subterranean crypt hollowed out in the travertine. I had scarcely glanced at my surroundings when I heard my men shouting my name. I realized that once I had entered the second aperture they had lost sight of my torch, and accordingly feared that I had either been buried in rubble or could not find my way back. I retraced my steps, and to their great relief, emerged into daylight, and as soon as I had assured them that I was all right, I told them to widen the opening. The Etruscans had carved out the vast crypt, some fifty palms long by thirty-five wide, in order to protect the *hypogeum* which lay immediately beneath from falls of earth and humidity.[3]

When we read this graphic account, we are reminded of the thrills, the disappointments that speleologists experience, but the eyes of Francois and des Vergers were dazzled, not with the wonder of icy cascades and exquisite formations of crystal, but by the marvel of a new world. Des Vergers has often described the moment when they penetrated into the tomb:

A final blow from the pick axe, and the boulder that sealed the entrance to the *hypogeum* split asunder. The light of the torches shone on the vaulted roof of the chamber where darkness and silence had reigned unbroken for more than twenty centuries. Nothing had been disturbed since the day when the entrance to the chamber had been sealed up, and ancient Etruria appeared before our eyes as it was at the height of its splendour. On their couches lay warriors with their shields and weapons who seemed to be sleeping after the bloody combats with Romans and Gauls, but theirs was the sleep of death. Shapes, clothing, materials, colours glimmered for a few moments, then, as the air reached the chamber, our torches flickered wildly and guttered out. The evocation of the past had been briefer than a dream, and as if to chastize us for our intrusive curiosity, it vanished.[4]

The wall-paintings found by Francois and des Vergers in the tomb were destined to rank with the most celebrated examples of Etruscan art, not because of their beauty, but because of the subjects they depicted. On the fresco on the left side of the chamber were portrayed not only scenes from the Greek epic—for example, Ajax snatching the hapless Cassandra from the foot of Athene's statue, and the death-struggle between Etiocles and Polynices— but silhouettes of heroes: Amphiaraus, Sisyphus, Nestor, Phoenix. From this extraordinary juxtaposition, we can only suppose that what the artist had in mind was an image of the underworld peopled by the illustrious shades of every cycle. In this infernal domain, pictured in all its horror, we see Achilles offering up human sacrifices to the *manes* of Patroclus. Achilles is about to thrust his sword into the throat of one of the Trojan victims whose eyes are convulsed with terror, while two demons of death await the soul that is about to be liberated.

(179)

On the opposite wall are scenes of a national character. The names painted by the figures identify them, and they are not altogether unknown to us. Some of them are mentioned by the classic writers, and also by Claudius in his famous *Discourse of Lyons* (the bronze tablet on which it was recorded was found in 1524). But the frescoes of Vulci have a particular value: they are first-hand evidence of events that were later pieced together by Roman historians who patriotically made them appear in a suitably flattering light.

The paintings show us two friends, Caelius Vibenna (also known as Vipenna) and Mastarna. Vibenna has just snatched Masterna from his Roman captors, and is inflicting fearful slaughter on the enemy. One of his warriors has flung a Roman, Gnaeus Tarquin, to the ground, and is about to plunge his sword into his throat.

It is difficult to reconcile this version of the incident with the account given by Varrus in Book V of his *Treatise on the Latin Language*, in which the same Caelius Vibenna appears as the ally of Romulus, who had rallied to his support when he was hard pressed by Tatius and his Sabines. Possibly Varrus is referring to another incident in the life of Vibenna, but if not, we must give credence to the painter of the Vulci fresco rather than to the historian, since his portrayal of the episode is far more in keeping with the revolution that swept Servius Tullius to power. We know from the *Discourse of Lyons*, in fact, that Servius was an Etruscan and was originally called Mastarna, and it is extremely probable that after the murder of the first Tarquin he was imposed on the Romans by the Etruscans of Vulci. Supposing this to be true, Livy's account of Tarquin's assassination and the accession of Servius Tullius would be a much-watered-down version of an event that was infinitely brutal, infinitely more discreditable to the Romans. Be that as it may, the fresco of the Francois Tomb is incontrovertible proof of Etruscan intervention into the affairs of Royal Rome. This painting gave the Moderns even more cause to doubt the authenticity of the ancient historians, and plunged archaeologists into further uncertainties, since the problem they were wrestling with was far too complex to be explained away by a single episode portrayed on the fresco of a single tomb.[5]

While one discovery after another was being made in central Italy, chance led to the extension of etruscology in the region of the Po. There was textual evidence that both slopes of the Apennines had been included in ancient Etruria and that Bologna had been an Etruscan city, but nothing of a confirmatory nature had come to light, nothing had been found that could compare with the marvellous tombs of southern Etruria. But in 1869 a number of artifacts dug up by peasants close to Bologna aroused the interest of the municipal engineer, Antonio Zannoni, and accordingly he decided to explore the terrain.

In August of that year, Zannoni uncovered the necropolis of the ancient Etruscan city of Felsina (the modern Bologna). Unlike his predecessors in central Italy who had been more concerned with harvesting a rich crop of treasures than with studying a site, Zannoni conducted his excavations with extreme precision, proceeding by a method that could truly be called scientific. He wrote a detailed description of each grave, catalogued the objects found in it, taking care to keep them separate from those from other graves, and scrupulously identified the various levels. Such meticulousness was rare indeed at this date, and was in striking contrast to the confusion that persisted for many years on sites where qualified archaeologists were at work.

Zannoni's researches brought out the real significance of an exploration carried out four years earlier by Count Gozzadini in the Reno valley, twenty-four miles from Bologna on the Pistoia road. The Count, who was an eminent archaeologist and had already won fame for his discovery of the necropolis of Villanova, believed he had laid bare in this valley, close to the modern town of Marzabotto, a second and identical necropolis. Actually, as Zannoni's explorations proved, Gozzadini had, in fact, disclosed the site of an Etruscan city. His mistake was due to the fact that during the first campaign the pickaxes of his workmen had encountered tombs, but when the excavations were resumed it soon became apparent that this was no place of burial. Gradually, an Etruscan city began to emerge in its entirety—it remained until quite recently the only Etruscan city known to archaeologists.

This city, called for the sake of convenience Marzabotto—we have no idea of its real name—was apparently a fortified post which had been set up to guard the main road between southern and Paduan Etruria. It was captured and laid waste by the Gauls in the fourth century B.C., hence only its ruins remain to us. The ravaged city was never rebuilt. After the Roman conquest the line of communications was shifted southward, running between the two spurs of the hills that overlooked the Tyrrhenian Sea and the Mediterranean respectively, and since Marzabotto no longer had any strategic value, it was abandoned for good. In Marzabotto, we have a miraculously preserved Etruscan site, unlike the sites of other Etruscan cities on which Roman cities were sometimes superposed and much more frequently, medieval towns. Marzabotto still retains many secrets, but its discovery marked another stage in etruscology, since it greatly enlarged its scope; at long last there had come to light in Etruria a world of the living, a domain of the Etruscan people.

Prior to the revelation of Marzabotto, knowledge of the Etruscans had been almost completely confined to their necropoles situated outside the city walls, whose tombs were buried so deeply in the earth (sometimes at a depth of ninety-five feet) that they had escaped destruction. Of their way of life, of the kind of houses they had lived in, archaeologists had not the slightest idea. The almost exclusively funerary character of the documents of etruscology has given the impression that the Etruscans were a gloomy people, preoccupied by thoughts of the next world and haunted by death. But when we begin to think of it, is this impression really justified? Even though we must refrain from all anachronistic comparisons, the care taken by the Etruscans to decorate their tombs (at least, at a certain date), the profusion of funerary offerings which makes each *hypogeum* a true dwelling for all eternity, cannot but convince us that their belief in survival was absolute. Can it really be asserted, then, that a people who cherished such a hope had a fundamentally pessimistic outlook? If we go still further and point out that the Etruscans made every provision to ensure that the after-life should be as cushioned as possible, can we not draw the deduction that they were a *bourgeois* people who placed a high value on their creature comforts and enjoyed to the full the sensual pleasures? Would they have expected the dead to savour the sweets of mortal existence in their tombs if they had not experienced the *ioie de vivre* in this world?

Although the exploration of Marazbotto could not in itself reverse the commonly expressed opinion that the Etruscans were a dour and gloomy people, it enriched our knowledge of their urban civilization and revealed, not only the influences that had led to its formation, but those which the Etruscans in turn exerted over Rome. The plan of Marzabotto tells its own story. While the line of the walls is irregular and purely conforms to the exigencies of defence, the city has a regular rectangular grid of streets. It lies at the foot of an *arx* on which stand several temples. The *cardo*, axed north-south, is forty-six feet wide, and is intersected at right-angles by two roads of equal width. The rectangles are made up by a number of alleys no more than sixteen feet wide. Neither Norba nor Ostia were known at this time; the Greek colonies of Southern Italy and Sicily had yet to be discovered but it was immediately noted that the plan of Marzabotto closely resembled that of the typical Roman city described by classic writers, and approximated very closely to the layout of cities that had been disengaged in the provinces, Timgad, for example. At first, Marzabotto seemed to confirm the traditional belief that the Etruscans had been the master-builders, but as archaeological data in fields outside etruscology accumulated, the problem became more and more complicated, and once more doubts arose. In fact, Marazbotto is a question-mark, and the answer is still beyond our reach.

The geometric plan of Marzabotto conforms exactly, not only with the plans of Norba and Ostia, but also with those of contemporary Greek cities: Selinonte (destroyed by the Carthaginians in 409) and Agrigente (whose plan has recently been established by aerial photography) in Sicily; Metaponte and many other cities in Magna Graecia. We also find it in the East, in Priene, for example, in Asia Minor; Priene was entirely rebuilt during the fourth century B.C. on the rectangular grid. These comparisons (only a few of which could be made at the beginning of the present century) lead us to believe that the Etruscans cannot be credited for having invented the grid plan, any more than they can be credited with having invented the techniques of ceramics, sculpture and painting, even though the ancient historians affirm that the geometric plan was bound up with the Etruscan mystique of city building.

Are we to take it, then, that the celebrated 'Etruscan ritual' adopted by the Romans when they founded their colonies in Italy and overseas, is only an Italianized version of the Hippodamian plan, the plan that Hippodamus of Miletus put into use in the Piraeus, in Thourioi and Magna Graecia? This hypothesis is far from satisfactory. When and how did the Hippodamian plan become charged with the religious significance that is attributed to the Etrusco-Roman rectangular grid? Does it follow that Romulus, tracing with his plough the outlines of his square Rome was, although he was quite unconscious of the fact, the disciple of a Greek architect?

Present-day archaeologists incline to the opinion that the rectangular grid was not invented by Hippodamus; they believe it to be an Eastern concept, possibly Babylonian, which ultimately reached the West, and spread throughout the Mediterranean Basin. If the Etruscans were of Lydian origin, they may well have introduced it into Italy, but even if we take the view that they were not Lydian, that their civilization evolved in Italy under the influence of Eastern Hellenism, the plan of Marzabotto testifies to the existence of a community with a Mediterranean culture (in the widest sense of the word) prior to the Roman conquest. Vases and statues can find their way from one shore of a sea to the other while potters and sculptors remain in their native countries, but whereas trade routes are easily established, the planning of a city is complex to a degree; it presupposes the conscious imitation of a model, the arrival of an army of technicians and that of an intellectual and artistic community.

Much more was learnt from the exploration of Marzabotto. On the *arx* dominating the city the remains of at least five temples were identified; these dated back to the close of the sixth century B.C., when the Etruscans first established themselves on the site. The most important of these sanctuaries might have been expressly built to illustrate Vitruvius's description of a temple in the Etruscan tradition; like the capitols of Rome and Roman cities, it was tripartite, but whereas in the former there was only one Capitolium, on the citadel of Marzabotto there was a second, smaller sanctuary with three *cellae*. From this we assume that two distinct triads were installed on the *arx*, the first of which united the Etruscan equivalents of the three major deities, Jupiter, Juno, and Minerva, while the second probably united the divinities corresponding with the Latin triad of Liber, Ceres, and Libera. In Rome, the temple of this minor triad was at the foot of the Aventine, and in classic times, Liber, Ceres, and Libera became Dionysos, Demeter, and Persephone. The temple of Marzabotto strongly suggests that the Roman grouping of the lesser triad was due, not to Greek, but to Etruscan influence.

Another somewhat mysterious feature of Roman religion had its counterpart in Marzabotto. In front of the altar of the larger temple was a ditch covered with a slab, at the bottom of which human bones were found. This was undoubtedly a *mundus*, the opening which put the world of the living in communication with that of the dead. Ancient texts refer to the *mundus* on the Palatine, and one of these sacred ditches was found by Boni beneath the Palace of Domitian. Now, the *mundus* has often been considered as one of the most strictly national institutions of Roman religion; must we, then, conclude from the *mundus* of Marzabotto that it was, in fact, borrowed from the Etruscan religion? The answer is no. The *mundus*, linked to the cult of the dead, is not peculiar to Etruria. It is mentioned in that episode of the *Odyssey* when Ulysses conjures up the spirit of the soothsayer Tiresias, further-more it has been found on many sites of archaic Greece, notably Mycenae.

Once again, as the result of research into affiliations and influ-ences, oversimplified unilinear hypotheses had to be discarded; the outcome of a single exploration, however conclusive it may seem, is not enough to establish a truth. Indeed, far from provid-ing the solution to a problem, it adds to its complexity and restates it in completely new terms.

FROM SATRICUM TO VEII

At the time when Italy was still divided and there was no central authority the non-political *Istituto die Corrispondenza Archeologica*, played a most valuable part and was, in fact, the unofficial ministry for archaeological research. After 1870 the State took over, and every site in the country came under its strict control. Gone were the days (theoretically, at least) of the amateurs, the treasure-seekers and those menaces, the traffickers in antiquities. Erudite scholars still carried on their researches in the provinces, but gradually they were replaced by qualified archaeologists. Un-doubtedly, undercover operators continued their activities, for no security measures are completely watertight; the treasures these illegal digs bring to light benefit the antique market, and ultimately enrich the world's museums, that is, if they are not acquired by private collectors, a total loss to the rest of us. The rigorous steps taken to prevent clandestine researches, however, led to their marked decrease, and in the new climate archaeology began to attach far less importance to the study of artifacts, more and more to the study of sites.

Objects that could be classified with near accuracy and whose provenance was practically assured went to the regional museums. The excavations of Lombardy enriched the museum of Bologna, those of Tuscany, the museum of Florence. To house the treasures that came to light in Southern Etruria and Latium, the Villa Giulia (built for Pope Julius III between 1550 and 1555 on the outskirts of Rome, immediately north of the Borghese Gardens) was converted into a museum which soon surpassed all the rest. A few years earlier, in 1876, an archaeological periodical had come into existence that published up-to-date bulletins of the progress of the excavations that had been undertaken in various parts of Italy. This periodical, *Notizie degli Scavi*, was sponsored by the *Accademia dei Lincei* and was included in its articles; special issues of *Notizie* appear today.

Up to this time, with the exception of Marzabotto, etruscology had confined itself almost exclusively to the exploration of necropoles. Once the State had assumed control, however, archaeologists paid much more attention to the ruins they uncovered, no matter how vestigial they were, and examined each level exhaustively. As a result there came to light, not only tombs but temples whose precious terracotta revetments were successfully reconstructed, thanks to a laborious game of patience.

The first sites to benefit from this new and meticulous approach were those in the vicinity of Rome. In 1886, at Civita Castellana on the borders of Etruria and Latium, the ancient city of Falerii was laid bare. A few years later discoveries made by archaeologists of the French School shed valuable light on the obscure centuries between the foundation of the Urbs and its capture by the Gauls at the beginning of the fourth century B.C. The explorations of Stephane Gsell at Vulci were followed by those of Graillot at Conca, the ancient Satricum.

The discovery of Satricum showed that the domain of the Etruscans had extended even farther south than had been thought. Satricum was not, in fact, situated on the right bank of the Tiber, but, as we now know, in the heart of Latium, at the extreme limit of the Pontine Marshes. It was here that in 1896 archaeologists became cognizant of a site that was clearly Etruscan: an *arx* that covered some four hectares and on which the remains of Cyclopian walls had always been visible. F. Graillot earned the distinction of disengaging close to this *oppidum* a temple whose sub-foundations were also Cyclopian. Undoubtedly, this was an Etruscan sanctuary, oriented from east to west, and answering to Vitruvius's description: 'One of those squat, broad, massive and severe temples with a protuberant roof and projecting pediments supported on heavy columns.' Graillot's vivid impression of the original aspect of the sanctuary anticipated the graphic reconstruction that became possible a little later on. He only uncovered a few elements of the temple: the subfoundations of a wall, the base of a column, a few scattered stones, but by calling on the help of his imagination he was able to picture silhouetted against the sky, the outlines of a massive temple decorated in brilliant colours, which had dominated the plain—an Italic version of the Greek temples which, at the time of the Etruscans, were being constructed on the eastern shore of the Ionian Sea, as well as in southern Italy and Sicily.

The discovery of this site, apart from its geographical importance, was of particular value because of the large number of architectonic terracotta fragments which were found amongst the debris—fragments of flat tiles, reliefs and statues that had formed part of the temple's exterior decoration. F. Graillot was not given the time to reconstruct them; the authorities who had granted him permission to excavate the site early in January, anxious to reserve the fruitful terrain for Italian archaeologists, ordered him to cease work. His researches only lasted for a few weeks; nevertheless, even in this short space, they completed and confirmed the discoveries at Civita Castellana, and disclosed for the first time, in all its reality, early fifth-century Etruscan art.

Carried away by excitement, lacking sufficient standards of comparison, Graillot pre-dated the temple by fifty years. But this mistake was relatively unimportant, since archaeologists realized immediately that Graillot's discovery took them back to the era of Royal Rome in a region that she had either already subjugated or was shortly to include in her Empire.

Up to this time it had been possible to believe that the Etruscan cities had formed a world apart, a world inimical to Rome, constantly threatening, constantly under threat. From now on, however, it could no longer be doubted that the Etruscans had left their mark on Latium; moreover, they had imprinted this mark at the traditional date of the advent of the Tarquins and during the reign of Servius Tullius, who, in the light of the Francois Tomb, may very well have been imposed on the Romans by the Etruscans of Vulci. Indirectly, the true face of Rome, the Etruscanized Rome of the sixth century B.C. was beginning to reappear. The descriptions by classic writers of the temples with terracotta revetments that were once raised in Rome, the laudatory sentiments of philosophers and rhaetors who extolled the age of the gods of clay, gods infinitely purer than those of marble and gold, assumed a new significance that rang with truth.

Not many years were to pass before these few glimmers of light were transformed into a dazzling illumination. In March 1913, seventeen years after Graillot's exploration, the Department of Archaeological Research for the province of Rome initiated a campaign in the locality known as Isola Farnese. This systematic series of excavations led to one of the most amazing discoveries in the history of etruscology. While it was not entirely revolutionary, since the way had been paved by the explorations of Civita Castellana, Conca, and various other sites, the dazzling beauty of the treasures it revealed raised the glory of Etruscan art to a far higher pinnacle than that to which it had been elevated by the funerary paintings, and fully justified the inclusion of Etruscan sculptors in the most eclectic of museums. The breath-taking moment of discovery equalled that when, on a never-to-be-forgotten day in February, on the Acropolis of Athens, north-west of the Erechtheum, the group of *Kore* came to light. On the site of Isola Farnese, as on the site of Greece, two *favissae* yielded up their treasures, and archaeologists gazed with wonder and awe at masterpieces of an art that up till then had been buried in oblivion.

The excavations at Isola Farnese had been undertaken in the hope of finding the lost city of Veii, which was known to have stood in this vicinity. The archaeologists had little to go on, for at this date, only the site occupied by the Imperium Municipium had been established. Clandestine researches in the course of the nine-teenth century had scratched the surface and revealed the vestiges of the township set up during the reign of Augustus on the terri-tory of Veii, Rome's most deadly rival. These same researches had also revealed the presence of a few tombs, amongst them, the Campana Tomb, a clear indication that there was an Etruscan level in this locality. A few exploratory digs in 1888 and 1889 had confirmed these meagre facts, but of Veii itself, there was not a sign.

This, then, was the situation in 1913. During the opening phase of the campaign, the trenches only disclosed tombs, but these were so numerous that they testified to the existence of a very large community on the site during the Etruscan era. In three years 1,200 tombs of every period, every type, were disengaged. Amongst them were cremation graves, and at the bottom of these small circular wells were cinerary vases, some of which were Villanovan whilst others were hut urns similar to those found in the necropoles of Latium and in the necropolis of the Sacred Way. At a very early date, inhumation *fossae* had made their appearance amongst the cremation graves, and had then multiplied to such an extent that they had almost supplanted the latter. Chamber tombs were also disengaged, but the majority of these had been ransacked, and so it was difficult to date them.

After long and patient research, however, archaeologists succeeded in establishing a chronology for the graves, which ranged over an unbroken period of time from the tenth century B.C. down to the fall of Veii, traditionally ascribed to the year 396 B.C. There was not the slightest evidence of any violent upheaval; clearly, it was a single civilization that had evolved in the locality, from its remote Italic origins up to the era when the Etruscan Empire had reached its zenith. There was absolutely nothing to suggest that another people had established themselves there, had gained the ascendancy and imposed their rites, their customs, their own cultural forms on the original inhabitants. The Greek influence, Oriental to begin with, and then Attic, had exerted itself continuously and pacifically. All this surprised a good many of the historians who favoured the hypothesis of an Etruscan invasion and were not at all willing to accept the idea of such a perfect cultural continuity from pre-history to history. Yet, since they had to admit that archaeology had furnished the proof of this continuity, did it necessarily lead, they asked, to the conclusion that the Italic peoples had been progressively civilized by the Etruscans? If it did, would it not raise an even more difficult problem? Would it not be tantamount to asserting that the Veiians were not true Etruscans but an Etruscanized people? Traditional evidence afforded no grounds whatsoever for doubting that the Veiians were not authentic members of the Etruscan nation.

Once again, scholars found themselves faced with the infuriating problem of the origin of the Etruscans. The archaeologists who were working on the site wisely refrained from tackling it in its entirety. Warned by all the polemics this subject had given rise to in the past, they did not advance a new theory based on a single exploration, but restricted themselves to pointing out that the Hellenization of Etruria had not, it seemed, been due to an invasion or a massive colonization, but to a slow and pacific infiltration of merchants, and possibly artists, from Asia during the period of the orientalizing phase of Etruscan art, and later, by a similar infiltration from Greece, notably Attica. It was tacitly assumed that the Etruscans were an offshoot of the Villanovans; traces of these people who cremated their dead had been found in the vicinity of Bologna. As we shall see, this opened the way for a number of extremely shaky hypotheses which have few adherents today.

The first exploration of Veii led to another, equally important issue. To the surprise of the archaeologists, there came to light the type of grave, the type of funerary furnishings that had hitherto been held to be peculiar to the Latin provinces. This discovery dealt a shattering blow to the dogma which maintained that the cultures of pre-Roman central Italy had formed strictly separate compartments. Archaeological criteria alone warned historians not to differentiate too sharply between the various peoples. The funerary furnishings of a grave were evidence, not of a particular race, but of a particular culture, using the word culture in its widest sense, and there was nothing to prove that race and culture were synonymous. On the contrary, there was every indication that at a very early date, in the very heart of the much larger Mediterranean communities there existed, as had been suspected, a community whose culture was Italic.

While the excavations of the necropolis continued, the ancient Etruscan habitat of Veii was also being explored. In 1913 and 1914, on the hill that is traditionally considered to be the acropolis of the ancient city, hut foundations were laid bare; these dated back beyond the eighth century B.C. and appeared to be similar in all respects to those of the Palatine. In the level immediately above, vestiges of the stone houses that had succeeded the archaic cabins were found; sherds of orientalizing pottery enabled archaeologists to establish a chronology that oscillated between the eighth and sixth centuries B.C. Veii yielded a succession of levels comparable to those which clearly appear today in the soil of Rome.

By the beginning of 1914 the archaeologists in charge of the excavations on the site of Veii could congratulate themselves on the outcome of the work with which they had been entrusted. In addition to locating the ancient city, they had established several facts whose consequences were to be far-reaching. Nevertheless, one of these archaeologists, E. Gabrici, was not satisfied. He was convinced that the site had not yielded up all that might have been expected—no temple, for instance, had come to light. He therefore resolved to carry the researches a little further, and opened up several trenches in an area where ex-votos had frequently been found. The dig disclosed a great many more of these ex-votos, as well as artifacts of a similar nature, but no sign of a temple. In August 1914 Gabrici was appointed Director of the National Museum of Palermo; to his bitter disappointment, the sanctuary had failed to come to light. G. Q. Giglioli, his successor, decided to pursue the quest. Giglioli had noted that all Gabrici's finds had come from a particular spot at the foot of a hill, and it had struck him that the ex-votos, the fragments of tiles, statues and painted terracotta jumbled together in a heap might have fallen from a height. Giglioli had formed the impression, therefore, that the temple from which they obviously came was situated on the hill, and as it turned out, he was right. Half-way up the hill, on a terraced slope overlooking the valley of a tributary of the Cremera, he soon disengaged a wall constructed in massive tufa blocks, at the foot of which there came to light a large deposit of fragments of every kind. Plainly he had found the long-lost temple.

In the meantime, Italy had entered the First World War, and Giglioli was called up. Veii was very much in his mind, and on 18 May 1916 a period of leave enabled him to return to the site. It was now that he reaped his reward. At the time when he had disengaged the first wall, he had ordered a series of trenches to be dug, and we can imagine his excitement when one of these trenches pushed along another wall (subsequently identified as the northern boundary of the sacred precinct) encountered an amazing deposit of terracotta statues. All were faceless but one, that of a young god standing erect, his lips curved in an age-old, hieratic smile.

Immediately, with infinite precautions, the statues were taken to the Villa Giulia to be restored. The largest was that of the youthful deity who was beyond all doubt Apollo, the son of Zeus.

Apollo is tall (the statue is about six feet high, though it appears to be a little less as the head is bent slightly forward); the supple folds of his knee-length tunic barely conceal the lines of his body. When the statue was found, both arms were missing, but subsequently the upper part of the right arm was recovered; it is stretched out as if the god is about to strike at an enemy, and balances the line of the left leg. Apollo's face is utterly serene, a serenity that contrasts curiously with the vigorous forward-striding sense of movement that his figure conveys, the impetuous onrush that has moulded his tunic so closely to his form. The god's flesh is painted the copper-red of archaic convention; his shoulder-length ringlets and his eyebrows are black.

The other statues found in the deposit (this went back to Roman times, when what remained of the temple's decorative elements had been reverently assembled and covered over) were not nearly so well preserved, but by using their imagination the archaeologists concluded that the group represented Apollo and Heracles fighting for possession of the hind, Ceryneia, watched by Hermes and a goddess, possibly Artemis—this interpretation is now generally accepted. The discovery in 1939 of the statue of a woman accompanied by a youth shed some doubt on it, but it may be that this piece of sculpture did not form part of the group. At one time it was thought that the Veii statues stood on bases in front of the temple; in fact, they surmounted the roof and were outlined against the luminous sky. At least, it would seem so, since terracotta sockets resembling saddles on which they no doubt rested, have since been found.

Never before had the soil of Etruria yielded up such a marvel. The group of statues not only confirmed but surpassed all the concepts of the vitality of Etruscan art during the archaic period of Greek sculpture. When the Apollo of Veii is compared with certain reliefs of the Siphnos treasury at Delphi, it can plainly be seen that it cannot date back beyond the closing years of the sixth century B.C., and that its style is unmistakably Ionic. But comparisons, while they reveal influences, do not explain everything. In the case of the Apollo of Veii, they do not explain why, for so large a statue, the sculptor elected to use terracotta. That he did so proves that there was a school of sculptors so highly skilled in the

POMPEII The Via Stabia

POMPEII The House of the Moralist. The Triclinium

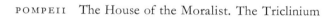

SICILY, TAORMINA View of the Greek theatre with Etna in the background

techniques of this extremely difficult medium that they were able to cope with the problem of baking a piece of such large dimensions. As we have said, the Greek influence is obvious, but for all that the statue is purely Etruscan. The vigour with which it is executed, the slight heaviness of the musculature, the dramatic, almost brutal, sense of movement it conveys are evidence of a spirit entirely unrelated to that which informs archaic Greek sculpture.

With the discovery of the Apollo, a new chapter in the history of ancient art was opened. Here was confirmation of a most striking order that the classic writers were not romancing when they spoke of a school of Veiian sculptors who specialized in life-size terracotta statues. We know from these same writers that the most celebrated of these sculptors was Vulca, who was commissioned by Tarquinius Prisca to sculpt the statue of Jupiter for the Capitolium.[6] Pliny tells us that this statue was in terracotta and painted red. Plutarch adds that the terracotta sculpture of a chariot and horses which surmounted the Capitolium was also the work of Etruscan craftsmen.[7]

After Giglioli's discovery of the Apollo group, it was no longer possible to doubt the evidence of the ancient texts. This, in itself, was of considerable value, but it was by no means the end of the story. The date ascribed to the Apollo of Veii led inevitably to the conclusion that the Veiian school had come into existence at a very early period, at latest, the close of the sixth century B.C., and that the Apollo, far from being an experimental work, was the outcome of years of experience. Now, according to tradition, it was precisely at the end of the sixth century B.C. that, after the fall of the Tarquins, the Capitolium was dedicated. This dealt a shattering blow to hypercritic historians, who maintained that the Capitol had only become the pre-eminent hill in Rome after the Gallic invasion in the fourth century B.C.; the structure they had built up so carefully collapsed. Moreover, it was recalled that on the Capitol, not far from the Temple of Jupiter, fragments of a painted terracotta antefix had been found. (Antefixes were ornamental devices used to cover the ends of half-round roof-tiles.) The antefix in question, the head of a woman, proved the existence of an Etruscan temple, proved in addition that the ancient history of Rome was not a mere tissue of legends. Insidious arguments that opened with: 'Does it not appear more likely . . .' had to be abandoned, chronological certainties retracted in the face of the archaeological evidence. As Gigliogli put it:

Just as epigraphers who rightly and properly doubt the authenticity of an inscription of which they only possess an ancient copy, refuse to include it in the corpus, just as they revise their views when the original inscription comes to light, so, after the Veii discoveries, I am certain that the erudite scholars of Roman history who, confining themselves to the texts, believed that traditional evidence was utterly unreliable, will re-examine and modify the conclusions that stringent criticism of this evidence has led them to draw.

THE AENEAS STATUETTES

Veii had another startling surprise in store for archaeologists and historians. The legend of the Trojan origins of Rome: the coming of Aeneas, son of Venus and Anchises, to Italy, the colonization of Latium by the immigrants from Asia, was generally believed to have sprung from Roman pride, or, rather, the false pride of an upstart nation with no ancestry. The myth was thought to have been born at the time when Rome, mistress of Italy, was faced by a second Achilles in the person of Pyrrhus, King of Epyrus, the first Hellene to oppose her designs on Magna Graecia. But suddenly, in our own century, there emerged from the Etruscan soil of Veii statuettes of Aeneas with Anchises on his shoulders.

These statuettes (the news of their discovery in 1938 was abruptly announced at the Archaeological Congress held in Berlin in 1939), suggested that historians should trace the Aeneas legend still farther back. Admittedly it is difficult to date these examples of popular art of no particular style, which were probably more or less mass produced for a hundred years or so. Italian archaeologists are inclined to ascribe them to the second half of the fifth century B.C., while a number of French archaeologists believe that they should be dated fifty years later; still others are of the opinion that they are considerably earlier and regard them as Hellenistic. The margin of error may be a couple of centuries or even slightly more, but even if we accept the earliest possible date (the close of the fourth century B.C.), the dissemination of the Aeneas statuettes at Veii would still be anterior by at least a generation to the day of Pyrrhus.

Leaving aside the question of the date of the Aeneas statuettes, it is absolutely certain that a legend associated with a place of pilgrimage could not possibly have been a sudden improvisation, least of all the improvisation of a people inimical to Veii. Conversely, it is hardly likely that the faithful who honoured the memory of Pious Aeneas were desirous of flattering Roman vanity. Rome may have accredited herself with the Trojan myth (other cities in Italy and Sicily had done so, for example Capua and Segesta), but she could never have invented it; indeed, the Aeneas story had grown up long before her time. The discovery of the Veii statuettes focused attention on a number of earlier finds that archaeologists had not been able to place, amongst them, a red-figured Etruscan amphora in the Munich Museum and an intaglio in Paris, undoubtedly the work of a sixth-century Etruscan craftsman. A study of these objects proved that the political ambitions of the Romans had not been responsible for the introduction of the Aeneas legend into Italy. Furthermore, the Aeneas episodes in the wall-paintings of Etruscan tombs had made it apparent that this legend, as well as many others, was known in Italy long before the Roman legionaries marched towards Magna Graecia; once again, then, the Etruscans had acted as intermediaries between Greece and Rome.

The progress of etruscology did much to demolish the structure of reason so laboriously raised by the hypercritics; the ancient historians, scornfully dismissed as 'naïve' finally triumphed over their modern colleagues. The etruscologists proved conclusively that Rome had not existed in a vacuum, that she had not been spontaneously generated and born out of the blue; they proved equally conclusively that the Sovereign People had not vegetated for several centuries in a hopeless mediocrity, groping about in darkness until such time as the first direct contacts with southern Italy redeemed and lighted them.

With each new archaeological conquest, it becomes increasingly clear that from the time when the Urbs was founded Latium formed a cultural community around it and that it was precisely at this moment that the seeds of its future greatness were sown. The religion of Rome was gradually enriched with beliefs of Eastern origin; the Roman deities, while they remained recognizable, were clothed in plastic forms that imbued them with new life. The Latins experienced an evolution similar to that which transformed the Achaean immigrants when they came into contact with Aegean culture on the shores of the Mediterranean; the vitality, the vigour of the Etruscan conquerors so vivified the heritage of the past that the Romans gladly accepted it, adapting it to their own traditions. From all this we see that the chain of circumstances which led to the Roman miracle was not so very different, after all, from that which produced the miracle of Greece.

VOLSINII AND TARQUINII

Twentieth-century etruscology can boast of more than the discovery of Veii. Only a few years ago R. Bloch and a number of young archaeologists of the French School shed fresh light on one of the most important sites of southern Etruria, that of the ancient city of Volsinii, at one time the capital of the Etrurian world. The conquering Romans had destroyed Volsinii and expelled its inhabitants, and for a long period of time historians had not been able to determine where it had stood; a large number, as the result of following a misleading trail, believed that Orvieto had been built on its site and that Volsinii was buried for ever beneath the medieval town. Today we know for certain that Etruscan Volsinii was erected on the slopes of the hills that dominate Bolsena. The Romans had contented themselves (as they had contented themselves in Gaul and elsewhere) with compelling the vanquished to descend from their acropolis, and had then driven them to the shores of Lake Bolsena. Volsinii was abandoned for good.

The first vestige of the lost city to come to light was its wall, whose contour had been established by preliminary digs. Like that of Marzabotto, it was irregular and did not conform with the rectangular grid. As one might have expected, the religious mystique had had to give way to the exigencies of defence, nevertheless, this fact had certain consequences: the interpretation of the traditional accounts of Rome's foundation appeared in a doubtful light since the line of its fortifications had been equally irregular.

Volsinii's wall, constructed with massive, matching blocks of stone, seems to have been similar to the type that became common after the Gallic invasion in the fourth century B.C. Plainly, however, Volsinii must have had defences prior to this date, and indeed, archaeologists noted that some sections of the wall noticeably resembled the fortified walls of Magna Graecia which date back to the sixth century B.C. Several explanations can be put forward; for instance, the Etruscans may well have incorporated part of the original wall in the course of repairing the fourth-century wall, or the fourth-century wall may have replaced fortifications of an earlier date. That the techniques of Greece should have prevailed in Volsinii from the fifth century onwards is not at all surprising. Greek influences are equally apparent in Marzabotto, whose plan was plainly inspired by that of the Greek cities of southern Italy.

Amongst the Etruscan cities explored in recent years is Tarquinii. This exploration, directed by P. Romanelli, has gone a long way towards revealing the true face of ancient Etruria. A campaign on the site had been initiated in 1934, but in 1938, it was suspended; the excavations were resumed by Romanelli in 1946. At this time, all that was known of Tarquinii was its necropolis, but thanks to Romanelli, we have evidence of the domain of the living. True, the research has not yet been carried to its logical conclusion, and the data so far acquired may be filled out and completed in the future, but already we have valuable information. Romanelli succeeded in tracing the entire line of the wall, and we now know that its perimeter was approximately five miles. The city occupied an area of some 320 acres, a very considerable area when we remember that it was only one third less than that occupied by Rome at the time when the Servian Wall was built. The wall of Tarquinii, constructed in freestone, is very similar to that of Volsinii, and archaeologists therefore tend to ascribe it to the fourth century B.C. As at Volsinii, however, this date is open to doubt, and so far nothing has come to light that would allow it to be fixed. Nevertheless, the exploration of a well whose opening had been partly covered by a later wall, proved that the site was already occupied in the sixth century B.C., and it seems probable that from this era, Tarquinii had a system of defences.

During the 1934–8 campaign an equally important discovery had been made. Shortly after it had begun archaeologists became aware of the presence of a vast monument, to which they gave the popular name of the *Ara della Regina*, the Altar of the Queen. Soundings had been carried out at various times, but had been so rapidly abandoned that it had been impossible to form any idea of what this monument was; at one time it had been taken to be a tomb, at another, part of the fortifications. Today we know it was a temple. In the course of the excavations of 1938 there came to light a sufficient number of elements to allow us to form a clear and precise picture. The temple, raised on an immense terrace and approached by a monumental flight of steps, was composed of a *cella* surrounded by a portico. The sanctuary itself was 140 feet long and slightly more than eighty feet wide; its elongated shape suggested a Greek rather than an Etruscan temple. Of the decorative features that were found, the most remarkable is the pair of terracotta winged horses in high relief which came from the temple.

The sanctuary dates back either to the close of the fourth century B.C. or to the beginning of the third century B.C. and the Greek influence is unmistakable in its shape and its decoration. The temple of Tarquinii exemplifies an extremely interesting attempt to combine to the religious tradition according to which temples were always built on lofty terraces so that the presiding deity could look down with a protective eye on the entire city, with the ideal of the new Greek-inspired architecture whose aim was to create a harmonious whole that would blend perfectly with the city and its surroundings. At Tarquinii, then, we see a new form of urbanization in the process of developing, and this at a time when Rome had not even begun to think of enhancing herself with monumental ensembles; once again, and even more clearly, the Etruscans emerge as the intermediaries between Rome and Greece. They acted in this capacity not only by increasing the flow of trade between Greece and Italy, and multiplying the Greek image on vases, in paintings, statues and reliefs, but also by furnishing the master-craftsmen of Rome with models that were all the more attractive because, in the course of time, they had become naturalized, had been partly assimilated by the Italic tradition, and far from clashing with religious sentiments, responded to the needs of the religious rites. The *Ara della Regina* (we do not know to which deity the temple was dedicated, and the theories based on the winged horses of the pediment are all very doubtful) seems to have replaced an earlier sanctuary which may have dated back to the sixth century B.C. If so, the decline of the Etruscan Empire and its disintegration during the last years of the fifth century B.C. could have had little effect on the prosperity of Tarquinii, since, a hundred years later, its citizens were able to build the magnificent temple whose style furnishes the proof that they were in continuous contact with the provinces of Greece.

THE ETRUSCAN LANGUAGE

Although our knowledge of the Etruscans continues to increase, they still remained enigmatic, they still retain that aura of mystery that so fascinated the Romantics. Two outstanding problems remain unsolved: the problem of their origins and the problem of their language.

From time to time someone claims to have deciphered the Etruscan language, but so far no system has stood up to expert criticism. Although it is technically undecipherable, however, this does not mean that the Etruscan language is the closed book sealed with seven seals that it was in the early day of etruscology. Even though its structure escapes us, certain parts of speech have been analysed, and we know the meaning of many Etruscan words. Our ignorance is only relative, therefore, and we are like travellers in a foreign country who, by a particular inflexion in the context of a phrase can catch the general drift of what is being said; even though this does not enable us to penetrate very deeply into the thoughts of the foreigners, we are not altogether baffled and mystified.

The Etruscan inscriptions we possess are mainly epitaphs. They are usually very brief, and with the help of the few lists of Etruscan words drawn up by Latin authors, and by means of Graeco-Latin glosses, we can arrive at the gist of these summaries of the lives of the dead. In a sense, the epitaphs have only a limited interest, and if we could interpret them word for word, while we should un-undoubtedly acquire a little more information about Etruscan institutions, about family, political and social life in Etruria (a recent study has shown what might be gleaned from these meagre facts by the application of a safe and judicious method), we should learn nothing new, nothing that we do not already know of the spiritual life of this people; the epitaphs are not literature, and consequently they do not reflect a personality, an aesthetic or a tradition.

True, we possess several larger documents, two of which would undoubtedly be particularly informative if only we could decipher them more completely. One of these is a text written on the linen wrappings of a mummy discovered in Alexandria and taken to the Zagreb museum, where it was perceived that the language was Etruscan. How did this linen book find its way to Egypt, how did it fall into the hands of the embalmer? There are no answers to these questions. Naturally, in the course of its metamorphoses, it was badly mutilated; only some 1,200 words remain, but from these philologers have been able to establish that it is a kind or sacred calendar, indicating the days on which such and such a sacrifice had to be made to this or that divinity.

Sacred calendars were by no means uncommon in central Italy, Umbria and Rome. Most of them are engraved on bronze or stone, and the Zagreb mummy has provided us with the only example of a linen-book calendar. The *libri lintei* were simply bands of linen wound round spindles; at a very early date, the Romans used them to record events of importance in their history, mainly events of religious significance. We know that the *libri lintei* were one of the sources from which the ancient historians drew their information.

The second inscription, the Tile of Capua, is engraved on a terracotta plaque. Also of a sacred character, it refers specifically to the ceremonial of burial.

That the two longest Etruscan inscriptions are both concerned with religious observances is quite certainly not due to sheer coincidence. In the days of antiquity, the Etruscans were regarded as a deeply devout people, who, ceaselessly seeking to propitiate the gods, conformed meticulously with the rites prescribed by an extremely strict tradition—the Etruscan religion was said to owe its origins to a divine revelation. Even though our understanding of the inscriptions is imperfect, we can nevertheless form some idea of the effect this sacred literature produced on Roman religion, the part it played in shaping its most ancient ritual. In the light of what we know, we can no longer consider as typically Roman the religious formalism that is found in the prescribed cults and in the works of such writers as Cato; above all, we cannot link it to Indo-European survivals, since philologers now agree unanimously that the Etruscans had absolutely no connexion with these Aryan immigrants. It was in the interior of the peninsula, in the heart of the Mediterranean community which embraced such widely divergent ethnic and cultural elements, that a great part of the Roman religion was formed and developed.

THE ORIGINS OF THE ETRUSCANS

What were the origins of the Etruscans? Even in the days of

Antiquity this question had been asked, and had elicited very different answers. To the explanations of Herodotus and Dionysos of Halicarnassus, modern historians added theories of their own—theories that changed as linguistic and archaeological discoveries made fresh facts available. The light is still so dim, however, that many scholars fight shy of the problem or else restate it in completely new terms.

There is one fact of which we have irrefutable evidence: from the seventh century B.C., a people with a brilliant culture whose art revealed a predominantly Eastern influence was established in Italy. Most of the Italic populations, the Latins, the Oscans, the Umbrians and the Venetans, used Indo-European idioms and their languages formed part of the great Indo-European family, but the language of this people, a language apparently confined for years to its own domain, was unique and could not be linked to any linguistic group. Where did this people originate? When did they establish themselves on Italian soil?

According to Herodotus, the Etruscans were Lydian invaders (or, properly speaking, colonists) who had left their country during the heroic age towards the twelfth century B.C., and had settled in Italy. From traditional sources we learn that a people related to the Etruscans had settled in Lemnos, but were ultimately forced to quit the island in the fifth century B.C. by Miltiades the Younger and the Athenian colonists. In 1885 the discovery at Lemnos of an inscription in an Etruscoid language confirmed this story; other inscriptions written in the same language have since been found on the island. It seems very probable, therefore, that the Etruscans—or, at any rate, certain elements of the Etruscan people—were the offshoot of a pre-Hellenic people of whose existence we find proof in a number of legends originating in Greece and the Cyclades. This people, submerged by the wave of Indo-European immigrants from the north, only survived in a few isolated groups; of these, the principal group was Etruscan.

Even though this seems to be probable, grave difficulties arise. As we have already said, the excavations of the Veii necropolis proved that the Villanovan culture had preceded without any break in continuity the appearance of the first Etruscan tombs, and it is difficult to reconcile this fact with the theory that the Etruscans were of Eastern origin. There is absolutely no evidence of a sudden, violent upheaval, an invasion. Furthermore, as the

Villanovan culture, characterized by the biconical urns in which they placed the ashes of their dead, has long been thought to be that of a people coming from the north, a number of scholars formed the opinion that the Etruscans were of northern origin and had penetrated into Italy via the Alps. But this second hypothesis leads to still greater difficulties. Where, for instance, did these proto-Etruscans come from, and when did they break away from the Villanovans who were undoubtedly the ancestors of the Umbrians and even of the Latins, for the culture of Latium was also an off-shoot of the Villanovan culture?

Today, there is little support for the idea that the Etruscans were invaders who imposed by force of arms their language, customs, and religious beliefs on the Italic peoples of the peninsula. Indeed, it is now generally accepted that the culture of the entire Mediterranean community was formed by influences exerted from within the country. Supposing this to be true, the Villanovan culture would not be an historically homogenous phenomenon, but the outcome of an evolution peculiar to Italy, possibly affected by currents from the north, which integrated extremely diverse ethnic substrata. In this complex whole of Italic peoples in the process of evolution, these or those elements would have become predominant according to the geographical location. In southern Etruria, Eastern influences and the language of the Tyrrhenians (those great seafarers whose traces have been found throughout the Mediterranean basin) would have predominated, whereas in Latium, Latin, the language of certain Aryan elements, would have prevailed. Then, towards the seventh century B.C., as the result of closer ties formed at a given moment between the Etruscan people and the peoples of the eastern Mediterranean, there would have been a cultural awakening in Etruria, and it would have been at this time that the orientalizing style, the oustanding style during the seventh and sixth centuries, would have made its appearance. To sum up, the brilliant culture of the Etruscans was not, according to this hypothesis, a pre-formed culture imported in one piece into Italy, but the outcome of a regional quickening, a sudden acceleration similar to that which, at about this same time, the Greek world, in the throes of emerging from its dark ages, was experiencing.[8]

Whether this theory is correct or not, the Etruscan phenomenon played a significant part in the development of pre-Roman

history. Before the foundation of the Urbs, the Etruscans represented Italy in the heart of the Mediterranean community. It was
towards Etruria, particularly southern Etruria, but also towards
the great port of Spina at the mouth of the Po, that maritime trade
was directed. The Etruscans shared with the Phoenician colonists
of Carthage the benefits derived from the exploitation of the East;
indeed, the Etruscans enjoyed what was virtually a monopoly until
they were forced to give way to the Greeks, who had established
their cities along the coast of southern Italy and Sicily. The
Etruscan Empire extended from the banks of the Po to the shores
of Campagna, but excluded from it were vast zones mainly peopled
by Indo-European elements destined in the course of the centuries
to supplant the Etruscans. The might of the Etruscan Empire lay
mainly in its command of the sea. The 'Tyrrhenain pirates' left an
imprint of terror on the minds of the classic Greek historians, but
for all that, it must not be supposed that they were no more than
bloody freebooters. Like the Phoenicians, many of the Etruscan
seafarers were pacific traders who helped to create prosperity on
both shores of the sea.

The Etruscans derived most of their wealth—the wealth that
was undoubtedly the major factor in the rapid evolution of the
Italic peoples—from their mineral resources, copper, lead, tin,
and above all, iron ore of which there was an abundance on the
Tyrrhenian coast. The centre of the mining industry was the city
of Populonia (Piombino) where the raw materials, some of which
were imported from Elba, were smelted down. The methods used
were primitive; clay and stone furnaces were stoked with wood,
but the heat was not great enough to allow more than a fractional
amount of metal to be extracted. At the beginning of this century
engineers carried out experiments with the ancient slag, and by
crushing and electromagnetic separation, found that it still contained up to 60 per cent metal. The Etruscans sold their mineral
products in Italy and also in Greece, where they bought in exchange exquisite vases, gold ornaments, and the various treasures
that have come to light in their chamber tombs.

As Etruria prospered, so the skill of her craftsmen increased.
In addition to the brilliant school of sculptors of which we have
already spoken, there were gifted potters who copied Greek
models and who succeeded in perfecting archaic ceramic forms,
the black *bucchero*, for instance, whose sheen endows it with a kind

of beauty. Goldsmiths created masterpieces of jewellery in their workshops. Ivory workers used a technique of engraving that had probably originated in Cyprus but was firmly implanted in Etruria. A speciality of Etruscan domestic art was the fabrication of metal mirrors. One surface was polished, and the non-reflecting surface engraved with various scenes, usually episodes from Greek mythology. These scenes were derived at first from Greek vases, but later, they were inspired by the great paintings. By way of these mirrors, turned out in countless numbers from the seventh century onwards, Greek mythology was diffused throughout Italy. The episodes were sometimes inaccurately depicted or were portrayed in obscure forms, probably local variants, but nevertheless, when classic Hellenism penetrated into second-century Rome, the legends round which the Attic poets wove their verses were already known; through the craftsmen of Etruria, they had become familiar to the Romans.

We see, then, what a major part etruscology played in filling out, both in time and space, the face of ancient Italy. The mysteries it has not yet succeeded in elucidating are as nothing compared to the brilliant light it has shed over centuries which as late as Winckelmann's day were plunged in almost total darkness. In no other domain perhaps has archaeology so strikingly manifested its might or given so many proofs of its power to bring the past to life and annexe new kingdoms. The revelations of the Etruscan world ranks as large in the history of Ancient Rome as does that of Crete in the annals of archaic Greece. We have more, much more to learn from both Etruria and Crete. Each year, new explorations are carried out that yield further data, raise the traditional problems, resolve some of the riddles and help to dissipate the mystery that still shrouds pre-Roman Italy and the pre-Hellenic East.

CHAPTER EIGHT

The Greek Colonies and Cities

TOWARDS THE MIDDLE of the eighteenth century cultured
Europeans suddenly became aware that there were temples at
Paestum and, just as suddenly, succumbed to their beauty. No one
knows exactly how they were discovered. In his *Paestenae Dissertationes*, F. A. Paoli, a contemporary historian, claims the honour
for Felice Gazzola, a gentleman of Piacenza and the commander of
King Charles of Bourbon's Royal Artillery. He does not tell us,
however, what drew Gazzola's attention to Paestum. Probably it
was simply the climate of the day; at this time, when all eyes were
on Alcubierre and his excavations at Portici and Torre Annunziata, archaeology was uppermost in men's minds, not only in
Naples itself but in Tuscany and Umbria, and ruins that had
previously been dismissed as mere heaps of stones had suddenly
assumed importance.

Gazzola made no immediate mention of his discovery, and in
fact, some time before Paoli attributed it to his friend, the wonder
of Paestum was described by two English travellers, Patrick
Brydone and W. H. Swinburne. Brydone's effusion was probably
inspired by the purely imaginary story, no doubt told by some
local guide, of an artist who was hunting in the woods and who
followed his dogs to a clearing where he beheld the marvel of
Paestum. Now let us listen to Brydone:

Some of these forests are of a vast extent and absolutely impenetrable;
and no doubt conceal in their thickets many valuable monuments of its
ancient magnificence. Of this, indeed, we have a very recent proof in
the discovery of Pestum [*sic*] a Grecian city, that had not been heard of
for many ages; till of late some of its lofty temples were seen, peeping
over the tops of the woods; upbraiding mankind for their shameful
neglect and calling upon them to bring it once more to light. . . . [1]

Alas, for the artist and his dogs, alas for Brydone's lofty sentiments, Paestum was never surrounded by woods; it stands now,
as it stood then, amongst cornfields and pastures. We cannot be
certain that Brydone ever visited Paestum, but Swinburne, who
did, has left as a more authentic account:

(205)

We are not therefore to suppose that Paestum had remained unknown, buried deep in impervious forests, and hidden for ages from the sight of man; it certainly never was furnished with woods; and between the walls and the sea, a bare, sandy down reigns along the coast. The pillars of Pesto have long been, and are to this day, a landmark for sailors, and are seen, as I can witness, from every part of the extensive gulph of Salerno. . . . [2]

Swinburne might have added that the temples never had been buried and that as their plan could clearly be seen there was no need for excavations. Indeed, the sole object of those recently undertaken at Paestum is to lay bare the ancient city. But it is truly extraordinary that although, as Swinburne tells us, the columns of the temples had been visible for years, no mention was made of them till the middle of the eighteenth century; the only explanation that can be advanced is that amongst all those who must have seen them there was not a single person who thought them of the slightest interest. But once attention was called to them the enthusiasm they roused more than compensated for the long years of oblivion and incredible neglect; every traveller who visited Naples felt it was his bounden duty to take the Salerno road and make the pilgrimage to Lucania.

The impression made on artists and writers by the temples of Paestum can be gauged from the following extract from Goethe's *Travels in Italy*:

The first sight of them excited nothing but astonishment. I found myself in a perfectly strange world; for as centuries pass from the severe to the pleasing, they form man's taste at the same time—indeed, create him after the same law. But now our eyes, and through them our whole inner being, has been used to, and decidedly prepossessed in favour of, a lighter style of architecture; so that these crowded masses of stumpy conical pillars appear heavy, not to say frightful. But I soon recollected myself, called to mind the history of art, thought of the times when the spirit was in unison with this style of architecture, and realized the severe style of sculpture; and in less than an hour found myself reconciled to it—nay, I went so far as to thank my genius for permitting me to see with my own eyes such well-preserved remains, since drawings give us no true idea of them; for in architectural sketches, they seem more elegant, and in perspective views even more stumpy than they actually are.[3]

The Age of Enlightenment had suddenly come face to face with the Doric Age.

For a considerable time, the temples of Paestum were regarded as outstanding examples of Doric architecture. In his *Antichità Romane*, Piranesi writes:

Informed travellers assure us that if we wish to see the finest examples of the classic Greek style, there is no need to undertake a long and fatiguing journey, since the temples of Paestum far surpass those of the same majestic architecture in Sicily and in Greece itself.

At this time there was little knowledge of the architecture of the Parthenon, and it is strange that an understanding of the Doric order should have been acquired through the study of a building, the great Temple of Poseidon at Paestum, in which it had not reached full maturity. But possibly the very imperfections, the slight clumsiness of the temple's proportions, the lack of harmony in its rhythms were so foreign to eyes accustomed to more gracious forms that they made the revelation even more complete. This style of architecture was a far cry from the facile flawlessness of Greek sculpture. It affected Piranesi in much the same way that it had affected Goethe, as we can gather from the commentary that accompanies his engraving of the Temple of Poseidon:

Nevertheless, this austere architecture is not to the taste of all those who visit Paestum, for many of them prefer the more gracious styles such as the Ionic, the Corinthian and the Composite which please the eye. Indeed, when the Romans became wealthy, they chose to enhance their city with the Composite, a style of which they made more use than any other nation, for the richness of its ornamentation, far exceeding the value of the materials, befitted, in their eyes, their high estate. The Greeks themselves sought to soften the severity of the Doric Order with a few embellishments, but the Romans in following their example enhanced it to excess.

When travellers arrived at Paestum they felt as if they had left Roman Italy behind them and stepped straight into Greece, and since Greece was the mother, the sacred source of art, Paestum became one of the most revered sites in Italy. But though the atmosphere was Greek, the soil was the soil of Italy, and artists familiar with the landscapes of Italy were perfectly at home. Beneath the same sky, they gazed on the same wide sweep of pastureland whose vast solitude was only broken by flocks of sheep and their shepherds. The scenery of Paestum was deliciously romantic, and it is in this romanticism that the engravings and paintings of the day are steeped.

THE DISCOVERY OF SOUTHERN ITALY

For many years, Paestum was more or less journey's end. In addition to the fact that there were no facilities for travel, the interior of Calabria was inhospitable and fraught with danger. Those who wished to visit Sicily took the boat from Naples, and few ventured by road to the southern coast. No doubt, the fact that there had once been prosperous Greek cities along the shores of the Tyrrhenian and Ionian seas was known, but the tales of a handful of bold travellers who had halted briefly at Metaponte or Heraklea taught the historians nothing—indeed, they appear to have ignored these sites for years. Here is just one example of this neglect. In 1813 the French Institute in Rome offered a prize to members of the Ancient History and Literature class for the best thesis on all that could be learnt from the ancient writers and from monuments and ruins of the history of the Greek colonies. The prize was awarded to Raoul-Rochette for his *Histoire Critique de l'Etablissement des Colonies Grecques*. Now, in the four volumes of this exceedingly erudite work, there is no mention of the monuments and ruins that testify to the Greek colonies in Italy; all the information has been drawn from literary sources. The broad outlines of the history of Greek colonization in Italy were not to emerge until the close of the nineteenth century, and even today this history is far from complete.

By the third century B.C., when the Romans set forth on their long series of conquests, the Greeks had been installed on the shores of southern Italy and Sicily for four or five hundred years. Some of their cities had been occupied by peoples from the interior, but from the long-established colonies the Hellenic influence was exerted throughout the peninsula. Even in those cities where the political power was wielded by Italians, Greek nuclei survived, as did the monuments raised during the period of independence, for the new overlords adhered strictly to the cult of the Greek divinities. Naturally, it was in Sicily where certain powerful states, for example, Syracuse, had succeeded in establishing protectorates over a wide domain, that Hellenism had been most strikingly conserved, indeed, when Roman governors arrived in Syracuse, it seemed to them that they were actually in Greece. Most of these governors showed a true respect for a civilization that commanded their admiration; they revered the

SICILY, SYRACUSE The Roman amphitheatre

CERVETRI   Aerial view of the Etruscan Necropolis

CERVETRI   Interior of the Regolini-Galazzi Tomb

temples of the gods—in their eyes, it would have been sacrilege to despoil them. For these reasons, the principal features brought by the Greek colonists from their native country or created by them on the shores of Southern Italy and Sicily, survived the Roman domination.

Undoubtedly, Cicero's eloquence has linked for-ever the name of Verres to the looting that took place in Roman Sicily, and it is certain that the treasures of Sicilian temples, as well as those from the sanctuaries of Magna Graecia, were removed and transported to Rome, where they enhanced this monument or that, or disappeared into private collections. As far as pillaging went, the Greek cities of Sicily fared no better than the more distant Eastern cities, but for all that, it must not be supposed that Sicily was entirely stripped. Verres, the praetor-aesthete, acquired many of his treasures legitimately, and a large number of those that had been torn from the temples were subsequently restored. The Romans followed the example set by their forebears after the Second Punic War, when they restored to Sicily the statues and works of art that Hannibal had borne away.

We learn of one instance of this restitution from Livy. In this particular case the scene was not Sicily but southern Italy, and the incident he relates is concerned with the Temple of Hera Lacinia, the federal temple of the Achaean colonies at the extreme tip of the Gulf of Taranto. In 173 B.C., G. Fulvius Flaccus, the Censor, stripped the marble tiles from the roof of the temple, since they were just what he needed for the roof of the sanctuary to Fortuna he was raising in Rome. But when the Senate learnt of his impious act he was severely reprimanded and ordered to replace the tiles immediately. Flaccus was forced to obey, but to fit them back required exquisite precision, and as he could find no workmen capable of carrying out this delicate operation, they were neatly stacked up in the sacred precincts, and the temple was re-roofed with common or garden tiles.

Shortly after 1870 a huge deposit of carefully arranged marble tiles was found close to the Temple of Hera Lacinia; undoubtedly, these were the very ones that the Censor had been obliged to return and which had remained undisturbed since 173 B.C. Need we add that many of these relics of the past were immediately sold to marble-workers and limestone-burners, while the rest were dispersed into this or that private collection. The history of the marble tiles of the Temple of Hera Lacinia is characteristic of the long night of neglect that closed in after the second century B.C., when the fortunes of the Greek colonies declined for ever. True, the cities of these colonies survived, and remained prosperous for many years to come. In almost every case it was the Saracen invasions, and to an even greater degree the Norman conquest, that led to their ruin, and in certain instances their total destruction. The endless wars, the massacres, the heavy tribute demanded by each successive government that imposed or superposed itself, impoverished and thinned out the population, until at last, with the exception of a few isolated urban centres, the country was transformed into a desert. The peasants of the mountain villages, almost constantly in a state of revolt against the wealthy landowners, became outlaws, brigands who swooped down from their fastnesses and took toll of hapless travellers. The ruins of the past were left in utter solitude, but even though this abandonment was a kind of protection in so far as no living being had designs on the land they occupied, it did not entirely safeguard them from the hands of marauders.

What had taken place in Rome was now repeated in southern Italy and Sicily; from the dawn of the Renaissance wealthy noblemen and rich religious orders treated the ancient monuments either as quarries that would furnish the materials they needed for their palaces or monasteries, or explored them with the sole object, it need hardly be said, of discovering treasures. The Jesuits of Policoro in Calabria, for instance, systematically exploited the site of Heraklea, and De Non, the French Chargé d'Affaires, who travelled through Calabria shortly after Swinburne, roundly accused them of having 'clandestinely explored the ruins of the city with the sole aim of enriching themselves. They bore off all the material they could utilize, and so transformed it that it shed not a ray of light on the site where it had been found.'[4] The only excuse we can find for the Jesuits of Policoro is that round about this same time the Abbé Rancoureil was similarly engaged on the Palatine, but whereas the curiosity of Roman scholars had effectively prevented him from keeping his activities secret, the Jesuit Fathers in the semi-solitude of Policoro were safe from prying eyes and could do as they pleased at Heraklea.

Not far from Policoro, the Temple of Hera Lacinia, on which the senators of Cato's day had kept so watchful an eye, had survived the barbarian ages, and remained more or less intact. It was still standing at the beginning of the sixteenth century, and Capo delle Colonne, the modern name of Cape Lacinion, comes from its forty·eight columns. Its doom was imminent, however, for it occurred to Bishop Antonio Lucifero that its material would be extremely useful for the episcopal palace he was building at Cortona. The temple was demolished between 1510 and 1521; and only two of its columns were left standing, one of which subsequently collapsed as a result of the earthquake of 1638. The Temples of Paestum met with better fortune; their columns were in travertine, of too little value to appeal to prospective builders.

Up to the close of the fifteenth century little interest had been evinced in the ruins of southern Italy and Sicily. Only two contemporary historians, Felino Sandeo and Michele Riccio, allude briefly to the former. The antiquities of Sicily, however, were found worthy of a little more notice. Before long, in fact, each of the principal cities of the island rated at least one learned monograph. In 1470 Pietro Ranzano wrote a book on the origins and early history of his native city, Palermo; it was not published until 1737, but was widely circulated while still in manuscript form. Messina found an annalist in Bernardo Riccio, a pupil of Lascaris; Mathias Corvo of Padua composed a topography of Syracuse. All these sources of information were drawn on by Sicily's first historian, Father Tommaso Fazello, who spent more than twenty years writing his *magnum opus*, on which he had begun to work when he returned to the island from Rome in 1535. The book was not published until 1558, but it was so successful that two years later a second edition was brought out, and in 1574 a third edition was published in Venice. The history outlived the historian by almost three hundred years; in 1830 it was translated into Italian and, greatly enlarged, was published in Palermo under the title of *Due Decche sulla Storia della Sicilia*.

In order to make his history as complete as possible, Padre Fazello had scoured the villages and countryside of the island for vestiges of the past. In his preface, dedicated to King Charles V he claims that he has restored to the cities of Sicily their true names, names that had either been forgotten or corrupted out of recognition, and expresses his patriotic sentiments:

If a cruel tyrant allows illustrious men who have rendered their country signal service to be put to death [he writes], it would be an act of even greater cruelty to suffer the total destruction of the country that gave me and my fellow Sicilians birth. . . .'

and he goes on to congratulate himself on having re-articulated, like a second Aesculapius, the scattered members of Sicily, and on bringing the decently-restored corpse back to life!

Despite his excellent intentions, Father Fazello was frequently led astray by erudite excesses and tempting etymological fancies. Not only did he echo ancient myths which obviously he was not in a position to evaluate, but he also embodied in his book legends of a more recent date, together with a few of his own invention.

Many temples in Sicily owe their names to Father Fazello, but although these have become traditional, we know today that a good many of them are baseless. An outstanding example is the Temple of Concord at Agrigente. A Roman inscription dedicated by the inhabitants of Lilyboeum to the 'concord of the Agrigenti' convinced Father Fazello that there was a temple to the Goddess Concordia in the city, and he concluded that it could be none other than the sanctuary adjoining the Temples of Hercules. Now this inscription which belongs to the first century B.C., as well as being several centuries later than the temple, did not even come from its site, and while it is not known exactly where it was found, we can take it as almost certain that it was a considerable distance away. At other times, Father Fazello advanced wild hypotheses. For instance, the temple in Agrigente known for no good reason as the Temple of Juno Lacinia was popularly called the *Turris Puellarum*, the Maidens' Tower, in the fifteenth century. This was quite enough for the learned priest to maintain that it was dedicated to the goddess Pudicitia mentioned by Diodorus!

Nevertheless, despite its faults, Father Fazello's book was for several centuries the standard work on the antiquities of Sicily. But while Father Fazello was an extremely conscientious antiquarian, he lacked skill as an historian; epoch follows epoch in the pages of *Due Secche*, one civilization takes the place of another, the names and dates of Carthaginian generals, Sicilian tyrants and Roman consuls are all given, but we cannot form a clear picture of the chronological development of Sicilian civilization in its historical perspective; it does not stand out in relief. Father Fazello and his contemporaries, as well as their successors for generations to come, could not 'live' history, and therefore they could not bring it to life. They set down facts, but they had no feeling for period, and the nuances that linked one epoch to another, the nuances that differentiated between them, escaped them altogether.

Due undoubtedly to the fact that the need to synthesize history was not realized at this date, Sicilian antiquities, knowledge of which had been spread by *Due Secche*, were regarded for years as merely local curiosities, of little interest except to erudite Sicilians. The relics of Ancient Rome benefited from the high esteem in which they were held; they were the mute witnesses of the all-conquering city, and it was easy to discover to what events of world importance they were linked. But when Sicily declined economically, when it became closed in on itself, and was no more than the appendage of a foreign kingdom, it was excized from history, and consequently the belief grew up that there was nothing to be learnt from the vestiges of the past scattered on the soil of Sicily. It was not until the middle of the eighteenth century when antiquarian societies flourished and multiplied that attention was once more drawn to the island.

The man responsible for this revival of interest was Padre Pancrazi, whose *Antichità Siciliane*, published in 1751, familiarized scholars with the temples of Agrigente. Apart from the excellent engravings, however, the book was not nearly as valuable as Father Fazello's *Due Secche*. Padre Pancrazi's knowledge of the subject was apparently confined to the Agrigente temples, and his references to the other ruins in Sicily were so vague that Winckelmann can be forgiven for writing in 1761: 'All the other monuments have been completely destroyed.' Nevertheless this ignorance on the part of the illustrious archaeologist (who was apt to lean too heavily on written evidence at times) seriously undermines his theories on the links between Roman and Greek art.

It is particularly surprising that Winckelmann should have been so ill informed at a time when travellers had begun to flock to Sicily, and accounts of Segeste, Selinonte, and Taormina multiplied.[5] These accounts dwelt far more on the poetic and pictur-esque aspect of the ruins than on their archaeological interest. At Selinonte, Swinburne, gazing with emotion at the scene before him, penned in his notebook: 'The remains lie in several stupen-dous heaps with many columns still erect and at a distance resemble a large town with a crowd of steeples,' and his final impression of Agrigente was that the 'view of the temple [the temple of Hera] and the delicious orchards that surround it are indeed precious to landscape painters.'[6] Once again, however, it is Goethe who voices most eloquently the emotions roused by the discovery of ancient Sicily. Strangely enough, it was not the ruins that fired the imagination of the Sage of Weimar, but a medallion. The poet-philosopher was in Palermo, and on 12 April 1787 he made the following entry in his diary:

Today we have been shown Prince Torremuzza's cabinet of medals. I went there in a certain degree against my will, I am too little versed in these matters, and a mere curiosity-mongering traveller is thoroughly detested by all true connoisseurs and scholars. But as one must in every case make a beginning, I made myself easy on this head, and have derived both gratification and profit from my visit. What a satisfaction, even cursorily, to glance at the fact that the old world was so thickly sown with cities; the very meanest of which has bequeathed us its precious coins, if not a complete series, yet at least some epochs of its history of art. Out of these cabinets, there smiles upon us an eternal spring of the blossoms and flowers of art—of a busy life ennobled with high tastes, and with much more besides. Out of these form-endowed pieces of metal the glory of the Sicilian cities, now obscured, still shines forth fresh before us.

Unfortunately, we, in our youth, had seen nothing but family coins, which say nothing, and the coins of the Caesars, which repeat to satiety the same profile—portraits of rulers, who are to be regarded as anything but models of humanity. How sadly had our youth been confined to a shapeless Palestine and to a shape-perplexing Rome! Sicily and Nova Grecia give me hopes again of a fresh existence.[7]

The coins of Sicilian cities with their beauty, their many different designs bring the past vividly to life and we can understand Goethe's disappointment when at Segesta he saw nothing but a desolate wilderness of ruins. He was equally disillusioned at Taormina:

The wearisomeness of winding through the insignificant ruins of a theatre took away from us all the pleasures we might otherwise have had in visiting the remains of the ancient city. . . .[8]

Goethe could not bear to gaze at Taormina any longer, and left his illustrator, Kniep, to record the spectacle:

Kniep . . . cannot be praised enough for relieving me of a burden which would have been intolerable to me, and which goes directly contrary to my nature. He is gone to sketch in detail the objects which yesterday he took a general survey of. . . . In a sorry and neglected peasant's garden, I have seated myself on the trunk of an orange-tree, and lost myself in reveries . . .⁹

Few possess the genius which enabled Goethe to relive the past by gazing at a medallion, and while the poet-philosopher gave himself up to dreams, other travellers in Sicily tore themselves away from the enchantment of the luminous sea, and pursued patient researches that were ultimately to lead to the resurrection of Greek and pre-Hellenic Sicily—the Sicily we know today. The fervour for archaeology that swept through the West in the mid-eighteenth century reached the island, and in 1748 Prince di Biscari obtained permission from the municipal authorities to explore the territory of Catania. Before long he was joined by Prince Torremuzza, the owner of the medallions which Goethe had so greatly admired. The chance discovery of some ancient coins on one of his family estates had roused in Prince Torremuzza a passion for archaeology. In 1755, following the example set by the academicians of Herculaneum, the two princes brought out an archaeological periodical *Memoria per servire alla Storia Litteraria di Sicilia*, to which many eminent European scholars contributed.

The archaeology of Sicily soon received the Royal support, and the year 1779 saw the beginning of the first official campaign. The princes were appointed directors in different zones; under Torremuzza, the vital work of restoring the Temple of Segesta, the Temple of Juno Lacinia and the Temple of Concord at Agrigente, was carried out, while di Biscari directed the explorations in the theatre and forum of Catania and in the necropoles close to Camarina.

The age of excavations had dawned in Sicily—excavations whose one aim was to acquire knowledge of the past, unlike those Alcubierre had pursued at Herculaneum in the hope of gain and glory. The treasures that di Biscari brought to light formed the nucleus of the museum of Catania, and the medal struck in 1757 to commemorate its foundation bore this significant device: 'PVBLI-CAE VTILITATI PATRIAE DECORI STVDIOSORVM COMMODO'—almost a model programme for scientific research. The antiquities collected by Torremuzza enriched the Palermo museum. So, while Goethe was pursuing his travels through Sicily, paying no heed to the ruins scattered around him, these same ruins were gradually being explored and disengaged; slowly, such vestiges of the past as the Amphitheatre of Syracuse and the Temple of Zeus at Agrigente were returning to life.

THE METOPES OF SELINONTE

In 1823 a discovery was made whose nature was such that it not only contributed greatly to Sicilian archaeology but led to a better understanding of the whole art of Greece. Two young English architects, William Harris and Samuel Angell, in the course of an authorized research at Selinonte, had the good fortune to lay bare three archaic metopes in the ruins of Temple C. These metopes opened a new chapter in the history of Greek sculpture. Here was the first evidence of a style which had not reached the ease and amplitude that Winckelmann and his disciples considered inseparable from Greek art; these reliefs were compelling in their barbaric beauty, their very clumsiness added to their power. Indeed, they were so imbued with life and movement that they captivated the romantics, sick to death of academic perfection.

The expedition cost William Harris his life. Before he could reconstruct the metopes, he contracted a pernicious fever in the unhealthy marshland of Selinonte, and died at a tragically early age. There were fifty-nine fragments of the quadriga metope, thirty-two of the Medusa, and forty-eight of the Hercules; these were successfully put together by Angell and the Sicilian archaeologist Pietro Pisani. The full significance of the Selinonte metopes was only understood many years later when the excavations at Corfu brought to light an archaic temple whose decoration bore obvious similarities to that of Temple C, but even though the technical interpretation was not established until the beginning of the present century, the importance of the metopes was immediately grasped and the zeal of Sicilian archaeologists was greatly stimulated.

In 1827 a Commission of Antiquities and Art was set up in Sicily. Its president, the Duke of Serradifalco, a Mycaenas as energetic as he was generous, promptly resumed the explorations that Harris and Angell had initiated with such signal success.

The tidings of the first victory appeared in *Ceres*, Sicily's national newspaper, on 9 December 1830, and in November of the following year Serradifalco sent a detailed report to the Istituto della Corrispondenza Archeologica. In this report he he stated that before returning to England, Angell had indicated the presence of two more metopes flattened beneath a huge mass of columns and architraves. He, Serridifalco, had been prevented from pursuing the excavations for a considerable period of time, but the moment that he was free to do so, he had returned to Selinonte, accompanied by the architect, Domenico Cavallari, and in addition to finding the two metopes to which Angell had drawn his attention, he and Cavallari had become certain that further metopes could be recovered from Temple C.

The research had, in fact, yielded five more metopes. The first of this series is severely mutilated; it may depict Apollo pursuing Daphne. The second portrays an episode from the Battle of the Giants in which we see Athene fighting with Enceladus; the third shows the hounds devouring Actaeon while Artemis looks on; the fourth, the combat between Heracles and Penthesilea, Queen of the Amazons; the fifth, the sacred nuptials of Zeus and Hera. These metopes date back to the middle of the fifth century, less than fifty years before Selinonte was razed to the ground by the Carthaginians. They prove how rapidly local sculptors mastered their art, that the ateliers of Sicily did not lag behind those of Attica and that the Greek miracle was not an exclusively Athenian phenomenon.

Sixty years later another series of metopes was to come to light in Selinonte, but in the meantime, the exploration of the city was continued with unabated vigour. The inclusion of Sicily in the kingdom of Italy was of great benefit to the archaeology of the island. In 1862 the post of Director of Antiquities of Sicily was created, and the man chosen by Amari, the head of the State, to fill it was Francesco Saverio Cavallari, a former pupil of Serradifalco and the brother of Domenico Cavallari, who had participated in the discovery of the metopes of Temple C. Cavallari, who had served as a staff captain in the insurgent army of 1849, was in Mexico, where he held the post of curator of the Academy of Fine Arts at the time of his appointment. He returned to Sicily at the first possible moment and immediately took charge of the Selinonte excavations, in which he was passionately interested. Before long he was rewarded by the discovery of still more metopes, elements of statues, fragments of reliefs and several inscriptions, the most notable of which enumerated all the deities of the pantheon of Selinonte and was the key to the religious life of the city. He also succeeded in disengaging several small temples whose presence had previously been unsuspected. The broad outlines of the topography of the south-west quarter of Selinonte, the sacred quarter, had begun to appear.

The excavations were carried out under considerable difficulties. The wreckage of the buildings destroyed by the Carthaginians in the fifth century B.C. had been flung hither and thither by earthquakes, and the chaos of Selinonte was indescribable. In his preliminary report Cavallari had stressed the need for mechanical equipment, and a light railway had been constructed on the site.

Alas, funds ran short, and despite Cavallari's bitter complaints, this most useful line was closed for two years. The earth and debris of the Harris-Angell excavations had, however, been removed, and the level of the ancient roads leading to the gates of the city had been reached. The results obtained by Cavallari and the dates ascribed to the monuments that had been disengaged were confirmed later. At the time of the campaign, however, a fact emerged whose importance has only recently been grasped: at the close of the sixth century, a hundred years before Hippodamus of Miletus, the grid plan had made its appearance on the acropolis of Selinonte. The traces of the *decumanus* and *cardo*, some thirty feet wide, were visible, as were those of the secondary roads, no more than ten feet wide, which made up the rectangles. This discovery staggered archaeologists, who for years refused to believe that the grid plan had been used for the original city and asserted that it had been adopted when Selinonte was rebuilt after the year 409 B.C. Since their day the grid plan has appeared elsewhere; it has been found in Sicily itself, in certain quarters of Syracuse, at Megara Hyblaea, and in the city explored by Paolo Orsi on Monte Casale, between Acri and Giarratana.

The exploration of Selinonte revealed the rapidity with which the city had developed from the time of its foundation, a striking instance of the remarkable power of expansion unique to Hellenic populations at the beginning of the fifth century B.C. The original site, almost a quarter of which had been marked off as a sacred zone where temples were raised, soon ceased to be adequate, and buildings spread out in all directions; as at Athens, the old acropolis became little more than the city of the gods, while the city of the living extended north, east and west, even beyond the mouth of the Selinus, where new quarters were erected along the coast.

The rapid growth of Selinonte was confirmed by Cavallari's

discovery of two vast necropoles. At the beginning of 1872 the earlier of the two, north of the city in the locality of Galera, yielded an extraordinarily abundant harvest of proto-Corinthian and Corinthian vases dating back to an epoch not much later than that when Selinonte was founded. As Cavallari observed, ten times as many might have been found but for clandestine researches. At this particular time the sale of antiquities was one of the most flourishing concerns of the island; the traffickers, picturesque and well-known characters, were slippery customers who almost invariably succeeded in outwitting the law.

The second necropolis, the necropolis of Manicalunga on the west of the city, was also laid bare in 1872. Cavallari asserted that he had deduced its presence from erudite studies, but as a matter of fact, peasants in the locality had turned up coins and fragments of pottery for years, and it had frequently happened that their ploughshares driven in with more than usual force had split open stone slabs and revealed human bones. The excavations at Manicalunga brought to light a quantity of Attic vases whose date oscillates between the first and last quarter of the fifth century B.C. Unfortunately, when winter was at its height, funds again ran out, and work had to be suspended. Cavallari, however, had no intention of remaining idle in the wastes of Selinonte, and accordingly he decided to try to trace the road leading from the city to the necropolis of Manicalunga. It was while he was pursuing this research that he discovered a group of temples in the heart of the wilderness, close to the Gaggera farm. At the time of this first, very incomplete campaign, the full significance of the ensemble was not grasped, but thanks to the eminent archaeologist, E. Gabrici, we now know that it is a document of the utmost importance in the history of the religious cults of Sicily.

The ensemble, situated far from any human habitation, consisted of two enclosures, one embracing the other. Adjoining the propylae which gave access to the sacred precincts was a chapel, probably dedicated to Hecate, the goddess of the underworld. At the extremity of the inner enclosure stood the temple of the principal deity who, as we know from an inscription discovered on 13 April 1889, was the goddess Malaphoros. It was shaped like the ancient *megaron*, and had replaced an earlier, identically shaped sanctuary which had been demolished to make room for the larger temple. Finally, at the northern end of the outer enclosure, a temple dedicated to Zeus Meilichios was identified.

The votive offerings and funerary furnishings found on the site proved that a complex cult which had retained many archaic features had existed from the time when Selinonte had been founded. Possibly it had been preceded by an indigenous cult, in which case Malaphoros (the Lady with the Fruits, the Honey Bearer, the Sicilian equivalent of Demeter) would have been some great fertility goddess worshipped by the Siculans. But this is far from certain, and while the offerings of the faithful, the extremely curious steles dedicated to Zeus Meilichios, do not appear to conform to the rules of Greek art, this may simply be because they adhere to sacred prescriptions of which we have no knowledge.[10]

Whatever the case may be, the Temple of Malaphoros affords us a particularly precious example of the type of sanctuary that by the seventh century B.C. was already a survival of past ages, and so takes us back to the epoch that preceded the beginnings of Doric architecture. We must search the Peloponnese, Sparta and Olympia for other instances of this traditional form, for the Dorian colonists brought it from their native land. When the Temple of Malaphoros is compared with the other temples discovered in Sicily at the end of the last century, it is seen to be the first of a series that allows us to follow the birth and evolution of the classic Greek temple in a Dorian country. The discovery of a temple similar in type, together with a great abundance of architectonic terracottas, close to the south-west corner of the Olympieion of Agrigente, allows us to form an exact idea of the violently coloured revetments that characterized Sicilian temples before ornaments sculptured in stone and marble became common.

In 1892, the Acropolis of Selinonte yielded up a fresh series of metopes that illuminated an earlier stage of Sicilian sculpture. Two were in a fair state of preservation, and the subjects were immediately recognizable; one relief showed a sphinx in profile, the other, Europa mounted on the bull. The third metope was severely damaged, but the figures of a man and an animal can be made out—possibly the scene depicted is Hercules fighting some monster. The fourth metope, which was reconstructed many years later, portrays the Delian triad, the goddess Latona with Apollo and Artemis, her children. These four metopes are plainly inspired by Ionian art. This may be accounted for by the proximity of Rhodian elements and that of the Chalcidic colonies whose metropoles were in closer contact than the Dorian cities with the East, but the source of this Ionic influence may equally well be attributed to the religious traditions of the federal temples; since Delos was at all times open to the cultural and religious currents from the East, is it not significant that the Ionic metopes should have given such prominence to the Delian triad?

The discovery in 1892 in the rampart of the Acropolis of Selinonte of the the relief of Eos and Cephalus confirmed that archaic Sicilian sculpture had been influenced by Ionian art. The treatment of the drapery is almost identical to the treatment of the folds of material on the throne of the Venus Ludovisi.

The excavations of Selinonte which best exemplify the work accomplished by Sicilian archaeologists during the nineteenth century and the beginning of the twentieth demonstrate the wide perspectives that were opened out, not only on the history of the whole of Greek art, but also on the history of Italy at the time when Rome was experiencing her first growing pains. Already at this epoch, in Sicily, in Magna Graecia, as we shall see later, throughout the Campagna to the borders of Latium, the powerful religious currents from the Aegean had created a spiritual ambience in which Rome was, as it were, immersed. Today it is quite conceivable that the Veiian sculptors whose work ornamented the temples of Rome, were in direct contact with the sculptors of Sicily. It may well have been through this intermediary that Rome participated in the vast Mediterranean community from which was to surge forth the marvellous Age of Pericles.

THE EXPLORATION OF SICILY

After the expulsion of the Bourbons, every city, every site in Sicily became the object of systematic researches by Sicilian archaeologists. In 1861 Giuseppi Meli explored the temple of Himera, and initiated a series of excavations on the site of the Carthaginian city of Solonte. Other campaigns were begun at Gela, Megara Hyblaea, Palermo, and Taormina. The results of all these researches were either published in the form of monographs or in important syntheses by eminent German scholars, amongst them, J. Schubring and A. Holm who at one time had been professor of Ancient History at the University of Palermo. But in 1899, a new personality appeared on the scene; this was none other than Paolo Orsi, who was to stimulate Sicilian archaeology to a truly remarkable degree.[11] For the next fifty years he visited every site on the island; he resumed excavations that others had begun, opened up completely new fields and uncovered cities so archaic that their very names had been forgotten. They are known to us by the names of the nearest villages: Caltagirone, Terravecchia di Grammichele, Licodia, Monte Casale, and so on. But the most striking feature that Orsi introduced into his vast programme was the stratigraphical study of the soil which revealed traces of the indigenous civilization that preceded the Greek colonists.

True, not all the problems relating to the earliest peoples of Sicily from the palaeolithic age onward have been solved, for in Sicily, as elsewhere, prehistory is shrouded in darkness. But as we move forward through the centuries and milleniums, a few glimmers of light appear. From the stratigraphical excavations begun by Orsi and carried out by his successors (notably by Barnabo Brea), we know that long before the Greek colonization, probably as early as the fourteenth century B.C., there were links of trade, and hence cultural links between the Sicilian populations and the Aegeo-Mycenaean world.[12] The most significant facts came to light quite recently; in 1946 on Panares, one of the smallest of the Lipari Islands, a deposit of indigenous ceramics and Mycenaean sherds was found, and four years later, a similar discovery was made on the acropolis of Lipari.

These two discoveries confirmed others of the same kind that had been made much earlier, but which had been differently interpreted.[13] We can now take it as almost certain that when the heroic age of Greece had reached its apogee, Sicily (and southern Italy which, with Sicily, forms a cultural whole) was in continuous contact with the Aegean world, and this compels belief in the traditions according to which the Achaean heroes, when the Trojan war was over, founded actual colonies in Sicily and Magna Graecia.[14] The Lipari Islands were, in fact, so the legend tells us, the domain of King Aeolus, who had quitted his former realm in Greece, and Aeolus was reigning over his new kingdom when Odysseus put in, seeking the way to Ithaca.

At a later date relations between the western and eastern Mediterranean were interrupted, and were not resumed until the seventh century B.C.; this break, of which we have written evidence, is confirmed by the superposition of the archaeological levels. We now have less reason than ever to believe that the Italic world was isolated; from the dawn of protohistory the soil of Ausonia was, so to speak, a crucible in which the most diverse elements were melted down, an infinitely slow process of fusion that finally gave rise to the civilization of Rome.

Obviously, within the space of this book it is impossible to describe or even enumerate all the explorations that have taken place in Sicily during the past twenty years, every one of which has been fruitful. The slow and infinitely careful work of archaeologists constantly brings to light ancient cities that up to the moment of discovery were little more than names, and others of whose existence we had previously been totally unaware. The work of Paolo Orsi has been carried on throughout the island,[15] and as data accumulates the picture becomes more fluid than was at first supposed. The discovery of a deposit of ceramics, for instance, may cause a revolution, and shed doubt on conclusions that seemed certain, probably because these were drawn from insufficient facts. The accurate identification of a fragment of pottery is an event of capital importance whose consequences are far-reaching. The most logically built-up structure may collapse when, in the light of freshly acquired information, it becomes clear that a factor which has been taken as proved is no more than a flimsy hypothesis.

Concrete evidence of the past is provided by the discovery of ancient buildings masked by modern edifices. Almost every year, for instance, archaeologists succeed in revealing yet another aspect of Syracuse. No doubt the island of Ortygia, the cradle of the Greek city, still holds certain secrets, but not nearly as many as it held thirty years ago. The disengagement of the theatre of Taormina (the ancient city of Taurominium) is also past history; the theatre, with its tiers of seats rising above the orchestra, has been brilliantly reconstructed, and the gigantic mass of Etna looming in the background forms a marvellous natural décor. Quite rightly, the archaeologists decided not to rebuild the high Roman wall that shut out the landscape; perhaps it was on this very stage, amidst the awe-inspiring scenery, that Aeschylus first produced his *Prometheus*.

Those who can read in the stones the superposition of the various levels can follow the long chain of civilization in Sicily, can see the changes brought about by a conquest that did not result purely and simply in a foreign domination, but which had the radical effect of liberating the subconscious tendencies of the conquered. Gradually, the Sicilian people emerge more and more clearly, the people who were neither wholly Roman nor wholly Greek, but an autonomous reality.

THE VILLA OF PIAZZA ARMERINA

Quite recently the soil of Sicily yielded up a monument which had long been the object of partial researches; none the less, its disengagement aroused in archaeologists the most lively surprise. As far back as the eighteenth century illicit treasure-seekers and local scholars had been aware that not far from the little town of Piazza Armerina, on the right bank of the River Gela in eastern Sicily, a vast ensemble was buried, on the site of which quantities of coins and fragments of every kind were found. In 1812 an archaeologist, one Sabatino del Muto, had uncovered a mosaic paving which must have fared extremely badly when it was exposed to the light, since it has vanished without trace.

Sixty years later the municipality of Piazza Armerina carried out a series of systematic researches. Pappalardo, the engineer in charge of the operations, was fortunate enough to lay bare other mosaics whose beauty and delicacy spoke eloquently of the splendour of the mysterious monument. But the excavations failed to uncover it, and the trenches were closed in. Individual attempts were made to solve the mystery, but these were completely unmethodical, and although fragments of mosaics were found, they deteriorated rapidly, since no steps were taken to protect them. In 1929 Paolo Orsi himself undertook a number of soundings, but while the archaeological authorities were convinced of the richness of the site, they also realized that it could only be explored at vast expense; an immense amount of earth would have to be banked up and in addition, costly equipment would have to be provided for the immediate protection of mosaics that might be uncovered. The history of the exploration of Piazza Armerina became one long, slow administrative struggle to obtain the expropriation of a huge tract of land and to raise the necessary funds; long before there could be any return, an astronomical sum had been expended. The campaign was opened in 1935, but it was not until fifteen years later that archaeologists reaped the reward of their labours and finally glimpsed the ensemble.

SICILY, PIAZZA ARMERINA Detail of a mosaic

FLORENCE Archaeological Museum. The Chimaera

SICILY, PIAZZA ARMERINA   Detail of a mosaic

As we know today, it was a villa, but so vast, so magnificent that archaeologists were convinced that its owner had been no private citizen. Paolo Orsi, after he had carried out soundings on the site, had expressed the view that, in its original state, the villa went back to the second century B.C., and that it had been destroyed at the close of that century by the slaves who had risen against their masters. There is, however, nothing to confirm his hypothesis, and we have every reason to believe that the villa was adapted, if not specially built, for Maximian, co-Emperor with Diocletian during the last years of the third century A.D.

At the time of the discovery the palace at Spalato (Split) to which Diocletian retired was already known. The villa of Piazza Armerina was utterly different from this austere stronghold. While Diocletian had planned his residence on the Dalmatian coast on the lines of a military camp, Maximian had chosen to re-create the gracious traditional villa of the spacious days of Domitian and Hadrian—a country residence with its landscaped garden where fountains played, its tiered terraces, its porticoes that opened on to exquisite scenery, its salons (*ceci et diatetae*) richly adorned with precious mosaics. There is no sign at Piazza Armerina (as there is at Spalato) of foreboding, no sense of awareness that a beleaguered world, a world with an army perpetually on the point of revolt and with invaders already fighting on its frontiers, was about to come to an end. In southern Italy, and above all in Sicily, the *pax romana* still reigned, and it was good to be alive.

We would be quite wrong to picture the villa as an enchanted palace, a refuge where its owner might forget the grievous cares of the day. The deliberate choice of subjects for the mosaics of the great apartments tell us that this was not so. One entire series portrays with a wealth of detail the Labours of Hercules, and we might be tempted to believe that this imagery was the last belated manifestation of an art incapable of renewing itself if we did not recall that it was precisely Hercules who was Maximian's chosen patron and the third member of the Maximian—Diocletian-Jupiter tetrarchy. We see that the ancient Roman ideal of *virtus*, symbolized for century after century by Hercules Triumphans, to whom the charioteers paid homage before entering the Circus Maximus, had remained a living reality on Sicilian soil.

Undoubtedly it is to the same imperial mystique that we must attribute the great mosaic of a chariot race in the Circus. We know that the true import of these races in the life of Rome, far from being mere spectacles staged for the diversion of the idle plebs, was the communion offered up by the entire population to the cult of Victory. It is significant to a degree that such a minutely detailed representation of one of the great moments in the public life of Rome should have been found in this particular villa.

Of equal significance are the *venationes*, the hunting scenes of the great mosaic that paves the corridor. Even in Hadrian's day the imperial *virtus* was symbolized in a series of medallions in which the Emperor was shown subduing wild beasts, imposing on brute nature the immense intellectual might of the new Hercules. These medallions which Constantine expropriated for his arch are recalled by the mosaics of the Piazza Armerina, where they helped to create an ambiance of unswerving belief in the invincibility of the Emperor, Lord of Creation. In the great villa the panegyrics extolling the Imperial might take on their full meaning; even as the shadow of doom fell inexorably over the Roman Empire, the monuments of that Empire continued to affirm the deathlessness of the Roman spirit, and so assured its survival.

THE PROVINCES OF TERRAFERMA

While archaeology was achieving all these brilliant results in Sicily at the close of the nineteenth century, the balance-sheet had not been nearly so favourable in the 'provinces of terraferma': Lucania, Calabria and Apulia. With the exception of the outstanding explorations of the Campagna, there had been little activity in southern Italy. Nevertheless, a few chance discoveries had given archaeologists an idea of what systematic excavations might disclose; gradually, they formed the opinion that the culture brought by the Greeks to the indigenous peoples had flourished even more in this part of the country than it had in Sicily.

We know from literary sources that it was in southern Italy that Pythagorianism was strongest, and the few existing texts by philosophers from Magna Graecia prove how deeply they were imbued with mysticism. But until the close of the nineteenth century, what these mystical influences were, whether they extended beyond philosophical circles and affected the daily lives of the people, were questions that could not be answered.

In 1836 the bulletin of the *Istituto di Corrispondenza Archeologica* drew attention to a curious document whose full significance was not immediately understood. This document, a flat gold leaf on which was an inscription in Greek, had been acquired in the antique market and was said to have come from Petalia, not far from Catanzaro. The circumstances in which it was found were not known. The epigraphers who first deciphered the dozen verses of the inscription unanimously agreed that they were the response of an oracle, which they unhesitatingly declared to be the Oracle of Trophonius in Boetia. The text ran as follows:

In Hades, thou wilt find on the left a spring, and near the spring, a white cypress. Go not nigh. Thou wilt find another spring, an icy spring that hath its source in the Lake of Mnemosyne, and before it, thou wilt behold guards. Then shalt thou say to these guards: 'I am a son of the Earth and the Starry Sky, but I come of the race of gods as ye know; my lips are parched, I am dying of thirst—oh, hasten, give me to drink of the icy water of the Lake of Memory.' And they will allow thee to drink from the sacred source, and when thou hast drained each drop, thou wilt reign with the other heroes. . . .

Here the epigraphers had been forced to stop, for the gold leaf was badly mutilated. They had, however, made out some kind of signature in the final three lines, probably that of the writer—no doubt, he was boasting in this last stanza that he had visited the underworld and returned unscathed to the land of the living.

The gold leaf of Petelia remained an unsolved mystery until 1879, when the outcome of an excavation threw further light on the text. This excavation was notable for the precautions that were taken to keep marauders from the site.

In March 1879 an exploration was in progress in Lucania on the territory of the ancient city of Sybaris. The work was slow and laborious because of the heavy clay soil, but the presence of bramble roots and black cinders mingled with fragments of pottery indicated to the archaeologists the presence of a tomb. They had to dig to a depth of twenty-five feet before it appeared, and to reach the slab that sealed the entrance took a further two days of hard digging. When the end was in sight the engineer in charge wisely took the precaution of detailing men to keep watch at night, and to make assurance doubly sure, he set 'persons of the locality' to guard the guards, who might otherwise have succumbed to temptation, since at this time trafficking in antiques was a lucrative source of revenue. At last the moment came for the slab to be raised. The mayor of the village was sent for, and that worthy arrived hotfoot, accompanied by a crowd of villagers, all agog with excitement.

When the slab was lifted from the tomb, charred bones were seen lying on a shroud of white linen which fell to dust the moment it was exposed to the air. Several chests had been placed by the cremated corpse, but nothing remained of them but the metal locks and hinges. This appeared to be all; a final look round, however, led to the discovery of a piece of gold leaf folded into seven lying near the skull. The archaeologists emerged from the tomb, and were instantly surrounded by the villagers. 'As it would not have been wise to unfold this precious leaf in the presence of over a hundred curious spectators who would certainly have tried to snatch it away and pass it from hand to hand,' we read in the official report, 'we showed it to them, told them it was a gilded ornament, and guarded it zealously.' When at last they were alone and free to examine the treasure they saw that there was an inscription on the gold leaf, and we can imagine their excitement when, in its folds, they came upon, a second, smaller gold leaf, also with an inscription in Greek.

Despite the fact that many of the characters were blurred and several words misspelt, epigraphers soon succeeded in deciphering the inscriptions; both were extracts of a similar nature from a sacred book analagous to the Egyptian Book of the Dead. The folded gold leaves were amulets of incorruptible metal bestowed during the funeral rites in order that the spirit of the dead might without fear confront the deities of the infernal regions. The following is the text of one of these amulets:

I come pure, born of a pure mother and father—oh, behold me, Queen of the Underworld, and thou, Illustrious One, and thou, Good Counsellor, and all ye immortal deities. I am of thy happy race and therefore am I glorified, but I have been broken by Fate and by the other immortal deities and by the astral flashes of the thunderbolt. I have fled far from the circle of pain, and on swift feet I have attained the longed-for crown; I have found shelter beneath the robes of the Mistress, the Queen of the Underworld.

Holy and happy one, thou shalt be no longer mortal, thou shalt be divine.

Kid, I have fallen into the milk.

Taken in conjunction with the gold leaf of Petelia, the amulets of Sybaris threw a totally unexpected and singularly revealing

light on the religious life of southern Italy. Thanks to the methodical direction of the Sybaris excavations, it was possible to arrive at
the approximate date of the tomb. From fragments of pottery, it
was established as not earlier than the fourth century B.C. and not
later than the third; hence the amulets take us further back into
the past than the literary texts, most of which belong to the fifth
century B.C.

From the amulets of Sybaris and the gold leaf of Petelia, which
are inspired by orphic beliefs, we can form an idea of the spiritual
milieu in which the Romans found themselves when, at the time of
Pyrrhus, their legions were forced to make war on the Greek
colonists of Calabria. Orphism was a living religion whose initi-
ates were assured of immortality provided that they were ritually
pure, followed the sacred way to the underworld and pronounced
the prescribed formulae when they crossed its threshold. The spirit
of the dead addressed itself to Persephone, but since it was taboo
to invoke the great goddess by name, it might only use her ritual
titles. The same was true of Dis, her husband, the king of the
infernal regions; Dis was 'The Illustrious One'. To this divine
couple, the faithful added the 'Good Counsellor', the Orphic
Dionysos who had first taught mankind how to overcome death.

While we do not know exactly how these beliefs originated, it
is certain that the essence of the doctrine to which the amulets of
Sybaris and the gold leaf of Petelia refer, was imported from
Greece and was linked to the Eleusynian Mysteries. It may have
undergone certain changes in Italy, but whether it did or not, the
existence of a living faith in pre-Roman Italy can no longer be
denied. Between the funerary realism of Etruria and the mystical
orphism of the south, the religion of Rome could not fail to be
enriched by all the ritual currents that flowed into the valley of the
Tiber.

The few glimpses afforded by the discoveries at Sybaris of the
richness and complexity of the civilization of Magna Graecia prior
to the Roman conquest were to be greatly amplified by a small
number of archaeologists in the course of explorations in Calabria,
similar in character to those which had been undertaken in Sicily.
In his account of his Calabrian journey, Lenormand had drawn
attention to a number of sites, but a solitary archaeologist, even
though he was thoroughly familiar, as Lenormand was, with all
the erudite works on this province which lack of communications

had cut off from the rest of Italy, could do no more than indicate the presence of scattered ruins and prepare the way for his successors. All the excavations carried out at the end of the nineteenth century were controlled by the regional authorities and directed by Italian archaeologists, and while this limited the work of non-nationals, it lessened activities of a destructive character, and ensured concentration on the major sites.

One of the first to be opened up was Locri, not far from Gerace Marina. A few excavations had been carried out by the Duke de Luynes in 1830, and various random digs by local inhabitants had brought to light a number of terracotta plaques. In 1879 Lenormand had drawn attention to the presence in this locality of ruins that were apparently Greek. Encouraged by these facts, Petersen, who was then the principal of the German Archaeological Institute in Rome, decided to undertake more extensive researches.

In the summer of 1889, Petersen identified the vestiges of a temple, and an expedition was immediately dispatched to the site under the leadership of Paolo Orsi; Orsi had explored Megara Hyblaea in Sicily, but this was his first campaign. To the surprise of all, the temple, unlike the other temples in the south, turned out to be not Doric but Ionic. True, only a few elements were discovered: the lowest drum of a column and its base, part of a central drum, a fragment of a capital decorated with lotus flowers, and finally a fragment of the flutings of a column. From these, however, Petersen recognized the affinity of the style with that of the Erechtheum and that of the Temple of Hera at Samos, and he was thus able to achieve a complete reconstruction of the temple. Two identical statues, each of a youth mounted on a steed led by a triton, were also found; the youths were undoubtedly the Dioscuri, the twin gods of Sparta. The statues had originally surmounted the roof of the temple which had been raised by the people of Locri to mark their gratitude to the Spartans who, according to a soundly-based tradition, had fought on their side against the warriors of Crotona at the battle of Sagras, and despite the enemy's far superior forces, had turned the tide in their favour.

In the course of these excavations there came to light beneath the Ionic temple, which cannot be earlier than the close of the fifth century B.C., the foundations of another temple. This archaic sanctuary dates back to the origins of Locri, that is, to the seventh century B.C.

From 1908 onwards the site was the scene of numerous campaigns directed by Paolo Orsi, campaigns which revealed the aspect of Locri and disclosed valuable evidence of the city's religious and cultural life. In a temple partly buried beneath a modern building, a block from the pediment supporting the figure of a rider mounted on a sphinx was found. This temple ,which appears to date back to the middle of the fifth century B.C., is a curious mixture of the Doric and Ionic styles; it marks a transitional stage in the architectonic evolution of the purely Ionic temples of Locri. Two further temples were also discovered and explored; the first was dedicated to Athene Promachos, Protectrix of Cities, the second was the celebrated *temenos* of Persephone.

Truth to tell, the *temenos* long sought for by archaeologists who knew of its existence through literary texts, proved to be a disappointment. It was not, as had been expected, a monumental temple, but simply a treasury no more than twenty-five feet long, with terracotta revetments. The disappointment was somewhat mitigated by the discovery of a considerable number of terracotta plaques, votive offerings to the goddess which had originally been deposited in the treasury; damaged during the course of a reconstruction in the middle of the fifth century B.C., they had been removed and buried a short distance away. The earliest of the plaques date back to the middle of the seventh century B.C. They form a series and are decorated with bas-reliefs (originally these reliefs were painted in brilliant colours, only traces of which remain) of scenes of the underworld in which Persephone and Dis, as well as other deities, appear. These terracotta plaques were by no means the first of their kind to come to light; in the course of the years clandestine researchers had uncovered many others that as usual had passed into the hands of dealers in antiquities or had been acquired by private collectors. It could now be established that all these plaques had come from Locri, and that the curious bas-reliefs were related to certain religious beliefs peculiar to the Locrans; at Locri, as at Sybaris, Orphism had left its mark on the religious life of the entire region.

At the beginning of the twentieth century, while Locri and a few other important sites had been explored, southern Italy, in particular Calabria, still remained almost without a past. But in 1908 the disastrous earthquake focused the attention of patriotic Italians on the misery of the southern provinces which had been so shamefully neglected, and thanks to Umberto Zanotti-Bianco, the National Association for the Promotion of the Interests of Southern Italy was formed. Convinced that one of the great assets of the south lay in its archaeological treasures, the committee immediately approached Paolo Orsi, who had not confined his activities to Sicily, and who, in 1908 had been appointed Director of Archaeological Research in Calabria. A programme for the restoration of the various ruins was drawn up, and despite violent local opposition, it was decided to found a museum worthy of the name in Reggio di Calabria.

At the close of 1920, after the interruption caused by the First World War, a new society for the promotion of the south came into being. Its main objective was to encourage archaeological research in this part of Italy, and like the National Association, it owed its existence to Zanotti-Bianco, who travelled up and down the country to enlist support. Eleanora Duse was a member of the original committee, and some of the most resounding names of the Italian aristocracy figured in the list. The distinguished and enthusiastic patrons reposed all their confidence in Paolo Orsi, certain that he would fulfil their hopes for Calabria. The association which took the title of the Magna Graecia Society stimulated the archaeology of the southern provinces through its publications and through the explorations it initiated and financed.

The first excavation to be carried out under the auspices of the Society was in the province of Catanzaro, at Monteleone, the Hipponium of the Greeks, the Vibo Valentia of the Romans. Here, in addition to a remarkably fine well, part of which had been identified during an earlier research, a number of temples were uncovered, amongst them an Ionic temple—Hipponium and Locri furnished the only instances of sanctuaries of this style. The exploration of Hipponium, following that of Medma, the present Nicotera (the excavation of Medma, also directed by Orsi, was begun in 1913), showed the extent of the Empire of Locri on the west coast. The terracottas of Hipponium and Medma (the latter are a little earlier than the former) are analogous with those of Locri, but the Ionic temple is evidence of the influence Locri exerted towards the end of the fifth century on this city which was undoubtedly the site of an Italic pre-colonization.

While Orsi was exploring Hipponium, the Magna Graecia Society financed an exploration at Taranto which led to the discovery of a magnificent Greek tomb containing a rich collection of funerary furnishings and Greek vases of exquisite beauty. From this time on archaeological activity in Calabria and Apulia was intensified, thanks to the inexhaustible energy of Paolo Orsi. Now that he could count on the unstinting and generous support of the Magna Graecia Society, Orsi was no longer cramped, as he had been under the administration, by shortage of funds. On 28 March, for instance, he sent an urgent telegram to the Society: 'Request sum of 10,000 lire. Remarkable discovery in Calabria'. The money was wired to him by return.

Orsi's remarkable discovery was the Temple of Apollo Alaeos near the ancient city of Crimisa, the modern Punta del Alice north of Crotona on the Ionian Sea. In this temple, half Greek, half Italic in addition to Greek ceramics, a number of notable pieces of sculpture were found; these included antefixes, votive statuettes in gold, silver and bronze, and an *acrolith* (a corner stone). The discovery of this temple had been wholly unexpected. Its remains had been concealed behind a dune some ten feet high, and it so happened that men who were carrying out the work of soil improvement (*bonifica*) in the locality needed sand to fill in marshy depressions. They promptly battered down the dune with their spades, and unfortunately they battered down the ruins as well. The debris had to be meticulously sifted for small objects and fragments of terracotta which would otherwise have been lost. The task took endless time and patience, and in this malarial part of the country conditions were far from pleasant, but the results obtained were an ample reward. They afforded the evidence of another phase of the Hellenization of the Italic populations, this time, within the orbit of Crotona. Yet one more document was contributed, one more stone added to the reconstruction of the history of the Greek colonies of Calabria.

It is impossible to list in this book all the sites opened up by Orsi along the Calabrian coast. At the close of 1915 he definitively identified the site of Caulonia (this had previously been highly debatable) on the Ionian coast, some twenty-five miles north of Locri. Sherds of geometric pottery dating back to the seventh century B.C. were proof of an Italic pre-colonization. Later, no doubt towards the middle of the sixth century B.C., the site had been occupied by Achaean colonists who settled there under the protection of Crotona. Caulonia enjoyed its greatest period of prosperity round about the middle of the fifth century B.C. We can form a picture of the city, thanks to the magnificent architectonic terracottas turned up by some peasants who were planting a vineyard at the beginning of April 1913; the site where they were discovered was thoroughly explored by Orsi. These terracottas together with those from other parts of southern Italy, notably Paestum (the Paestum terracottas, locked away for years, can now be seen by visitors) and Sicily, enable us to picture more clearly the ornamentation of the temples built by the Greek colonists between the sixth and fourth centuries B.C.[16]

The architectonic terracottas make it apparent that while the Doric temples conformed to fairly strict architectural rules which gave them a more or less uniform appearance, the style of their revetments differed greatly and gave each sanctuary, each city a completely individual character. Techniques varied from epoch to epoch, and the occasional survival for a fairly long period of an archaic style, the introduction of new motifs, complete our knowledge of the schools of sculpture, the local ateliers, and enable us to follow to some extent the cultural history of a city. In archaic times, flat painting was predominant, but gradually more and more preference was given to reliefs accentuated by polychrome. Terracotta revetments seem to have persisted far longer in southern Italy than in Sicily, and this was undoubtedly due to the fact that the island possessed a far greater abundance of stone suitable for sculpture.[17] The influences that had stemmed from the ancient metropoles (Corinth, the Dorian cities of the Peloponnese) gave way to those emanating from the centres of orientalizing culture; the tremors that were shaking the Greek world made themselves felt in the Italic West, and their repercussions gradually affected the entire peninsula. There is no doubt whatsoever that the architectonic fragments found in Latium and Etruria are related to those of the south; possibly Selinonte and western Sicily were the sources of the cultural currents, or they may have reached Latium and Etruria more deviously, coming from Taranto, Locri, and Paestum.

THE HERAION OF PAESTUM

In the past, scholars had long racked their brains in vain over a passage from Strabo in which he refers to a temple dedicated to Hera, founded by Jason during his voyage on the Argo at the mouth of the river the Romans called the Silarus or Siler, and which is now known as the Sele. The few travellers who had adventured into this region, which is quite close to Paestum, had never mentioned any ruins, and what made the problem even more teasing was the fact that the temple, one of the earliest of the sanctuaries built by the Greek colonists, had seemingly survived to the days of Antiquity; it figures in Plutarch's list of temples looted by Cilician pirates in Pompey's day during the closing years of the Republic.

In 1934, Zanotti-Bianco, the founder and moving spirit of the Magna Graecia Society, decided to try and elucidate the mystery of the vanished temple. Accordingly, on 9th April of that year, with the help of a small working party, he carried out soundings close to the mouth of the Sele. This region is almost deserted; the earth is waterlogged and the fields are intersected with drainage canals; here and there, a few herds of buffalo lazily browsing add a vague touch of life to the desolate landscape.

After prospecting for several hours and carrying out two or three fruitless soundings at points where the conformation of the soil had suggested the possible presence of buried ruins, Zanotti-Bianco and his party came upon several blocks of limestone. Now this was not a limestone region, moreover, the blocks resembled those which had been used in the construction of the ancient temples of Paestum; here was proof, then, that an ancient monument had once stood in this locality. Furthermore, the blocks were extremely heavy, and it was clear that they could not have been moved very far from their original site. Much encouraged, the prospectors studied the terrain minutely, and as they approached the river they found more and more limestone blocks, a sign that they were nearing the site. By the time darkness had begun to close in, they had become certain that an ancient ruin was buried on the left bank of the Sele, approximately three miles distant from the river itself, for here, in addition to the limestone blocks, they uncovered fragments of tiles and pottery. Furthermore, the rusty remains of three ploughshares indicated unmistakably that their career of usefulness had ended when they had struck against slabs of stone lying just beneath the topsoil.

The party spent the following day, 10th April, in reconnoitring the river bank to check and confirm the results already obtained. On the morning of the 10th they began to explore the site; three simultaneous soundings were taken, one round a shapeless block of stone which seemed to be deeply rooted in the earth, the other two in those parts of the field which the peasants had prudently left unploughed. After a few hours, it became clear that the stone block was, in fact, an archaic type of Doric capital; the two other soundings led to the disclosure of a wall that was still intact. Moreover, just below the level of the soil, the party uncovered statuettes, sherds, and coins of the Hellenic period—offerings the faithful had brought to the temple. The exploratory dig had attained its goal, and the time had come to organize a full-scale operation.

The first campaign was opened on 12 May 1934, and resulted in the disengagement of the base of an archaic Doric temple and the discovery of a great quantity of architectonic fragments. At the same time, immediately north of this temple, the foundations of a small sanctuary were laid bare and two early metopes were found, one of which, in a very good state of preservation, depicted the giant Tityos bearing away Latona. The second campaign, which began in October 1934 and ended in June 1935, was equally fruit-ful; it brought to light more metopes, decorated capitals and in-numerable terracotta votive offerings which included a large number of female busts and the strange 'female flowers', faces of women crowned with a calyx of petals and frequently surrounded by volutes.

In the spring of 1935 the disengagement of the sacred precinct was resumed, and still another ruin was disclosed; this was identi-fied later as a portico where pilgrims to the temple were received. The portico which cannot date back beyond the fourth century B.C., had been constructed with material taken from an earlier building. Archaeologists had now come upon two distinct mo-ments in the life of the sanctuary: the archaic phase represented by the temple and its adjacent chapel, and a much later phase repre-sented by the portico and its annexes. Coins had been found beneath the portico with the device ΓʼΑΙΕΤʼ showing that they had been struck at the period when the Lucanians, the mountain peo-ple of the hinterland, were in possession of the Greek colony of Posidonia to which they had given the Italic name of Paestum.

The fourth campaign, which lasted from the end of October 1936 till February 1937, did not open up the site any further. Efforts were concentrated on completing the exploration of a *favissa*, begun during the summer and which had already yielded a number of important results. From these it had become quite certain that the temple was indeed the Heraion of Silaris; quantities of votive objects had come to light, scratched on which was the name of their 'owner', the goddess Hera. Even so, there remained many problems to be solved.

In 1938, while excavations were being pursued immediately west of the portico, a second and far earlier portico dating back to the seventh century B.C. was revealed. Beneath the foundations of the great Doric temple built a century later the vestiges of a sanctuary contemporary with this portico were identified.

From 1936 onward archaeologists had vainly sought for the altar of the temple which, in conformity with the prescribed plan, must have stood opposite its main façade. Meticulous exploration, however, had failed to reveal it, and it was not until the summer of 1949, during the course of a final search, that chance led to its location. An examination of the terrain showed that the altar had fallen into disuse long before the activities of the temple ceased; it was already in ruins in A.D. 79, when a rain of ashes from Vesuvius buried it completely. We may reasonably suppose that it was abandoned in 62 B.C. after the Cilician pirates had desecrated it with their bloody hands. The discovery during the campaigns of 1939 and 1940 of what seem to be the remains of the tower of a sacred precinct of Roman times suggests that after the devastation of 62 B.C., and, above all, after the destruction caused one hundred and twenty years later by the earthquake of A.D. 63, the seat of the cult was moved farther towards the south. Here undoubtedly the Roman portions of the temple still lie buried.

Unquestionably, the greatest revelation of the Heraion was that of its metopes. Some were intact, and in all, ninety-three fragments of others were found. They had been sculptured from the somewhat friable stone from a quarry in the vicinity, a fact that proved that they were the work of local craftsmen. The metopes, the first of which was discovered in June 1934, were fragile to a degree, and to extract them from the clods of earth in which they were embedded was by no means easy. Long planks of wood had to be hammered into the ground and slipped beneath them to act as a kind of stretcher strong enough to take their weight; they were then covered with straw-lined wooden cases and raised by tackles and pulleys. All the minute fragments were scrupulously collected and left to dry; when the stone had hardened, the slow work of reconstruction began, a laborious jigsaw in which each tiny piece had to be fitted into its right place in the right metope.

The metopes, which have been minutely studied, measured and compared, may come from at least five friezes, four of them archaic. This suggests that there were several other buildings in the vicinity of the temple, buildings that are still buried, and that the Heraion, like the Temple of Delphi, was surrounded by 'treasuries', chapels where the ex-votos offered to the goddess by this or that city were deposited. So far, only one of these treasuries has come to light; it seems fairly certain that it was raised to Hera by the people of Siris shortly before their city was abruptly destroyed between the years 570 and 566 B.C. The reliefs depict episodes from the Heraclean cycle, incidents of the Trojan War and scenes from various legends that appear to have little connexion with one another. Most prominence has been given to Heracles fighting the centaurs and Heracles overpowering the satyrs. It has been suggested that the choice of subjects was inspired by favourite themes in Western literature, and is to be attributed to the influence of Stersichorus, the poet of Himera. This is quite possible, and it gives us a good deal of satisfaction to imagine the people of Siris, proud of their Trojan origins, choosing for their metopes certain episodes of the Trojan War that were anything but flattering to the Achaeans, to whom their neighbours and rivals, the people of Metaponte, owed their descent.

The Heraclean episodes (particularly fitted to adorn a temple dedicated to Hera for whose glory Heracles had performed his labours) are followed by scenes of the death of Patroclus—one of the most grievous losses suffered by the Achaeans in the Trojan War: Andromache with the infant Astyanax in her arms, mourning over the corpse of Hector; Clytemnestra assassinating Agamemnon with a hatchet; Orestes and Aegysthus; Orestes pursued by a Fury; and finally an extraordinary relief of Odysseus riding on a turtle, apparently an Italic variant of one of the hero's innumerable adventures.

The nuptial theme recurs with particular insistence, perhaps because Hera was the presiding goddess of marriage. What led to the choice of subjects can only be conjectured, but the metopes are proof of the existence of a highly original school of sculptors who, as Zanotti-Bianco emphasizes, had at the close of the archaic era attained a mastery of their art that strongly invites comparison with the standard reached by the Greek sculptors of this period. From literary sources, we know that from the end of the sixth century B.C., Sicily and Magna Graecia were the centres of intense intellectual activity; the names of Pythagoras, Parmenides, Stesichorus, followed by that of Empedocles and others too numerous to mention, spring into our minds. The metopes of the Heraion, taken in conjunction with those of Selinonte, make it abundantly clear that the plastic arts kept pace with the development of philosophy, poetry, and music.

The resurrection of the Heraion which we have been privileged to witness has taught us yet another valuable lesson: we now know that from the remotest ages, as far back as we can go, the cultural exchanges between the East and the Hellenized West were extraordinarily ample and complex. To the Greek colonies established on Italian soil by the hardy adventurers who had sailed across the Ionian Sea, there flowed from the outset cultural currents, not only from Greece itself, but from every source of Hellenism—currents in which Asian influences, as well as Rhodian, Cypriot, Eubaean, and Achaean elements, were mingled. So it came about that far from waiting passively for one or two centuries for the Greek miracle which was slowly taking shape in Athens, Delphi, Olympia, in every city in Greece, the Greek colonies in southern Italy and Sicily activated progress in the very heart of the Mediterranean community towards which, before long, Rome was to be irresistibly drawn.

CHAPTER NINE

What is Rome?

ARCHAEOLOGISTS AND ANNALISTS who, in the last hundred years, have pursued the quest for Rome, have been spurred on, consciously or unconsciously, by an overriding ambition. Secretly or openly, they have sought to discover in the past of the city, with the help of their ever-increasing knowledge of its historical environment, the explanation of the Roman miracle. This miracle of a civilization that suddenly irrupted into history, of a city that established its spiritual, as well as its material domination over the the entire Mediterranean basin and extended it to the distant confines of the barbaric West, demands an explanation which is not to be found, as all agree today, in the old philosophical, moral, and religious structures.

We no longer believe, as Polybius believed, that Rome owed her greatness to the *virtus romana*, a genius inherent in her beginnings, a gift of the gods to the chosen people. The picture of Rome grows more and more complex, the problem has to be continuously restated in new terms as archaeologists set their sights higher. They no longer content themselves, as did the antiquaries of the eighteenth century, with amassing curious facts, poring over ruins, collecting medals and coins and building up romantic theories. Archaeology, sometimes called the handmaid of history, has acquired a kingdom, has itself become a history, the history of the craftsmen who sculpted stone, modelled in clay, turned the potter's wheel, traced exquisite designs on craters and amphorae, built, according to laws that we are learning to understand, temples to the gods, smelted bronze for *fibulae*, engraved rings, carved intaglios. The intense activity of the workshops, of the *tabernae* standing beneath the colonnades or crowded together at the foot of the hills, of the sites where Rome was expanding and her soul was taking shape—this is the profound reality, both everyday and solemn, that long years of patient research have brought home to us. Excavations have led to the discovery of objects and shapes that are in themselves matter for history and which take us back through time. We find ourselves in the setting familiar to the rhaetors and statesmen of Ancient Rome; we see

the city walls, the roofs of the houses, the temples of the gods—all
that the legionaries fought to defend. The very essence of the life
of their day informs the spirit of the Roman poets, a spirit we
must do our utmost to understand, since if we fail to do so, they
will remain locked up in a narrow prison of words. We shall learn
to understand it through archaeology which has given life and
substance to a civilization by probing deep into its subconscious.

But there is one illusion archaeologists must guard against:
however profound, however irreplaceable their analyses may be,
they must never be deluded into thinking that, by their own unaided efforts, by a miracle, they will suddenly find themselves in
possession of the key to a civilization. At the close of the nineteenth century an entire school of Italian archaeologists were
momentarily convinced that this miracle had taken place, that they
had found material traces of the Roman people, already a fully-
formed people with its own particular characteristics, its own
religious beliefs and fundamental rites, on the march towards the
site of the Eternal City. Today, this illusion is fading, but it is
worth while recalling what might be termed the romance of the
terremare, the more so because the wildest hypotheses have a grain
of truth hidden in them, and the heated discussions to which their
extravagances give rise bring out more clearly the facts on which
they are based.

It had long been the custom of the peasants in the country
round Modena, Parma, and Piacenza to fertilize their land with a
dark, greasy substance which they dug up at certain levels. When
sold, it fetched a high price, three times as much as the best
manure. Mixed in this compost called *marna* or *terra marna*, and in
Aemilian dialect *terramara*, were fragments of pottery and other
artifacts. Attention was drawn to these true archaeological layers
at the beginning of the nineteenth century, and the scholars of
Aemilia elaborated various extraordinary theories. According to
some, the decayed organic matter that had formed the compost
came from the bodies of the human victims sacrificed by the Boii,
the Gaulish people who inhabited this part of Aemilia at the time
of the Roman conquest; others averred that the *marna* came from
charnel heaps, *puticoli* similar to those found on the Esquiline; still
others maintained that they were the rotted remains of rustic
temples of some unknown cult, dedicated to equally unknown
gods. The first really scientific study of the *terremare* was carried

out by Bartolomeo Gastaldi in 1861. Gastaldi made a minute examination of the flint and bronze axeheads found in the *marna* in the vicinity of Imola, Parma, and Modena, and compared them with artifacts discovered in various localities over a wide area; his findings suggested that long before the First Iron Age a unique culture had existed in Aemilia. The following year, Pellegrino Strobel undertook the study of a *terramara* at Castione dei Marchesi, not far from Parma. The owners of the land had been digging up the *marna* for the past fifty years to fertilize their land, but it was so extensive that they had barely made an impression on it. In the two lowest levels, Strobel found the vestiges of a large number of stakes which had been driven vertically into the virgin soil, some of which had obviously served to sustain a horizontal plank. At the northern limit of these stakes was a row of gabions (wicker baskets) filled with clay and branches of trees, wedged together so as to form a barrier. The site of Castione was methodically explored by Strobel and by Pigorini, whose name is indissolubly linked to the study of the *terremare*.[1]

During this period explorations and discoveries multiplied, and the physiognomy of the culture of the *terremare* began to appear more clearly. At the same time, however, arbitrary interpretations deduced from facts that had not been sufficiently firmly established, were advanced; from each site came a crop of generalizations that had only a limited value. The classic example of this confusion of ideas is the *terramara* of Castelazzo di Fontanella in the commune of Fontenella some three miles from the Via Aemilia, excavated by Pigorini in a series of campaigns which lasted from 1886 to 1896. By 1892 Pigorini was convinced that he had discovered the layout of the site, and from this moment, the romance of the *terremare* was born.

According to Pigorini, the village had been circumscribed by a trapezoidal enclosure which was entirely surrounded by a moat, thirty feet wide and ten feet deep, filled with water by a rushing stream. Within the enclosure he claimed to have discovered a regular grid of eight roads. The main road, running longitudinally through the village, terminated at a drawbridge over the moat, the only access to this truly fortified post. On the transversal axis he fancied he had found a ditch with five sink-holes which he immediately likened to the *mundus* of Rome! Finally, on the east of the village, Pigorini stated he had found traces of an *arx* surrounded by a moat 100 feet wide, the seat of the cult and the last line of defence, which he averred was analagous to the capitol of a Roman city! In addition he affirmed the existence of two necropoles, one square, one rectangular, outside the village, which allowed it to be inferred that the inhabitants of the *terramara* already conformed with the fundamental prescription of Roman religion that forbade the burial of the dead within the precincts of the living. From this it was naturally deduced that the prehistoric villages of Aemilia were enclosed within a pomaerium (boundary), and that they were thus as Roman as the Palatine Rome of Romulus (whose reality none doubted at that time), *Roma Quadrata*.

Pigorini's illustrated reports on the *terramara* of Castellazzo were widely read, and even today many believe that his plan of the site was the typical layout of the *terremare* villages. Certainly, it contributed largely to the idea that the Roman civilization had been imported ready made into Latium by a people coming from the north, bringing with them their own religion, rites, social organizations, and language. In Pigorini's day archaeologists thought they could already discern in the *terramara*, the geometric plan of *decumanus* and *cardo*, the plan then held to be characteristic of Roman urbanization—a tempting but extraordinarily naïve reconstruction of a past which, as we are in a better position to assess today, was infinitely complex.

Pigorini's excavations at Castellazzo in no way justified these astonishing conclusions. The flimsiness of the facts on which he built up his hypothesis has since been demonstrated. Indeed, the objections that were immediately raised, the criticism to which his theory was subjected, are now extended to the grounds on which it rested. It is not true, for instance, that *terremaricoli invariably* built their lake villages on the same immutable plan; some are circular, others irregular, and so on. Furthermore, if this people gave rise to the Roman race, why do we only find traces of them in the valley of the Po? Did they cross at a single bound the entire expanse that separates Aemilia from Rome? The Latin villages of the region of Alba have nothing in common with those of Piacenza and Modena. In reality, the culture of the *terremare* was a strictly limited phenomenon, a phenomenon undoubtedly due to immigrants from central Europe who for a long period of time remained isolated from the rest of Italy. It is no longer possible to affirm that this immigrant people exerted any influence over the other peoples of the peninsula. We must renounce the old equation *terramaricoli* = proto-Latins from which so many falsely labelled truths have been drawn.

Nevertheless, the study of the sites occupied by the *terramaricoli* has not been without profit. It has taught us that from approximately the second millenary to the close of the seventh century B.C. a pastoral and agricultural people inhabited the valley of the Po. The discovery of terracotta vases pierced with holes tells us that they knew how to make cheese, and in all probability, they were also able to spin wool and thread, and weave materials. The shepherds had dogs (skeletons of these dogs have been found) to help them guard their flocks of sheep and cattle. There were two species of the latter animals, one large, and the other much smaller. There were herds of pigs round the villages, and quite likely, horses and donkeys were amongst the worldly wealth of this people which pursued its existence for more than a millenary and a half, maintained its own rites (notably the cremation of the dead), and only vanished when a second wave of invaders, the Villanovans, also incinerators, swamped the region.

Archaeological researches on prehistoric sites have revealed an extraordinarily complex picture of the vast number of cultural and ethnic groups into which the peninsula was split up. We can no longer ignore the importance of the populations which for a long period of time occupied a vast territory, Picenum, on the Adriatic coast between the region then inhabited by the Gauls north of Ancona and that of the Vestini on the south, almost on the same latitude as Rome. Whatever their origins were, whether they were the descendants of neolithic peoples or whether they were immigrants who arrived on this territory at a later date, it is certain that they came under influences exerted from the opposite shore of the Adriatic and that it was partly due to them that Balkan forms of culture were introduced into Italy.

In the mountains and mountain valleys of the Apennines, archaeological discoveries have been relatively rare. With a few exceptions, the ancient Italic cities remain almost unknown. Not so long ago, however, a chance find focused attention on these barely explored cantons. In September 1934, not far from the village of Capestrano, a peasant who was digging up his small plot of land in order to plant a vineyard turned up the scattered fragments of a strange statue. As they did not seem important to him, he did not bother to remove them, and for almost three weeks, they lay where he had found them, caked with earth and almost unrecognizable. A heavy shower of rain, however, washed away the soil, and the fragments caught the eye of the officer in charge of a near-by post of *carabinieri* who happened to be passing that way. On the largest piece he made out the outline of weapons carved in relief, and realized that the remains were those of an ancient statue. On his orders they were removed to a place of safety and the archaeological authorities notified; the news of the discovery was communicated to the Department of Antiquities of Rome, at whose direction the pieces of the statue were immediately taken to the national museum of Termae. In this way totally unexpected evidence, the most amazing evidence so far discovered, of pre-Roman Picenian culture was revealed to the world.

This statue, the Warrior of Capestrano, is of monumental proportions. The Warrior is of average height five feet eight inches, but his tall helmet, topped with a crest, increases his stature to over eight feet. He stands erect with his arms crossed, one hand resting on his breast, the other just above his stomach, his fingers spread wide. He wears a mask, through which his eyes gaze out with a strange fixity. His chest is protected by a cuirass, his belly with a kind of apron made of leather and metal. He is armed with a short sword in a sheath, a poniard and an *ascia*, the last, no doubt, not so much a weapon as an insignia of authority.

The figure is held upright by two stone supports, on each of which a lance is engraved. The Warrior's back is naked but for a metal disc that protects the vital region of the heart, and a leather triangle across the lowest ribs. On the left support there is an inscription in extremely archaic characters whose sense remains far from clear despite the many attempts made to decipher it.[7] Possibly the language belongs to the Osco-Umbrian group, and is one of the Indo-European dialects of the ancient Italic peoples, but as there are only some thirty-three letters in the inscription it is impossible to reach any firm conclusion. Fortunately, the date of the statue is less uncertain, and it is generally agreed that it can be ascribed to the latter half of the sixth century B.C. Plainly at this epoch Picenian sculptors were acquainted with works of Greek origin; the slender waist, the excessive development of the hips immediately bring to mind the figures in Aegean paintings, the rigid erectness of the pose evokes the *kouroi* of primitive Greek art.

The Warrior of Capestrano revealed an entire Italic culture and brought out the significance of the numerous sporadic finds made on Picenian territory at the end of the nineteenth century. We see the birth and evolution of this tough warrior breed against which the Roman might was to be hurled in the course of the fourth century B.C., and which in the day of Sulla, in the last throes of the Social War, was finally to become an integral part of Imperial Italy. In Picenum, through the immigrants coming from north, south, east and west, the most radical ethnic elements were united in conditions that we can barely glimpse. Before the arrival of the Romans the orientalizing influence had penetrated into the territory, possibly directly by way of the sea, possibly indirectly, from the Greek colonies of Magna Graecia, and also, so it would appear, through the intermediary of the Etruscan civilization. Picenum was a gigantic vat which produced a cultural fermentation that was not contained, as we are now beginning to see, within the limits of true Roman history: in the course of the eighth, seventh and sixth centuries B.C., a community was evolving that was to draw Rome irresistibly into its very heart long before she dominated it, and which was to contribute to her ultimate development.

Each new discovery on both sides of the Apennines brings further evidence of this community. The frescoes of the Oscan tombs which have been found and are still being found in the region of Padua, Cumae, and Paestum (where the discoveries are of more recent date) prove that Etruscan funerary art spread throughout central Italy. In these pictures that accompanied the dead to the other world we see warriors fighting, human victims being offered up as sacrifices during the funeral rites; these scenes are magnificent interpretations of the closing books of the Aeneid in which Virgil strove with the force of his poetic might to re-create Italy as she was in her earliest days, the Italy he imagined as coming to an end with the arrival of the Trojan civilizers, but which in fact survived for many centuries after the mythical founding of Lavinium.

In this resurrection, unhoped-for, indeed, hardly foreseen at the beginning of this century, there is much that still remains obscure; only the broad outlines of the picture are beginning to appear, and at every step, we encounter a thousand uncertainties. Nevertheless, the results that have been acquired even in regions that have scarcely been explored, give the greatest ground for hope.

So far we have dwelt on the material evidence of primitive Italic civilizations revealed by archaeologists, but it would be unjust if we did not emphasize the immense amount of work accomplished by linguists in the past hundred years. They have spent endless time and patience deciphering the inscriptions, many of them lengthy, on monuments that have come to light in almost every corner of Italy, and have made us acquainted with languages spoken by Italic peoples before Latin came into general use.

Linguists had begun by concentrating on the study of documents that had long been known. For example, it was only towards the middle of the nineteenth century that they succeeded in more or less translating the Engubine Tablets found at Gubbio—the ancient Iguvium—in 1444. On these five bronze tablets are inscribed the rules of an extremely archaic ritual, valuable subject-matter for historians of Roman religion that sheds light on the spiritual ambience of central Italy around the third century B.C. We learn from the Tablets how minutely the auguries were observed within a zone marked out with the strictest care. Furthermore we are astonished to find, not only that the rules are couched in terms similar to those of the stylistic religious and juridical language of Rome, but that these prescriptions to which it was essential to adhere rigidly lest any equivocation, any ambiguity, entered into the relationship between man and the deity are repeated again and again. The Engubine Tablets prove the hollowness of the theories of the Latinists of a former day who claimed they could deduce the elements of Roman religion from what they called the national character of the peasants of Latium, a character they defined as the pedantic determination to eliminate anything of a doubtful, and therefore dangerous, nature from the formula of prayer, the contract between human beings and the divinity.

What had once been held to be peculiar to the Latins, then, appeared at Iguvium. Moreover, at Iguvium a dog was sacrificed to Jupiter, and we know that every year the same sacrifice was offered up in Rome on the Capitolium, to recall *ad perpetuam*, according to tradition, the sin of the dogs who had failed to bark and warn the troops on the citadel that the Gauls were scaling the heights. This piece of folklore becomes meaningless when taken in conjunction with the Engubine text; we must leave it to the historian of religions to discover why the Jupiter of Iguvium and the Jupiter of Rome exacted the same victim!

The study of the dialects spoken in Italy in the days of Antiquity has afforded precious material for historians, but naturally its main contribution has been made in the sphere of linguistics; it has thrown light on the various influences that may have led to the formation of the Latin language and on its prehistory. The linguists have furnished us with a mass of material that has enabled us to make detailed comparisons, with the result that certain formations, once completely baffling, have now become comprehensible. In addition, we have learnt into what an extraordinary number of language groups the peninsula was split up. Side by side with the two great related linguistic groups, Oscan, spoken in southern Italy and to the south of central Italy, and Umbrian, represented par excellence by the Tablets of Gubbio, there were, as we know today, other languages, of which we have only fragmentary texts: Messapic, Ligurian, Venetan, and the mysterious rhetic language which seems to be a vestige of pre-Indo-European dialects and was spoken in the region between Lake Como and Lake Constance.

It is probable that the Etruscan language was in part formed in Italy through contact with the Italic dialects.[2] In this linguistic confusion Latin occupied a place apart; comparatively isolated, it was only related to a few sharply defined linguistic groups, such as Faliscan, the language spoken in the small town of Falerii close to Rome, etruscanized at a very early date, and possibly, from such faint glimpses as we have of it, Siculan.

From certain indications, it would seem that Latin detached itself more rapidly from the Indo-European dialects than the languages related to Oscan and Umbrian, possibly because it was introduced into the country by immigrants whose history went farther back than that of the other populations of central Italy. But this can only be surmised, since facts are few and far between, and even those we possess are far from being confirmed. The prehistory of languages leads to the same predicament as the prehistory of cultures. Only vestigial traces remain to us, and scholars, driven by the overwhelming urge to understand everything and explain everything, have elaborated theories on indications that could easily be combined in such a way as to contradict them completely.

SICILY, AGRIGENTE   View of the so-called Temple of Concord

SICILY, SELINONTE   Remains of the Temples

PAESTUM   The Temple of Poseidon. (From an engraving by Piranesi)

PAESTUM   Interior of the Temple of Poseidon

SICILY National Museum, Palermo. Two of the metopes found at Selinonte;
(*above*) Artemis and Acteon, (*below*) Herakles and the Cyclopes

The Warrior of
Capestrano

In particular, it is difficult to a degree to link together, even with the frailest of bridges, linguistic facts and archaeological facts. At one time, Latin was defined as the language of the *terramaricoli*, but now that the hypothesis advanced by Pigorini has collapsed, a completely new structure has to be raised. No attempts have yet been made to do so, for linguists and archaeologists have grown more cautious, and rather than risk falling into errors, prefer to wait until they have reliable information on which they can proceed to build. But this is not all. As both linguists and archaeologists readily admit, the ties that exist between a language and the various aspects of a civilization can be very different, and it would be dangerous to draw conclusions from data regarding the former to establish conclusions about the latter; the language of a civilization in process of evolution may not show any marked changes, while a new language may replace the old language without affecting the customs and usages of a culture. We may be said to possess several pictures of earliest Italy, all of them faithful; the trouble is that each of them represents a different aspect of reality, and as we cannot tell how far one is separated from the other, we cannot put them together. As yet we have not found the key that would enable us to assemble the entire mosaic.

Although, as we are forced to admit, our knowledge of the earliest Italy is sadly imperfect, the glimmers of light in the darkness so feeble that we can barely discern the seed of the Rome to be, none the less, in the course of the centuries the outlines of the picture have become more sharply defined, the canvas has been touched in and enriched. Since the days of Winckelmann and Goethe, countless discoveries have opened up new perspectives, dispelled doubts and replaced them with certainties. The science of Antiquity has been renewed by a multiplicity of monuments, documents, and facts, and long years of history have been rewritten beneath our eyes. Two or three centuries ago the Roman miracle was subject-matter for aesthetes, a reality without context, a phenomenon that took place suddenly out of the blue; today we can follow each successive stage that led to it, we can relive the great moments, and in the light of what we know the miracle begins to appear as what it actually was: a natural evolution.

Today Rome seems to be inseparable from pre-Roman Italy, inseparable from Hellenistic Italy and pre-classical Hellenism (for was it not partly in the environment of Italy that pre-classical Hellenism matured?), inseparable from the whole of the ancient Mediterranean culture which has left its imprints in the deepest layers of Italian soil. In retracing in broad outlines the history of so many discoveries, many of the old concepts, sound though they may seem, appear to be seriously endangered, in particular, the idea of race, an entity which, if it is isolated from its biological support, cannot be grasped, cannot furnish any testimony in the domains of art, religion, and linguistics. Nothing so simple as race is the key to the story: the *virtus romana* cannot be explained in terms of a special grace, a caprice of nature, or a gift of providence. The Roman mind, the Roman soul, was made up of countless tendencies—countless threads that crossed and recrossed till the pattern was complete. Beneath the shock of facts the concept of the Roman soul, composed, according to one particular school of thought, of all the virtues or all the vices, has crumbled to dust. From this point of view, as well as from the others, Rome appears as the outcome, temporary, accidental and variable, of an infinity of factors, some of which tend to be constant, while others are episodic and conflict with one another. Thus, in Roman civilization there are contradictions, unforeseeable retrogressions which can only be explained within the framework of an evolution outside the limits of Rome.

When Rome made her appearance in history she was already a city, but for long years her face remained hidden. Today, after so much patient research, after a century and a half of discoveries, some of them humble and of interest only to archaeologists, some of them so outstanding that they have caused the world to marvel, that face has become a little clearer. A few graves in the necropolis of the Sacred Way, a few hut-foundations on the Palatine, a stele beneath a paving of *lapis niger*: these revolutionized all our concepts of Royal Rome. A few temples discovered beneath a square in a corner of Baroque Rome, a façade concealed by parasitic buildings in the shadow of the Auberge of the Knights of Rhodes, two or three private houses, a palace buried since the days of Titus: these all formed part of the Queen of Cities, and without them the finest pages of Livy and Tacitus might be empty of meaning.

But Rome was also the capital of an empire, raised by the victories she won to the leadership of Italy and the world. The glory of her splendour, the glory that still dazzles us, was so refulgent that for centuries the lesser civilizations by which she was surrounded and to which she was indebted, were totally eclipsed. These civilizations that two hundred years ago were completely unknown or barely glimpsed have been brought back to light and the mystery in which their origins are shrouded has at least been partly dispelled. Etruscan tombs have opened wide, and for the second time life has triumphed over death; Etruscan necropoles have revealed themselves, and after this revelation of the domain of the dead the cities of the living have returned to life. From the alluvial soil of the valley of the Po, Spina is emerging; on the hills of Bolsena traces of the ancient religious metropolis of the Etruscan confederation are beginning to appear. The Etruscan temples are no longer empty and meaningless, for once again they enshrine their resurrected deities.

If we go southward, we see that it is not Pompeii alone that is struggling free from its winding-sheet of ashes; Herculaneum is emerging from its deeper tomb, that tomb sealed in beneath a sea of solidified mud. The past of Greek Italy is written in more detail, as page after page unfolds. Ostia, Rome's double, lives again in her lofty *insulae*.

Herculaneum is furnishing the proof that at the beginning of the Christian era the Campagna played an active part in the renewal of urban architecture, even if languorous Pompeii drowsed amidst the delight of her gardens and thermae and passed all her waking moments in a frenzy of pleasure and passion. The cities of Magna Graecia, already half-dead in Caesar's day, speak to us of the remote age of the first Greek colonists, of their contacts with the Italic peoples; their temples, many of them of breath-taking magnificence, tell us that the fruitfulness of Greek art lost nothing of its genius on Italian soil; through the votive statuettes we catch glimpses of the faith of a people, and we see in imagination endless processions of pilgrims making their way to the temples to implore a favour from the gods. If we go even farther, to the mountains overlooking the Adriatic, we shall find civilizations open for thousands of years to influences from the East which are just beginning to become known to us through the endless, the infinitely patient work of archaeologists.

The marvellous development of Italian archaeology during the past two centuries has resulted in upsetting all our preconceived ideas so that we now see chaos where we once saw an admirable simplicity. Rome is no longer the city of our schooldays, the city sung by Virgil and described by Livy; Rome has emerged from her isolation, and often our eyes can only perceive an image that is blurred; we stagger beneath the weight of new facts, we cannot relate them to one another, form a coherent whole. The riches that have been revealed have exceeded all hopes, surpassed the limits of human knowledge, the wealth of new discoveries has had the paradoxical effect from generation to generation of making the pattern seem still more incomplete. But we must not complain, for we know that, like Penelope's tapestry, the fabric of history must be endlessly woven and unwoven.

NOTES

CHAPTER ONE

1. For the study of the various building materials and methods of construction employed in Rome and the vicinity in the days of Antiquity, the following work is indispensable: *Ancient Roman Construction in Italy from the Prehistoric Period to Augustine*, by M. E. Blake, with an additional bibliography and a commentary on the studies by E. B. Van Deman dealing with building and building material in the late Augustan period, Washington, 1947.

2. Livy, Vol. XXIV, 47, 15.

3. Livy, Vol. XXVI, 27.

4. R. Lanciani: *The Destruction of Ancient Rome*, London, 1901, pp. et seq. A large number of the facts in this chapter have been taken from this book.

5. Grimaldi: *Diario della Distruzione di S. Pietro Vecchio,* Barberini MS. XXXIV, 50, quoted by R. Lanciani in *The Destruction of Ancient Rome*, pp. 31 et seq. For full details of Constantine's basilica and the recent excavations of the Confessional of St. Peter, see *Études d'Histoire Chrétienne*, by J. Carcopino, Paris, 1953.

6. For a detailed history of the Curia and a full description of the restorations effected after 1935, see *I lavori della Curia* by A. Bartoli, Rome, Instituto di Studi Romani, 1938.

7. In addition to the christianized temples mentioned in this chapter, we would draw the attention of readers to the following: Sta Maria Antica installed in the Temple of Augustus in the Velabrum; S. Lorenzo, in the Temple of Antoninus and Faustina, in the Forum Romanum; the chapel dedicated to St. Peter in the Temple of Venus and Rome on the Velia, and the Church dedicated to SS. Sergius and Bacchus in the Temple of Concord. There are, of course, numerous others.

8. R. Lanciani: *Ruins and Excavations*, p. 46.

9. *The Destruction of Ancient Rome*, pp. 58 et seq., in which R. Lanciani describes his personal experiences of the excavations of 1892.

10. R. Lanciani: *The Destruction of Ancient Rome*, p 208.

CHAPTER TWO

1. The clearance of the Forum was mainly achieved by the Comte de Tournon, who was Prefect of the Department of the Tiber during the French domination. Amongst the monuments de Tournon disengaged are the Temple of Vespasian, the Temples of Castor and Pollux, Antoninus and Faustina, Venus and Rome, the Basilica of Constantine; he also disengaged the Temple of Mater Matuta, the Temple of Portunus, the Janus Quadrifons in the Forum Boarium, and the Basilica Ulpia and part of Trajan's Forum.

2. R. Lanciani: *The Destruction of Ancient Rome*, p. 117.

CHAPTER THREE

1. Poggio Bracciolini, op. cit., pp. 503 et seq. *Nam ex publicis aut privatis operibus liberae quondam Civitatis interrupta quaedam et ea parva vestigia visuntur.* Half of the buildings cited as examples were constructed during the Empire, for instance, the Pyramid of Cestius (in the Protestant cemetery) which was believed by Petrarch to be the tomb of Remus, the brother of Romulus! It actually goes no farther back than the year 12 B.C., and belongs to the Augustan era. The Arch of P. Lentulus Scipio and T. Quinctius Crispinus on the Aventine, which Poggio took to be a 'Republican monument', was raised in the year 2 A.D.

2. The Reverend Edward Burton: *A Description of the Antiquities and other curiosities of Rome, from personal observation during a visit to Italy in the years 1818–1819*, London, 1828, p. 201. This book is a kind of encyclopaedia of all the archaeological facts that were known about Rome at the beginning of the nineteenth century. The usual traditional mistakes are found in its pages. Nevertheless, Burton, who took a deep interest in the excavations carried out in Napoleonic Rome, succeeded in drawing a little closer to the truth.

3. See E. M. Blake: *Ancient Roman Construction in Italy*, pp. 193 et seq.

4. R. Lanciani: *New Tales of Old Rome*, London, 1901, pp. I et seq.

5. For details on the ceramics found in Latium, see in particular W. R. Bryan: *Italic hut-urns and hut-urn cemeteries, a study in the early Iron Age of Latium and Etruria* (MSS. and Monograph of the

America Academy in Rome, Vol. IV, 1925).

6. E. Gjerstad: *Early Rome, I. Stratographical Researches in the Forum Romanum and along the Sacra Via* in *Acta Inst. Romani Regni Sueciae*, 4, XVII, I, Lund, 1953. See also Gjerstad: *Early Rome: The Tombs*, Lund, 1956. These two volumes are the first of a series on which Gjerstad is engaged.

7. This observation was made by G. Dumézil. See his *Naissance de Rome*, Paris, 1944.

8. Gjerstad: op. cit., p. 58.

9. See *New Tales of Old Rome*, by R. Lanciani, pp. I et seq.

10. See Lanciani's *New Tales of Old Rome*, pp. 22 et seq. Lanciani tales this date to be certain, and agrees with Ceci's interpretation of the inscription. (For further details of Ceci's interpretation see the article by Von Duhn in *Neue Jahrbucher*, 1899.) Ceci's version runs as follows: 'He who wishes to sacrifice a cow in calf must do so near the sanctuary. The ritual cakes must be brought by the *rex sacrorum* at the moment when the moon is full. He who desires to sacrifice a cow in calf or a sow in farrow must first obtain through the *kalator* the permission of the *rex sacrorum*, and before making the sacrifice, must consult the auspices and make the ritual offerings. He who desires to offer a sacrifice when the moon is in its first quarter must follow the same rules.' This picturesque interpretation is purely the romantic effort of an antiquary; the hypotheses advanced by Ceci to support the words with which he has filled in the Lacunde are insusceptible to proof. Here, as far as can be made out from the letters on the stele, is the text of the inscription: QVOI HOI . . . /SAKROS ESE ED SORD . . ./ . . . IA . . . IAS RECEI IO . . ./EVAM QVOS RE . . ./ . . . M KALATOREM HAI . . ./ . . . OD IO VXMENTA KAPIA DOTAV . . ./ . . . M I TER RIT . . ./ . . .M QVOI-HAVELOD NEQV . . ./ . . . OD IOVESTOD . . ./ . . . LOIVQVIOD . . .

Certain words in these mutilated lines are relatively clear: *iouxmenta*; *kapia* (d) (the d is the first letter of the next word); *Recei*; *kalatorem*; *quoi*; *sakros essed*; *iouestod*—equivalent to *jumenta*; *capiat*; *regi*; *calatorem*; *qui*; *sacer erit*; *justo*. see page 75.

11. Fr. Altheim: *History of Roman Religion*, London, pp. 230 et seq.

12. All these facts have been brought out by A. Piganiol in 'Les Origines du Forum' in *Mel. de l'Ecole Francaise de Rome*, XXVIII, 1908, pp. 250 et seq.; also my own study: 'Le Dieu Janus et les Origines de Rome' in *Lettres d'Humanité*, IV, 1945, pp. 15 et seq. In my view the location of the Temple of Janus, the subject of so many controversies, has been correctly fixed at the point where the Argiletum debouches into the Forum. See my article in *Mel. de l'Ecole Francaise de Rome*, 1952, pp. 39 et seq.

13. See Wagenvoort: *Roman Dynamism*, Oxford, 1947.

14. Nibby, in his revised edition of Famiano Nardini's *Roma Antica*, Rome, 1818, traces, very inexactly, the line of the Servian Wall, which he confuses at various points with the Aurelian Wall. (See map in Vol. I, pp. 49 et seq.) It was not until 1878, when H. Jordan's *Topographie* was published, that the line of the Servian Wall was more accurately drawn; even so, however, there were many mistakes.

15. G. Saflund has given a very full analysis of the identified vestiges of the Servian Wall in 'Le Mura di Roma Republicana' in *Acta Inst. Regni Suec.*, Lund, 1932. Saflund was convinced that the Wall did not go back to Royal Rome and his contentions raised the knotty problem of its date.

16. P. Quoniam: 'A propos du mur dit de Servius Tullius' in *Mel. de l'Ecole Francaise de Rome*, 1947, pp. 41–64.

CHAPTER FOUR

1. The Reverend Edward Burton: *A Description of the Antiquities and other curiosities of Rome from personal observation during a visit to Italy in the years 1818–1819*, London, 1828, p. 201. See Piranesi's famous engraving of the Forum.

2. The *atria* of Maenius and Titius—see Livey, Vol. XXXIX, 44.

3. During the recent excavations, reports of which have not yet been published.

4. For the sources from which the architectural style of the Imperial Fora was derived, see in particular A. Von Gerkan: *Griechische Städteanlagen*, Berlin-Leipzig, 1924. This subject was taken up after the later excavations by E. Gjerstad: 'Die Ursprungsgeschicte der

romischen Kaiserfora' in *Opusc. Arch. Inst. Rom. Regni Sueciae*, III, pp. 40–72. Gjerstad is of the opinion that the style had a double origin: Asiatic, through the Etruscan architectural styles and the Italic fora, and Hellenistic, since certain elements resemble the porticoes with peristyles of agoras such as those of Priene, Pergamo, etc. Consult also R. Martin: *Recherches sur l'Agora Grecque*, Paris, 1951.

5. Gn. Julius Agricola typifies these administrators of senatorial rank. He was the father-in-law of Tacitus, who wrote the history of his career in his *Life of Agricola*.

6. See my article in *Lettres d'Humanite* IV, 1945.

7. R. Lanciani: *Ruins and Excavations*, p. 143.

CHAPTER FIVE

1. See amongst others, R. Lanciani: *Wanderings in the Roman Campagna*, London, 1909; G. Tomassetti: *La Campagna Romana*, 4 vols., Rome, 1910–26; T. Ashby: *The Roman Campagna in Classical Times*, London, 1927; also the numerous articles by G. Lugli in *Bollettino della Commissione Archeologica Municipale*, 1913 et seq.

2. R. Lanciani: *Wanderings in the Roman Campagna*, pp. 121 et seq.

3. Thomas D. Price: 'A Restoration of Horace's Sabine Villa' in *Mon. American Academy in Rome*, X, 1932, pp. 135–42, pl. 34–42.

4. For the date of Ostia's foundation, see J. Carcopino: *Virgile et les Origines d'Ostie*, Paris, 1920. See also G. Calza's *Scavi di Ostia*, V.I., *Topographie Generale*, Rome, 1953.

5. A. Boethius: 'The Neronian Nova Urbs' in *Corolla Archeologica*, 1932, pp. 84–97. Re the possible Egyptian origin of the *insula*, see H. W. Fairman: 'Town Planning in Pharaonic Egypt' in *The Town Planning Review*, Vol. XX, 1949, pp. 32–51. See also L. Homo: *Rome Imperiale et L'Urbanisme dans l'Antiquite*, Paris, 1951.

6. For the history of the Roman aqueducts see T. Ashby: *The Aqueducts of Ancient Rome*, Oxford, 1935; E. B. Van Deman: *The Building of the Roman Aqueducts*, Washington, 1934.

7. T. Frank: 'Roman Buildings of the Republic' in *Papers and Monographs of the American Academy in Rome*, III, 1934;

E. B. Van Deman: 'The Methods of Determining the Date of Ancient Roman Concrete Constructions' in *American Journal of Archaeology*, Vol. XVI, 1912, pp. 230–41 and pp. 387–432; M. E. Blake: *Ancient Roman Constructions in Italy*; 2 vols. Washington, 1947–59; G. Lugli: *La tecnica edilizia romana con particolare riguardo a Roma e Lazio*, 2 vols., Rome, 1957; H. Bloch: *I Bolli laterizi e la storia edilitare di Roma*, Rome, 1947.

8. G. Schmiedt and F. Castagnoli: 'L'Antica Città di Norba' in *L'Universo*, XXXVII, 1957, pp. 125–48. For the technique of aerial photography in archaeological research, the numerous studies by Raymond Chevallier will be found useful, in particular *Les Leçons d'une recente Exposition*; 'Photographie Aerienne et Archéologie' in *Bollettino di Geodesia et Scienze affini*, XVI, 4, 1957; *La Photographie Aerienne au service de L'Archéologie*, Paris, Institut Pedagogique National, 1958.

CHAPTER SIX

1. The thickness of this shroud has been established by the latest geological researches. An article by G. de Lorenzo in *Nuova Antologia*, I, October 1909, encouraged for many years the belief that the layer of tufa which covers Herculaneum was formed as a result of the city's gradual burial beneath the cinders and *lapilli* which were soaked by rain and consequently became solidified. This theory conflicted with that of A. Lacroix, who, in 1908, had published his 'Les Dernier Jours de Herculanum et de Pompei interpretes à l'aide de quelques phenomenes recents du volcanisme' in *Bull. Soc. de Geographie*, XVIII, Paris. On the whole question, see two important studies by Professor Maiuri: Nuovi studi e Ricerche sul seppellimento di Ercolano in *Rendiconti Accademia di Italia (classe di scienze morali)*, 1940, and 'Geologia ed Archeologia ad Ercolano ed a Pompeii' in *Rendiconti dell' Accademia Archeologica di Napoli*, 1942.

2. Bayardi: *Le Antichita di Ercolano Esposto*, 8 vols., Naples 1757–92. This work was preceded by *Prodromi delle Antichita di Ercolano*, five tomes published in Naples in 1752 in which such knowledge as the author possessed of Herculaneum is submerged in a sea of decidedly dubious erudition. Bayardi's

books are interesting today because of their plates.

3. Actually, Winckelmann was referring to Herculaneum, as we can see from the rest of the letter. but the method he describes was also followed at Pompeii.

4. THERMAE/M (arci) CRASSI FRUGI/AQUA MARINA ET BALN (ea)/AQUA DULCI JANUARIUS L(ibertus). M. Licinius Crassus Frugi, consul in A.D. 64, executed by Nero in 68, is known to us through Pliny the Elder, who tells us there was a hot spring on his estate which gushed into the sea. We see that the great patricians were not above making a handsome profit out of their property through the agency of a freedman. Consult A. Mau: *Pompeii in Life and Art,* translated by F. Kelsey, New York, 1899, p. 400.

5. D. Comparetti and G. de Petra: *La Villa Ercolanese dei Pisoni,* Turin, 1883. This book contains the full story of the exploration of the villa.

6. *Herculanensium Voluminum, quae supersunt. Collectio Prior,* 10 vols., Naples, 1793–1850, and under the same title, *Collectio Altera,* 11 vols., Naples 1862–76. Other papyri from Herculaneum, now in the possession of the University of Oxford, have been published under the title of *Herculanensium Voluminum Pars Prima et Id., Pars Secunda,* Oxford, 1824–5, followed by *Fragmenta Herculanensia,* by Walter Scott, Oxford, 1885; *Herculaneum Fragments,* Oxford, 1891, the sequel to 9 vols, with the same title published in Oxford, 1880. See also D. Bassi: *Papiri Ercolanesi, Philodemos, sui Vizi e sulla Morte, Herculanesium Voluminum quae supersunt, Collectio tertia,* Milan, 1914. (This first volume was not followed by a second.) (On the work of unrolling papyri, etc., see Raf. Cantarella: 'L'Ufficio dei Papiri Ercolanesi dal 1923 at 1931' in *Rivista di Filologia Classica,* X, 1932, pp. 359–68, and Werner Liebich: 'Aus der Arbeit an den Papyri von Herculaneum' in *Wissenschaftliche Annalen,* II, 1953, pp. 304–13. It appears that at present there is no apparatus for unrolling papyri other than Padre Biaggio's 'cradle', by means of which all the rolls that were in a sufficient state of preservation have now been unwound. The technical details of the 'cradle' will be found in Winckelmann's *Letters,* pp. 135 et seq., and an even fuller account is given by A. de

Jorio in *Officiana de' Papiri descritta,* Naples, 1825.

7. Winckelmann: *Letters,* p. 139.

8. M. ARRIVS L(ibertus) DIOMEDES —SIBI SVIS MEMORIAE—MAGISTER PAG(i) AVG(usti) FELI(cis) SVBBRB(ani). Marcus Arrius was the president of the confraternity of the citizens of Augustus Felix, a suburb immediately west of Pompeii. The president of this confraternity was invariably a freedman.

9. Della Corte: op. cit., p. 11 (in 2nd edition). The formula *Oro vos factis* (I ask you to elect . . .) was usually abbreviated to OVF.

10. See my book *Les Jardins romains,* Paris, 1944.

11. Pliny: *Natural History,* Vol. III, p. 60.

12. The four arteries are: two *decumani* (oriented from east to west), the Via di Nola and the Via dell'Abbondanza (the former takes its name from the fact that it terminates at the Nola Gate in the direction of Nola, the latter from a painted notice), and two *cardines* (oriented south-north). The first *cardo* is the Via di Stabia, which links the Vesuvius Gate with the Stabiae Gate. The second *cardo* has not yet been disengaged, but we know as a result of the excavations of 1954 that it terminates at the Nocera Gate, immediately south of the Palaestra. (See A. Maiuri in *Saggi,* pp. 351–2) On the north this *cardo* led to the Capua Gate.

13. On the excavations of Herculaneum, see H. Marrou: 'Herculanum à la lumière des nouvelles fouilles' in *Annales des Hautes Etudes de Gand,* I, 1937, pp. 79–107; A. Maiuri: *Ercolano,* Rome, 1932, and the same author's 'La ripresa degli scavi di Ercolano' in *Saggi,* pp. 355 et seq.

14. On the early excavations of Stabiae, see M. Ruggiero: *Degli Scavi di Stabia del 1740 al 1782,* Naples, 1881; Cosenza: *Stabia,* 1907.

CHAPTER SEVEN

1. R. Bloch: *The Etruscans.*

2. For the story of the discovery of the vase, see *Annali dell'Istituto,* 1848, pp. 299–305. The vase, a black-figured crater dating back to the sixth century B.C., is in the Florence Museum.

3. Letter dated April 1857, quoted by Noel des Vergers in *l'Etrurie et les*

Etrusques, Paris, 1862–4, Vol. III, p. 17. See also *Bollettino dell'Istituto*, May 1857.
4. Noel des Vergers, op. cit., Vol. III, p. 47.
5. An inscription which came to light after the discovery of the Francois Tomb has confirmed the history of Aulus Vipenna. The inscription is votive and was found at Veii; it dates back to the middle of the sixth century B.C. See *Studi Etruschi*, XIII, 1939, pp. 455 et. seq.
6. Pliny the Elder: *Natural History*, Vol. XXXV, 157.
7. Plutarch: *Life of Publicola*, 13.
8. For the extremely complex question of the origin of the Etruscans, see M. Pallotini: *Etruscologia*, Milan, 1955.

CHAPTER EIGHT

1. Patrick Brydone: *Voyage in Sicily and Malta*, London, 1773, Vol. I, p. 47.
2. H. Swinburne: *Travels in the two Sicilies in the years 1777, 1778, 1779 and 1780*, London, 1783–5, Vol. III, p. 205.
3. Goethe: *Travels in Italy*, Dohn's Standard Library, p. 210.
4. H. Swinburne, op. cit., Vol. II, p. 193.
5. J. Hermann de Riedesel, who travelled through Italy between 1767 and 1770, addressed two letters to Winckelmann which were published in Zurich 1771 under the title of *Reise durch Sicilien und Grossgriechenland*.
6. Swinburne, op. cit., Vol. III, p. 367.
7. Goethe: *Travels in Italy*, Dohn's Standard Edition, pp. 237–8.
8. Ibid., p. 260.
9. Ibid.
10. T. J. Dunbabin: *The Western Greeks*, Oxford, 1948, p. 175; see also Charles Picard in *Revue de Philologie*, 1933, pp. 341 et seq.
11. See the most interesting book written

as a tribute to Paolo Orsi, the man and this work: *Paolo Orsi, 1859–1939* sponsored by *Archivio Storico per la Calabria e la Lucania*, V fasc. 3–4, Rome.
12. See J. Bérard: *La Colonisation Grecque*, 2nd ed., 1957, pp. 493 et seq.
13. An example of these discoveries is that of the mycenaean vases found in the Siculan necropolis of Thapsos. See *Monumenti Antichi . . . Lincei*, Vol. VI, 1895, pp. 89 et seq.
14. This thesis was advanced in 1941 by J. Bérard in *La Colonisation Grecque*, 1st ed.
15. For example, Orsi's work at Megara Hyblae was continued by F. Villard and G. Vallet. For these excavations, see *Melange de l'Ecole Française*, LXIII, pp. 7–52; the excavations of 1949 led to the identification of the original settlement, and made it possible to trace the history of the city from its foundation towards 728 B.C. up to the Roman epoch.
16. E. Douglas Van Buren: *Archaic fictile revetments in Sicily and Magna Graecia*, London, 1923.
17. This is the reason given by Paolo Orsi for the persistence of terracotta revetments in southern Italy. See *Caulonia, secunda memoria*, col. 478 et seq.

CHAPTER NINE

1. The *terremare* have been the subject of a large number of studies, all of which will be found in L. Pigorini's 'Terramare dell'eta di bronzo situata in Castione dei Marchesi (Territorio Parmigiano)' in *Atti . . . Accad. dei Lincei*, series III; see also *Mem. classe di Scienze Morali*, Vol. VIII, Rome, 1883, pp. 265 et seq.
2. For a description of the various languages of ancient Italy see Pisani: *Le lingue dell'Italia antica oltre il Latino*, Turin, 1953.

INDEX

Accademia dei Lincei, 186

Academy, the—*see* Hadrian's Villa, 117
of Herculaneum, later *Accademia delle Scienzi e delle Belle Arti* of Naples, 136, 144

Adrian I (Pope 772–95), 18

Aemilia, 12, 241, 242, 243

Aeneas statuettes, discovered at Veii in 1938, 194–5

Aeolus, King, 222

Agrigente, Sicily—Greek city built on the geometric plan, 183; Temple of Concord at, 212, 213, 215; Temple of Zeus at, 216; architectonic terracottas, 220

Agrippa, Marcus Vipsanius (63–12 B.C.), 31, 35–36, 45

Alaric, leader of the Goths—his sack of Rome, A.D. 410, 19

Alba, Lake, nineteenth-century discovery of a necropolis at, 47–48, 51

Alcubierre, Rocco Giocchino, appointed (1738) by King Carlos III to excavate Herculaneum, 136; excavation at Pompeii (1748), 137–9; at Herculaneum (1750), 139–44; at Stabiae 161, 205

Allobrogicus, Quintus Fabius, conqueror of the Allobroges, 121 B.C., 71

Altar of Peace, dedicated on 30 January 9 B.C., 106; remains found in 1568, 107; the work of reconstruction leading to complete restoration in 1938, 107–9

Amphitheatre, the—*see* excavations at Pompeii, 139, 144

Anaglyphus of Trajan, 73

Angell, Samuel, co-discoverer of the metopes of Selinonte, 216

Alexander VII (Pope 1599–1667), 16

ancilia—sacred shields, 61, 79

Antichità Romane, by Piranesi, 207
Siciliane, by Padre Pancrazi (1751), 213

Apollo, statue of, found at Veii, 192
Alaeos, Temple of, near Crimisa (now Punta del Alice), 233
Temple of, Pompeii, 155–6
Sauroctonus, 89

Apollodorus of Damascus, 84

Apulia, 226, 233

aqueducts—courses of those supplying Rome plotted, 130; *La Anunciada* and *La Civita,* Pompeii, 137

Ara Coeli, 42
della Regina (Altar of the Queen), temple at Tarquinii, 197–8

Arch of Augustus, 55, 72
of Constantine, 15, 23
of Fabius, 38
of Janus Quadrifons, 23, 39, 82
of Septimius Severus, 38, 57, 73
of Titus, 12, 22, 23, 70

Arezzo (formerly Arretium), 165

Argiletum, the, 45, 80, 83

Arretium (now Arezzo), 165

Ars Poetica, Epistle to the Piso family by Horace, 142

Athene Promachus, Temple of at Locri, 231

atria—
Tuscan, supported on beams, 152
Tetrastyle, supported on four columns, 152
Corinthian, supported on six columns, 152

Augustan Exhibition, 1938, 108

Augustus, Gaius Julius Caesar Octavianus (formerly Octavian), Roman Emperor, 63 B.C.–A.D. 14, 37; continued work on the Forum begun by Julius Caesar, 71, 76; Altar of Peace raised in his honour, 9 B.C., 106
Arch of, 55, 72
domus Augustii, 91–93, 97
Forum of, 72, 74, 78–79, 80, 81, 82, 83
Mausoleum of, 23
Rostra of, 73, 74

Aurelian Wall, 22; raised in the third century B.C., 65, 104

Aventine, the—buildings destroyed by fire, 213 B.C., 11; and again in A.D. 64, 12; plundered by barbarians, A.D. 408, 19, 22, 45; included within the Servian Wall, 64, 67

Baldelli, Abbé Onofrio, founder of the Cortona Museum, 174

Barbarian invasions of Rome, 19, 20

Barberini Museum, Palestrina, 127

Bartoli, A., Director of the Antiquities of the Palatine, 89

Basilica Aemilia, 14, 39; construction begun, 179 B.C., 45, 71, 82, 83
Julia, 14, 22, 24, 31; begun by Julius Caesar, completed by Augustus, 71, 83
of Constantine, 30, 33, 75
of Maxentius, 33
of the Porta Maggiore, 100, 104–6
of St. Peter, 15, 26, 29, 34
Porcia, built by Cato, 184 B.C., 70
Ulpia, 38

basilicas—their building begun in the second century B.C., 9–10, 70–71

Baths of Caracalla, 29

Bayardi, Monsignor, editor of *Le Antichità di Ercolano Esposto* (8 vols., Naples 1759–92), 136, 255–6

Bembo, Cardinal Marco, builder of the Priory of the Order of the Knights of Rhodes (1465), 78

Benedict III (Pope 855–8), 21
 XIV (Pope 1740–58), 28

Biaggio, Padre, Latin scribe in the Vatican library, 140

Bianchini, Monsignor—*see* excavation of the Farnese Gardens, 89–90, 96

Bigi Tomb, Corneto, 175

Biscari, Prince di, co-editor of *Memoria per servire alla Storia Litteraria di Sicilia*, 215

Block, R.—*see* excavation of Volsinii, 196–7

Bolletino delle Archaeologica Municipale, 43

Bologna (formerly Etruscan city of Felsina), 181, 190

Bomarzo, exploration of Etruscan tombs at, 175

Boni, Giacomo, Director of Antiquities of the Forum and the Palatine, discoverer (1902) of the Sacred Way necropolis, 48–50; directed excavations on the Palatine, 52–53, 55; uncovers a stele in the Comitium (1899), 57, 185

Boniface IV (Pope 608–15), consecrated the Pantheon, A.D. 609, 36

Bonifacio, the grammarian, 84

Borsari—*see* excavations at Ostia, 119

Buonarotti, Filippo, Florentine scholar, 166, 167, 169

boustrophedon ('in-and-out' writing), 57

Bracciolini, Poggio, Florentine worthy, 24, 25, 44

Bramante, Donato d'Agnolo (*c.* 1444–1514), Italian architect and painter, 30

Brea, Barnabo, 222

Brizio, collaborator with Pietro Rosa in archaeological research, 43

Brydone, Patrick, 205

Burton, Reverend Edward, 44, 45, 69

Byres, James, English painter, 168

Caecilia Metella, tomb of, 111

Caecilius, 148

Caelian heights, 13, 14, 17, 64, 67, 98, 99

Caesar, Gaius Julius (102 ?–44 B.C.), partially builds the Basilica Julia, 71; site and plans for a new Forum, 75–77

Calabria, 226, 229; excavations at Locri, 230–1; at Hipponium, 232; at Taranto, 233; discovery of the Temple of Apollo Alaeos by Orsi, 233; identification of the site of Caulonia (1915), 233–4

Caligula, Gaius Caesar, Roman Emperor A.D. 12–14, 15, 41, 95, 98

Caltagirone, Sicily, 222

Calza, Guido—*see* excavations at Ostia, 119–20

Campagna, the Roman, 110–33

Campana Tomb, Isola Farnese, 188

Campus Martius, 13, 21, 22, 23, 31, 32, 42, 72, 75, 77, 100, 108

Canina, Italian archaeologist, 96, 116

Canopus of Alexandria—*see* Hadrian's Villa, 117

Capestrano, the Warrior of, statue discovered in 1934, 244–6

Capo delle Colonne (Cape Lacinion), 211

cappellaccio (volcanic stone used for building), 10, 61, 63, 65, 67, 68

Capitol, the, 10, 11, 22, 24, 31, 32, 33, 38, 39, 42, 45, 60; political and religious centre of Rome, 63, 71; inside the Servian Wall, 64, 68, 73, 75, 77, 100, 193

Capitolium, the ('Tarpeian Citadel'), 19, 24, 25, 29, 45, 63; founded by the Tarquins, 64, 193, 247

Caracalla, Baths of, 29

Carcopino, J., 100, 104, 105

Carinus, Marcus Aurelius, Roman Emperor A.D. 283–4, 14

Carlos III, King, promotes excavations at Herculaneum (1738), 135–6; and at Pompeii, 137–9

Castelazzo di Fontanella, *terramara* of, excavated by Pigorini (1886–96), 242–3

Castellamare di Stabia, village on the site of Stabiae, 134

Castione dei Marchesi, *terramara* excavated by Pellegrino Strobel, 242

Castor, Temple of, 39, 70

Catania, Sicily, explored in 1779 under the directorship of Prince di Biscari, 215

Catiline, Lucius Sergius (*c.* 108–62 B.C.), 31

Cato, Marcus Porcius, 'The Censor' (234–149 B.C.), 10, 70, 210

Catulus, Quintus Lutatius (*c.* 120–61 B.C.), 71

Catullus, Gaius Valerius, lyric poet, 105

Caulonia, site identified by Paolo Orsi in 1915, 233

Cavallari, Domenico, architect, 217
 Francesco Saverio, appointed Director of Antiquities, Sicily (1862), 217, 218, 219

Celestinus II (Pope in 1143), 32
Ceres, Temple of, 18
Cermalus, the (western summit of the Palatine), 54, 89; hut foundations on, 52, 53, 96, 98
Cervetri, discovery of the Regolini-Galazzi Etruscan tomb at (1836), 175-6
Championnet, General, 144
Chaupy, Abbé Bertrand Capmartin de —*see* Horace's Farm, 113-15
Chimaera, statue of, found at Arretium, 165
Chiusi, exploration of Etruscan tombs at, 175; ceramic vase restored by Alessandro Francois, 178
Churches—
  S. Adriano (formerly the Curia), 16, 33
  S. Cesario, 22
  S. Cosmo, 33
  S. Damian, 33
  S. Lorenzo in Miranda (which incorporates the Temple of Antonius and Faustina), 38
  S. Nicola ai Cesarini, 100
  S. Nicola in Carcere (built on the site of three ancient temples), 18
  S. Pietro in Vinculo (raised by the Empress Eudoxia), 19, 33
  S. Pudenziana, 33
  S. Stefano delle Carrozze (formerly? temple of Hercules Custos), 17
  S. Stefano Rotondo, 17
  S. Theodore, 39
  Sta Lucia-in-Orphea (or Orphtea), 35
  Sta Lucia and S. Martino (formerly the Secretarium), 16
  Sta Maria Egyptiaca (formerly? temple of sea-god Portunus), 17-18
  Sta Maria in Cosmedin, built in sixth century, 18
  Sta Maria Maggiore, 28, 33
  Sta Maria Nuova (now Sta Francesca Romana), 27
  SS. Sergius and Bacchus, 32
Cicero, Marcus Tullius (106-43 B.C.), 31, 91, 94, 104, 110, 129, 143, 163, 164, 209
Circus Flaminius, 22, 32
  Maximum, 12, 21, 45, 89, 97, 225
Cities and Cemeteries of Etruria, The, by George Dennis, 177
City of the Forum, 62, 63, 64
Civita Castellana (built on the site of Falerii), 186, 187
Claudius, Tiberius Claudius Drusus Nero Germanicus, Roman Emperor from A.D. 41-54, 79, 95, 98, 105; constructed harbour at Ostia, 123; his historical study of the Etruscans,

163; the Discourse of Lyons, 163, 180
Clemens, T. Suedius, military tribune under Vespasian, 137
Clement XI (Pope 1700-21), 28
Clivus Argentarius (Ascent of the Bankers), 77, 83
  Victoriae, 98
Coke, Thomas, 166, 167
Cloaca Maxima, constructed 33 B.C., 45, 130, 171
Collectio Altera, series of eleven volumes of the deciphered papyri found at Herculaneum, 141
  Prior, series of ten volumes of the deciphered papyri found at Herculaneum, 141
Colosseum, the (Flavian Circus), 12, 13, 23; short history of, 25-29, 42, 85, 99
Colossus of Nero, 25-26
Column of Phocas, 15-16, 39
Comitia Centuriata, assembly of citizens enrolled to take up arms in time of war, 75
Comitium, the—political centre of the early Roman Republic, 20; excavated by Giacomo Boni, 57-60, 62, 68, 70; replaced by the Curia, 72, 77
Commission of Antiquities and Art, set up in 1827, 216
Commodus, Lucius Aelius Aurelius (169-92 B.C.), Roman Emperor, 14
Conca (formerly Satricum), terracottas of, 172, 186-8
Concord, Temple of, Agrigente, 212, 215
  Temple of, Rome, 74
Considérations sur les Causes de la Grandeur de la Décadence des Romains, by Montesquieu, 44
Constans II, Byzantine Emperor (630-68), 17, 20, 36
Constantine I (288?-337 B.C.), Roman Emperor, 15, 23, 30, 33, 73, 75, 226
Conviva, Aulus Vettius, 148, 149
Corso Umberto, built over the old Via Lata, 107
Corneto (former Tarquinii), 165, 167; discovery of Etruscan tombs in 1827, 175
Corte, Matteo della, Pompeiian epigrapher, 147, 148, 149, 150
Corvo of Padua, Mathias, author of a topography of Syracuse, 211
Crassus, Marcus Licinus (c. 115-53 B.C.), 94
Creto-Mycenaean civilization, 61, 62
Crimisa (now Punta del Alice), site of Temple of Apollo Alaeos, 233

Crotona, Etruscan Academy founded at (1726), 168, 174, 211
Pietro da (1596–1669), Italian painter and architect, 16
Crypto-Porticus (subterranean passage on Palatine), 41
Curia of Julia, 76
of Tullus Hostilius, 76
the, 14; became church of S. Adriano, A.D. 630, 16, 33; originally built to replace the Comitium, 72, 80, 83
Cybele, Mother of the Gods, 36; sacred stone of (*baetyl*), 96

De Etruria Regali libri septum, by Sir Thomas Dempster, 166, 167
D'Elboeuf, Prince, Austrian general who directed exploration at Portici, 135
Delbrück, author of a book on Praeneste, 127
Della magnificenza ed architectura dei Romani, by Piranesi, 171–2
Dempster, Sir Thomas, author of *De Etruria Regali libri septum,* 166, 167, 168, 169
Dennis, George, author of *The Cities and Cemeteries of Etruria,* 177
De Non, French Chargé d'Affaires, 210
De Rerum Natura by Lucretius, 142
dialects spoken in ancient Italy, 247–9
Diana, Temple of, at Norba, 132
Die Etrusker, by K. O. Muller, 177
Diocletian, Gaius Aurelius Valerius (A.D. 245–313), 13, 14, 76, 225
Diomedes, M. Arrius, 147
Dionysos of Halicarnassus, 38, 46, 201
Dioscuri, twin gods of Sparta, 230
Di Rossi—*see* necropolis at Lake Alba, 47
Discourse of Lyons, by the Emperor Claudius, 163, 180
Dissertazioni, issued by the Museum of Cortona, 174
dolia—terracotta vases, 47, 48
Domitian, Titus Flavius Domitianus (A.D. 51–96), Roman Emperor, 73, 82, 91
Palace of, 13, 52, 88, 94, 96–97, 99, 185
equestrian statue of, 55, 73
Forum of, 81–82
Domus Transitoria, built by Nero, 13, 41; damaged by fire A.D. 64, 98, 99
Doric Temple, Pompeii, 155–6
Drunken Faun, the, bronze found at Herculaneum, 139
Due Decche Sulla Storia della Sicilia, by Father Tommaso Fazello, 211–13
Duhn, Von, German archaeologist, 154
Dumeznil, G.—*see* interpretation of stele found on the site of the Comitium, 59, 60

Einsiedeln Itinerary, account of ninth-century Rome, 32, 33, 35
Empedocles, 239
Engubine Tablets, 166–7; found at Gubbio (ancient Iguvium) in 1444, 247, 248
Epicurean Circle, the, 142–4
Erzoch, architect, discoverer of part of the Altar of Peace in 1859, 107
Esquiline, the, 13, 22, 33, 35, 41, 42, 64, 67, 78
Etruscan Academy, Cortona, founded in 1726, 168
Etruscans, the, master builders, 46; first traces of their influence in Rome towards the middle of the sixth century B.C., 53, 56, 62, 64, 68, 113, 120; their occupation of Pompeii *c.* 530–474 B.C., 155–6; their discovery from the Emperor Claudius to modern times, 163–204; their alphabet, 173; mirrors and funerary urns, 176–7, 204; language, 199–200; origins? 200–2; mineral wealth and industries, 203–4
etruscology, funerary—*see* Etruscan tombs
Eudoxia, Empress, 19
Eugenius IV (Pope 1431–47), 17, 27
Evander, early Greek colonist, 164

Falerii (now Civita Castellana), discovered in 1886, 186
Farnese, Cardinal Alessandro (later Pope Paul III), 28
Gardens, laid out in sixteenth century; excavations in 1722 and 1728 carried out by Francis I, Duke of Parma, 89; further excavations under Pietro Rosa, revealing the House of Livia, 90–93, 96
Palace(present French Embassy), 28, 101
Villa, discovered in 1879, 101; its decoration, 101–4, 106
Fasti, by Ovid, 37
favissae (deposits of votive offerings), 188, 237
Fazello, Father Tommaso, Sicilian historian, author of *Due Decche sulla Storia della Sicilia,* 211–13
Fea, Carole, appointed Director of Antiquities in 1801, 38
Fede, Count Joseph—*see* Hadrian's Villa, 115–16, 118
Felsina (modern Bologna), 181
'Female Dancers', sculpture found at Herculaneum, 140
Festus, Sextus Pompeus, Latin grammarian of the second or third century A.D., 58

Ficorini, archaeologist, 41; *cestus* discovered at Praeneste, 168
Filarete, Antonio di Pietro Averlino (*c.* 1400–69), Italian sculptor and architect, 34
Fiorelli, Guiseppe, Director of Pompeiian excavations: his three rules for excavation, 145–7, 148, 150
Flaccus, G. Fulvius, the Censor, 209
Flaminius, Circus of, 22, 32
Flavian Circus—*see* the Colosseum, 25
Fontana, Domenico (1543–1607), architect to Pope Sixtus V, 28
Fora, the Imperial, 74–86
Forlivesi, Padre Gian Nicola, monk and author of vanished MS. on Etruscan tombs, 167–8
Fortuna Primigenia, Temple of, at Palestrina, 127–9
Forum Boarium, 23, 40, 44, 45
   Holitorium, 29
   Julium, 74–77, 83
   Romanum, 21, 22, 24, 33; plan as reconstructed by Nibby, 38–39, 40, 44, 45, 46–47, 52, 55; becomes the civic centre of Rome, sixth century B.C., 56, 57; 'City of the Forum', 62–64, 68, 69; its history in the light of modern exploration, 70–74, 75, 77, 80, 81, 82, 99
Forum Romanum, The, by Antonio Nibby, 37
Forum Transitorium, planned by Domitian, 22; completed by Nerva, 81
Francois, Alessandro, discoverer of the Francois Tomb at Vulci, 177–80; restorer of the Chiusi vase, 178
Frederick II, Holy Roman Emperor (1194–1250), 26
French Embassy (former Farnese Palace), 28
Frugi, M. Licinius Crassus, consul in A.D. 64, 139, 256

Gabii, ancient city of Latium, 110
Gabrici, E., Director of the National Museum, Palermo—*see* excavations at Veii, 191, 219
Gaiseric, King of the Vandals, sacked Rome A.D. 455, 19
Galazzi, General, discoverer with Archpriest Regolini, of the Regolini-Galazzi tomb, 176
Gastaldi, Bartolomeo—his study of *terremare,* 242
Gatti—*see* excavations at Ostia, 119
Gauls, the—their invasion of Rome, 390 B.C., 65–66
Gazzola, Felice, discoverer of Paestum, 205

Gerhard, Edward, founder of the German Institute in Rome (*Istituto di Correspondenza Archeologica*), 175
Germanicus, Caesar (15 B.C.–A.D. 19), 95
Giglioli, G. Q., archaeologist—*see* excavations at Veii, 191–4
Gjerstad, Einar, Swedish archaeologist, 49
Goethe, Johann Wolfgang von (1749–1832), 106; his description of the temples of Paestum (*Travels in Italy*), 206, 207; at Segasta and Taormina, 214–15, 249
gold leaf amulets, found at Petalia, 227, 228, 229; and at Sybaris, 228–9
Golden House, the, of Nero, 14, 33, 73, 83, 98–99
Gordian III, M. Antonius Gordianus Pius, Roman Emperor (224–44), 26
Gori, A. F., author of *Museum Etruscum,* 116, 168, 169
Gozzadini, Count, archaeologist, discoverer of an Etruscan city, now Marzobotto, 181–5
Graillot, F., discoverer of Satricum (modern Conca), 186–8
Gregory the Great, (Pope 590–604), 84
grid plan of city building, 132, 154, 155, 156–7, 159, 183, 184, 218, 243
Griffins, The House of the, partially excavated in 1722, and again between 1910 and 1913, 93–94
Grotta Oscura, volcanic stone used in Roman architecture, 10, 57, 58, 65, 66, 67
Gsell, Stephane—explorations at Vulci, 186
Guarnacci, Abbé Matio, founder of the Etruscan Museum of Volterra, author of *Memorie Storiche Etrusche sul piu antico Regnio d'Italia,* 170, 173–4

Hadrian, Publius Aelius Hadrianus (A.D. 76–138), 14, 15, 22
   Arch of, 15
   Epitaph of, 117
   Mausoleum of, 22
   Temple of Venus and Rome, 14
   Villa of, 115–18, 131
   Wall of, 15
Harris, William, English architect, codiscoverer of the metopes of Selinonte, 216
Hackert, Georg, engraver—*see* Horace's Farm, 114
'Head of an Athlete'—sculpture found at Herculaneum, 140

'Head of an Ephebe'—sculpture found at Herculaneum, 140

Henry VII (*c.* 1269–1313), Roman Emperor, 27

Hera, Temple of at Agrigente, 214
Temple of at Samos, 230
Lacinia, Temple of at Taranto, stripped of marble tiles by G. Fulvius Flaccus 173 B.C., 209–10; demolished between 1510 and 1521, 211

Heraion of Paestum, the, excavated by Zanotti-Bianco (1934–7), 234–9

Heraklea, Greek city of Calabria, 208, 210

Herculaneum, destroyed by volcanic action A.D. 79, 10; first excavations by Prince D'Elboeuf (1719), 135; work continued by Rocco de Alcubierre (1738), 135–7; Villa of the Papyri discovered (1750), 139–42; House of Argus partially disengaged (1825), 157–8; the characteristic features of Herculaneum as revealed by explorations from 1927 onwards, 158–61, 251

Hercules, Temple of, Agrigente, 212
Custos, Temple of, 17, 18, 100
Triumphans, Temple of, 18, 225

Hermes Resting—bronze found at Herculaneum, 139

Herodotus, 172, 201

Himera, Temple of, Sicily, 221

Hippodamus of Miletus, popularizer of the rectangular grid system of city planning, 156–7, 183, 184, 218

Histoire Critique de l'Établissement des Colonies Greques, by Raoul-Rochette, 208

Holm, A., one-time Professor of Ancient History at the University of Palermo, 221

Honorius I (Pope 625–38), 16

Horace's Villa (The Sabine Farm), 113–15, 142, 143

Hortensius, Quintus (114–50 B.C.), Roman orator, 91

borrea (warehouses) at Ostia, 124

House of Joseph II, Pompeii, 147
of Homer, Pompeii, 147
of Loreius Tiburtinus, Pompeii, in process of restoration, 152–3
of Lucretius Fronto, Pompeii, reconstructed by de Petra, 152
of the Centenary, Pompeii, 147
of the Coloured Capitals, Pompeii, 147
of the Crypto-porticus, Pompeii, 147
of the Farm, Pompeii, 147
of the Golden Cupids, Pompeii, work of restoration completed in 1902, 152
of the Little Bronze Bull, Pompeii, 147

of the Silver Wedding, Pompeii, 147; restored by Ruggiero in 1892, 151
of the Surgeon, Pompeii, 147
of the Two Coctii, Pompeii, 150
of the Vestals, 9; damaged by fire A.D. 191, 14
of the Vettii, Pompeii, 148, 151; *atrium* reconstructed by de Petra, 152

hypogeum (Etruscan burying vault or sepulchre), 171, 178, 179, 182

hut foundations, 52, 53, 54, 55, 96, 150
urns, 47, 48, 53, 189

inhumation *fossae,* 48, 49, 50, 51

Innocent IV (Pope 1243–54), 26
VIII (Pope 1484–92), 165

insulae (apartment houses) in Rome, 77; in Ostia, 124–6; in Pompeii, 160

Isis Pavilion, the, 94–95, 97

Isola Farnese, site of excavation undertaken in 1913 to discover the lost city of Veii, 188

Isolani, Cardinal Giacomo, 24

Istituto di Correspondenza Archeologica, 43; first meeting on 21 April 1829, 175, 176, 177, 185, 216, 226

Itinerary of Benedict, the, drawn up by Pope Celestinus II on twelfth-century Rome, 32, 33, 35

Janiculum, the, 81

Janus—
Arch of, 23, 39, 82
Gate of, 62
Temple of, 18, 20, 82

Josephus, Flavius, 41

Julius III (Pope 1550–5), 186

Juno Lacinia, Temple of, Agrigente, 212; restoration by Prince Torremuzza, 215
Lucina, Temple of, Norba, 132
Sospita, Temple of, 18

Jupiter Capitolinus (Optimas Maximum), 63, 64, 70, 72, 193
Stator, Temple of, 12, 70
temple of, 9, 24, 35; completed and dedicated in 509 B.C., 63, 70, 98, 193
Tonnans, Temple of, 39

Justi, biographer of Winckelmann, 174

Knights of Rhodes, 78

Kore, 188

Koste, G., compiler of volumes on Etruscan mirrors and funerary urns, 177

La Civita, locality near Pompeii, 134; scene of first excavation in 1748, 137–8

Lacus Orphei, 35

Lanciani, Rodolfo, Secretary of the Municipal Archaeological Commission, 41, 43, 46, 114; excavations at Ostia, 119

Lenzi, Abbé Luigi, author of *Saggio di lingua etrusca e di altri lingui antiche d'Italia*, 174–5

lararium of Domitian's Palace, 93, 96, 97

Largo Argentina, archaeological discoveries in 1927–8, 100–1

Lateran, the, 16, 26

Latin language—theories of its formation, 248–9

La Vega, succeeded Alcubierre as Director of Exploration at Pompeii in 1870, 144, 159

Lenormant, archaeologist—*see* excavations in Calabria, 229, 230

Leo IV (Pope 847–55), 22

XII (Pope 1823–9), 29

Lepidus, M. Aemilius, Roman censor 179 B.C., 71

libraries—
in Vespasian's Temple of Peace, 81
in Trajan's Forum, 83–84
at the Villa of the Papyri, Herculaneum, 140

Ligorio, 97, 129

Lipari Islands, 222

Lives of the Caesars, by Suetonius, 37

Livia, House of, excavated by Pietro Rosa in 1869, 90–93, 94, 97, 101, 102

Livy, 11, 45, 46, 48; his dating of the Servian Wall, 64–66, 70, 141, 164, 180, 250

Locri, explored from 1889 by Paolo Orsi, 230–1, 232

Lucania, 226; excavation at Sybaris, 227–9

Lucifero, Bishop Antonio, 211

Lucretius, Titus Lucretius Carus, Roman poet and philosopher, 142

Lugli, G.—*see* Horace's Farm, 114

Luynes, Duke de, 230

Lyceum, the—*see* Hadrian's Villa, 117

Macellum Magnum of Nero, 17

Maecenas, Gaius, Roman patron of letters, 113

Magna Graecia, 121, 183, 209, 222, 226, 229, 246, 251
Society, formed by Umberto Zanotti-Bianco in 1920, 232, 233, 235

Maiuri, Professor Amadeo, present-day Director of Excavations at Pompeii, 150, 155, 156

Majorianus, Emperor of the West (457–61), 19

Malaphoros, Temple of at Selinonte, 219–20

Mamertine Prison, 38, 44, 63, 70

Manicalunga, necropolis of—*see* excavation of Selinonte, 219

Marcellus, Theatre of, 23

Marcus Aurelius Antoninus (121–80 B.C.), 15, 31

Mariette, Jean-Pierre, opponent of Piranesi's theory of 'The Rome of the Tarquins', 171–3

Marius, Gaius (155–86 B.C.), Roman general, 79, 122, 131

Marliani, sixteenth-century archaeologist, 37

Mars Ultor, 78, 79

Martini, Francesco di Giorgio, 25

Martius, King Ancus, founder of Ostia in 325 B.C., 120

Marzobotto, site of former Etruscan city, 155; site disclosed by Count Gozzadini (1865), 181–5, 196, 197

Mausoleum of Augustus, 23
of Caecilia Mecella, 28
of Hadrian, 22

Maxentius, Marcus Aurelius Valerius, Roman Emperor (306–12 B.C.), 14, 33

Maximian, co-Emperor with Diocletian, third century B.C., 225

Medici, Cosimo de', 166

Medna (now Nicotera), excavations by Paolo Orsi begun in 1913, 232

Megara Hyblaea, Sicily, 218, 221, 230

megaron of Mycenaean palaces, 61, 219

Meli, Giuseppi, explorer of the Temple of Himera (1861), 221

Memoria per servire alla Storia Litteraria di Sicilia, first published in 1755, 215

Memorie Storiche Etrusche sul piu antico Regnio d'Italia, by Guarnacci, 170

Metaponte, city of Magna Graecia built on geometric plan, 183, 208

metopes of Selinonte, 216–17, 220–1; of the Heraion of Paestum, 236–9

Metrodorus, Greek philosopher, 141

Mills, Charles, 88, 95

Mezenius, Etruscan king, 164

Minerva, statue of, found at Arretium, 165
Temple of, 35, 81

Mirabilis Urbis Romae, 32, 35–37

Monte Casale, Sicily, 218, 222

Monteleone, Catanzaro (the Greek Hipponium, the Roman Vibo Valentia), explored by Paolo Orsi, 232

Monteverde stone, 57

Monumenti, journal of the Istituto di Correspondenza Archeologica, 175, 177

Moon, Temple of the, 12

Montesquieu, Charles Louis de Secondat (1689–1755), author of *Considéra-tions sur les Causes de la Grandeur de la Décadence des Romains*, 44, 45

Moretti, G., Curator of the Antiquities of Rome, 108

Mori, Benedetto, assistant to Piranesi, 89

Muller, K. O., author of *Die Etrusker*, 177

mundus, the opening linking the dead with the living world, 185

Museum Etruscum by A. F. Gori, 168

Muto, Sabatino del, archaeologist—*see* Villa of Piazzo Armerina, 224

Myron's Cow, sculpture in the Temple of Peace, 20

National Association for the Promotion of the Interests of Southern Italy, formed by Umberto Zanotti-Bianco, 232

necropolis—
at Lake Alba, Latium, 47, 51
at Veii, 189–90
at Selinonte, Sicily, 218
at Villanova (Etruria), 181
on the Quirinal, 50, 51
the Sacred Way, 48–49, 50, 51, 52

Neoptolemus of Parion, author of *Poetic Art*, 142

Nero, Claudius Caesar Augustus Germanicus, Roman Emperor A.D. 54–68, his 'New City', 9; Domus Transitoria on the Palatine damaged by fire, 13, 98; replaced by the Golden House, 14, 73, 83, 99; the Macellum Magnum, 17; restored Temple of Janus, 25; Colossus of Nero, 25; 'Obelisk of Nero', 34, 41, 107

Nerva, Marcus Cocceius, Roman Emperor (A.D.? 35–98), 31; completed Domitian's Forum Transitorium, 81

Nibby, Antonio, author of *The Forum Romanum;* his hypotheses concerning the Forum, 38–40, 70, 116

Nicholas V (Pope 1447–55), 27

Nobilior, M. Fulvius, Roman censor, 179 B.C., endowed the Forum with the Basilica Aemilia, 71

Norba, founded in 497 B.C., aerial survey of, 131–3, 157

Notizie degli Scavi, archaeological periodical founded in 1876, 186
degli Scavi di Antiquita communicate alla Reale Accademia di Lincei, 43

Numa, Pompilius, legendary King of Rome (715–672 B.C.), 12, 51, 61

Obelisk of Nero, or Terebinth Tomb, 34

Octavia, Portico of, 29

Octavian, later Augustus—*see* Augustus

Odeon, the—*see* Hadrian's Villa, 116

Orator, Statue of the, found (1556) at Lake Trasimene, 165

Orphism, 229, 231

Orsi, Paolo, 218; introduced the stratigraphical study of the soil, 222, 223; soundings taken at the Villa of Piazza Armerina, 224–5; directs campaign at Locri, 230–1; appointed Director of Archaeological Research in Calabria (1908), 232

Ortygia, Island of, 223

Ostia (founded 325 B.C.), after 1870 scheduled as a site of permanent excavation, 119–27; the *insulae* of, 124–6

Paestenae Dissertationes, by F. A. Paoli, 205

Paestum (Posidonia), ancient Greek city in Lucania, 205–7, 211, 234; discovery of the Heraion of Silaris, 234–9

Palace of Domitian, 13, 52, 88, 94, 96–97
of Tiberius, 41, 96, 97–98

Palaces, Imperial—
of Domitian, 13, 52, 88, 94, 96–97
of Tiberius, 41, 96, 97–98
Domus Aurea of Nero, 98–99
Domus Transitoria of Nero, 98, 99

Palatine, the, devastated by fire A.D. 64, 12, 13, 14, 22, 23, 33, 41, 42, 47, 48, 49, 50; systematic excavations carried on in the twentieth century, 51–54; the Palatine villages, 54–56, 60, 63, 64, 68, 69; earlier excavation from 1536 onwards, 86–95; the history of the Palatine as revealed by archaeology, 95–99

Palatium, the, 52, 53; site of Domitian's Palace, 96, 98

Palazzo Caffarelli, 63
Farnese (present French Embassy), 28, 101
Fiano, 107, 108
Maggiore, 86
Venezia (formerly Palazzo San Marco), 28

Palermo, 211, 221

Palestrina (formerly Praeneste), 112; excavation of the Temple of the Goddess of Fortune, 127–9

Palladio, Andrea (1508–80), Italian architect, 129

Palus Caprae (Marsh of the Goat), 45

Pancrazi, Padre, author of *Antichità Siciliane*, 213

Index

Pantheon, the, consecrated by Pope Boniface IV in A.D. 609, 17, 29, 35–36

Paoli, F. A., author of *Paestenae Dissertationes*, 205

Pallalardo, engineer—*see* Villa of Piazza Armerina, 224

Papyri, Villa of the, Herculaneum, excavated by Alcubierre and Carl Weber, 139–42, 157

Paribeni, R.—*see* excavations at Ostia, 119

Parcae, statues of the, 20

Parma, Francis I Duke of, carries out excavations at the Farnese Gardens in 1722 and 1728, 89–90

Parmenides, Greek philosopher, 239

Pasqui, A.—*see* Horace's Farm, 114

Panares, Lipari Islands, 222

Paul II (Pope 1461–71), 25, 28
III (Pope 1534–9), 24
V (Pope 1605–21), 81

Peace, Temple of, 20

Pelasgians, the first Greek settlers in Italy, 170

Pellegrini, collaborator with Pietro Rosa, 43

Persephone, *temenos* of at Locri, 231

Petalia, the gold leaf of, 227

Petersen, Secretary of the German Archaeological Institute of Rome—his attempted reconstruction of the Altar of Peace, 107–8; undertakes research at Locri, 230

Petra, Guilio de, his excavations at Pompeii, 150, 151; work of restoration of Pompeiian houses and gardens, 152

Philodemus of Gadera, 141, 142, 143

Phocas, East Roman Emperor (602–10), 17; the Column of, 15–16, 39, 74

Piazza Armerina, Villa of, Sicily, attributed to Maximian third century A.D., 224–5

Picenum, 244, 245, 246

Pigorini, 47, 52, 53—*see* study of *terramare*, 242–3

Piranesi, author of *Della magnificenza ed architettura dei Romani* and *Antichità Romane*, 89, 116, 207

Pisani, Pietro, Sicilian archaeologist, 216

Piso, L. Calpurnius, father-in-law of Julius Caesar, 141, 143

Pius IV (Pope 1559–65), 18
VII (Pope 1800–23), 29, 119

Pliny the Elder, 155, 160, 193
the Younger, 97

Plutarch, Greek biographer (*c.* A.D. 46–120), 46, 193, 235

Poecile, the (Painted Porch of Athens)—*see* Hadrian's Villa, 117, 118

Poetic Art, treatise by Neoptolemus of Parion, probable source of Horace's *Ars Poetica*, 142

Polybius, Greek historian, 240

pomaerium, spiritual limit of classic Rome, 50, 54, 64, 243

Pompeii, destroyed by volcanic action A.D. 79, 10; forum constructed in second century B.C., 76; first excavations by Alcubierre in 1748, 137–9; continued by La Vega—disengagement of Forum completed 1813, 144–5; Guiseppe Forelli appointed Director of Pompeiian excavations, 145; his cardinal rules for disengagement of a city, 145–6; the work of Della Corte in identifying villas, 147–9; restoration work by De Ruggiero and G. de Petra, 151–2; re-creation of gardens by de Petra, 152; the Greeks in Pompeii, 153–7; occupation by Etruscans *c.* 530 B.C. and 474 B.C., 155

Pompeiian architecture, classic, 92, 93, 94, 95, 153

Pontius Pilate, 31, 33

Ponzi—*see* discovery of necropolis at Lake Alba, 47

Pope, Alexander, 18, 19

Populonia, Etruscan centre of the mining industry, 203

Porta Ercolano, Pompeii, 139, 144, 155
Janualis (Gate of Janus), 62
Maggiore, the Basilica of, 100, 104–6
Pendana (the Gaping Gate), 62
Romana, 62
Salaria, 19
Vesuvio, Pompeii, 155

Portici, village on the site of Herculaneum, 134, 135, 205

Portico of Octavia, 29

Portunus, the sea-god, 17

Poseidon, Temple of at Paestum, 207

Posidonia, Greek colony renamed Paestum, 236

Pozzuoli, 123, 161

Praeneste (now Palestrina), excavation of the Temple of Fortuna Primigenia, 127–9; discovery of *cestus* (1738), 168

Praetors' Tribunal, 71

Price, Thomas D.—*see* Horace's Farm, 114

Priene, Asia Minor, Greek city built on geometric plan, 183

Prisca, Tarquinius, 63

Procopius, Byzantine historian, 20

Propertius, Sextus (*c.* 50–*c.* 15 B.C.), Roman elegiac poet, 68, 105, 111

Index

Puglisi, S. M.—*see* excavations on the Palatine, 53

puteus, small circular altar, 40

Pyrrhus, King of Epyrus, 194, 229

Pythagorian Basilica, 100, 106

Pythagoras, Greek philosopher, 51, 226, 239

Quirinal, the, 13, 23, 24, 42, 45, 50, 52, 64, 68, 82, 85

Rancoureil, Abbé, his excavations on the site of Domitian's Palace, 88–89, 210

Ranzano, Pietro, author of a history of Palermo (1470), 211

Raoul-Rochette, author of *Histoire Critique de l'Etablissement des Colonies Grecques* (1813), 208

Regia, the, 12, 60, 61, 62, 63, 71

Regolini, Archpriest, co-discoverer of the Regolini-Galazzi tomb, 175

Regolini-Galazzi Etruscan tomb, opened up at Cervetri (1836), 175–6

Resina, village on the site of Herculaneum, 134

Ricci, Corrado, excavator of Caesar's Forum (1930–2), 76

Riccio, Bernardo, author of a book on Messina, 211

Michele, historian, 211

Romanelli, P.—*see* excavation of Tarquinii, 197–8

Rome, early building materials, 10–11; damage by fire and flood, 11–14, 21; destruction of ancient buildings by the Roman Emperors, 15–16; transformation of temples into churches begun in the seventh century, 17–18; invasions by barbarians, 18–19; some work of restoration by Theodoric, 20; extension of existing fortifications in the ninth century, 22–23; systematic pillaging of ancient monuments for marble, 23–25; the Colosseum, 25–30; the beginnings of scientific research into the history of Rome after 1870 (unification of Italy), 32; Nibby's hypothetic reconstruction of the Forum Romanum based on existing accounts by earlier writers, 37–40; after 1870, part of Rome scheduled as an archaeological preserve, 42; origin of foundation of the Urbs discussed, 44–47; discovery of the Sacred Way necropolis (1902), 48; and of graves on the Quirinal, 50; systematic excavations on the Pala-

tine, 51–54; Palatine villages, 54–56; identification of the Comitium (1899), 57–60; the 'City of the Forum', 60–64; the Servian Wall, 64–68; rediscovery of the Forum, 72; the Imperial Fora, 74–86; excavations carried out on the Palatine, including the House of Livia in the Farnese Gardens, 90–93; the House of the Griffins, 93–94; the Isis Pavilion, 94–95; and the Imperial Palaces, 95–99; the ancient temples of the Largo Argentina quarter, 100–1; the Farnesina Villa, 101–4; the Basilica of the Porta Maggiore discovered in 1917, 104–6; the Altar of Peace—history of its discovery, excavation and restoration, 106–9

and Divus Augustus, Temple of, at Ostia, 123

Romulus, 34, 35, 39, 47, 48, 49, 51–52, 54, 58, 70, 96, 184

Rosa, Pietro, Director of Antiquities, 43; excavations at the Villa Farnese, 90–91; at Ostia, 119

Rostra of Augustus, 73, 74

Rufus, L. Varius, member of the Epicurian circle, 143

Ruggiero, Michele de, Director of Excavations at Pompeii (1875–93), 150, 151, 152

sacred calendars, 200

Sacred Way, the, 72, 73, 74, 83; discovery of necropolis (1902) by G. Boni, 48–49, 52, 53, 54; necropolis abandoned and built over in seventh century B.C., 55, 56, 58, 61, 189, 250

Saggio di lingua etrusca e di altri lingui antiche d'Italia, by Abbé Luigi Lanzi, 174

Sanctis, Domenico di—*see* Horace's Farm, 113–15

Sandeo, Felino, fifteenth-century historian, 211

Sangallo, Antonio, architect, 100

Saracens, the, their conquest of Rome (A.D. 846), 22

Satricum (modern Conca), discovered by F. Graillot (1896), 186–8

Saturn, Temple of, 15, 39, 45, 74

Schubring, J., German scholar, 221

Secretarium, annex of the Curia, later the church of Sta Lucia and S. Martino, 16

Segeste, Sicily, 213, 214

Selinonte, Greek city built on the geometric plan, destroyed by the Carthaginians in 409 B.C., 183, 213;

Selinonte, discovery of archaic metopes, 216–17, 220–1; further excavations carried on by Francesco Saverio Cavallari, 218–21, 234

Septizonium of Septimius Severus, 22; demolished by Pope Sixtus V, 28, 34

Serradifalco, Duke of, President of the Commission of Antiquities and Art, 216, 217

Severus, Alexander, 23, 26
Septimius, 22, 28, 34, 38, 57

Servian Wall, the, 10, 44, 62, 64–68, 96, 121, 122

Servius Tullius, King, 64, 66

Sleeping Satyr, the, bronze found at Herculaneum, 139

Sixtus V (Pope 1585–90), 28, 107

Smaragdus, Byzantine Exarch of Italy, 15–16, 74

Sogliano, A.—*see* excavations at Pompeii, 150, 154

Solonte, Carthaginian city in Sicily, 221

Spalato, Palace of, 225

Spes, Temple of, 18

Stabiae, 10, 119, 120, 157, 160, 161–2

Stackelberg Tomb, Corneto, 175

Stadium of Domitian (now Piazza Navona), 32

Statio Annonae, 18

Stesichorus (*c.* 640–555 B.C.), Greek lyric poet, 239

stone houses, rectangular, first appearance in sixth century B.C., 56, 61, 62

Street of the Tombs—*see* excavation of Pompeii, 138, 144, 147

Strobel, Pellegrino—his study of *terremare*, 242

Suetonius, Tranquillus Gaius (*c.* A.D. 70, d. after A.D. 122), Roman biographer and historian, 37, 41, 91, 95

Sulla, Lucius Cornelius (138–78 B.C.), Roman general and dictator, 9, 10, 79, 94; fortified Ostia in 1 B.C., 122, 123, 131, 132, 161, 246

Superbus, Tarquinius, 63

Sybaris, Lucanian, excavations in 1879, 227–9, 231

Swinburne, W. H., his account of Paestum, 205–6; notes on Selinonte and Agrigente, 213

Syracuse, 208, 211, 216, 218, 223

Tabularium (Records Office), dedicated 78 B.C., 71

Tacitus, Cornelius (*c.* 55–120), Roman historian, 11, 12, 141, 250

Taranto, discovery of a Greek tomb, 232–3

Taormina, Sicily, 213, 214, 221, 223

Tarquinii (now Corneto), 165, 167; excavations directed by P. Romanelli (1946), 197–8

Tarquinius Prisca, 63, 64, 193
Superbus, 63

Tartaglia Tomb, discovered in Corneto in 1699, 167

Taurus, T. Statilius, Roman senator, 105

temenos of Persephone, Locri, 231

Temple of—
Antonius and Faustina, 38, 48, 73
Apollo, Pompeii, 155–6
Apollo Alaeos, Calabria, 233
Athene Promachus, Locri, 231
Castor, 39, 70, 82
Caesar, 71–72
Ceres, 18
Concord, 14
Concord, Agrigente, 212, 215
Diana, Norba, 132
Doric Temple, Pompeii, 155–6
Fortune, 39
Goddess of Fortune, Palestrina, 126
Hera, Agrigente, 214
Hera, Samos, 230
Hera Lacinia, Taranto, 209
Heraion of Paestum, 234–9
Hercules, Agrigente, 312
Hercules Custos, 17, 18, 100
Hercules Triumphans, 18, 225
Himera, Sicily, 221
Janus, 18
Juno Lacinia, Agrigente, 212, 215
Juno Lucina, Norba, 132
Juno Sospita, 18
Jupiter Capitolinus, 9, 24, 35, 63, 70, 98
Jupiter Stator, 12, 70
Jupiter Tonnans, 39
Malaphoros, Selinonte, 219
Mars, 37
Mars Ultor, 78
Minerva, 81
the Moon, 12
Pantheon, 17
Peace, 20, 80, 81, 83, 84
Poseidon, Paestum, 207
the Regia, 12, 60, 61, 62, 63, 71, 72
Saturn, 15, 39, 45, 72, 73
Spes, 18
Venus and Rome, 14
Venus Genetrix, 76
Vespasian, 39
Vesta, 9, 12, 39, 40, 55, 60, 61, 62, 71, 72

Terebinth Tomb, or Obelisk of Nero, 34

terracotta ornamentation, 172, 186–8, 231, 232, 234

terremare—fortified villages, 12, 241–4

Terravechia di Grammichele, Sicily, 222
Theatre of Marcellus (site of the Savelli Palace), 23
of Pompey, built 55 B.C., 23, 123
Theodoric, King of the Ostrogoths (*c.* 454–526), 20, 26
Tiberius, Claudius Nero (42 B.C.–A.D. 37), Roman Emperor, 41, 74, 96, 97–98, 123
tibertinum, travertine stone, 34
Tigillum Sororium (The Beam of the Sisters), a postern gate dedicated to Juno, 62
Tile of Capua, terracotta plaque inscribed in the Etruscan language, 200
Timon's Tower—*see* Hadrian's Villa, 116, 117
Titus, Flavius Sabinus Vespasianus (A.D. 40 or 41–81), 12, 14, 22, 23, 70, 73, 80, 99, 134
Torre Annunziata, village on the site of Pompeii, 134, 144, 205
Torremuzza, Prince, co-editor of *Memoria per servire alla Storia Litteraria di Sicilia,* 214, 215
Tullus Hostilius, King, 58
Turnus, King of Ardea, 164
Trajan, Marcus Ulpius Trainus (A.D. 53–117), Roman Emperor, 22, 33, 72, 74, 125
Trajan's Anaglyphs, 73
Baths, 33
Column, 74, 84, 85
equestrian statue of, 83
Forum, 74, 82–86
Market, 33, 85–86, 126
Trasimene, Lake, 165
Treatise on Architecture by Vitruvius, 39
Triangular Forum, Pompeii, 155
trompe d'oeil window, 92, 94, 95, 102, 112

Umbilicus Romae, 32–33
Urbs of Romulus, 44, 48, 49, 51, 52, 53, 64, 68, 96, 164, 186, 195

Vaglieri, Dante, his excavations on the Palatine, 51–52, 53; at Ostia, 119
Van Duhn, German archaeologist, 107
Varus, Quintilius, 143
Veii, 57, 59, 66, 156, 172; excavated from 1913 onwards, 188–96; 201
Velabrum, the, 21, 39
Venus Genetrix, Temple of, 76
and Rome, Temple of, 14, 29

Vergers, A. Noel des, 178–9
Vespasian, Titus Flavius Vespasianus (A.D. 9–79), Roman Emperor, 83, 99, 137; his Forum, the Temple of Peace, 80–81, 83
Vesta, Temple of, 9, 12, 39, 40, 55, 60, 61, 62, 71
Vesuvius, eruption in A.D. 79, burying Pompeii, Herculaneum and Stabiae, 134, 143, 159, 160
Villa D'Este, Tivoli, designed by Ligorio, 129
Giulia, built for Pope Julius III, later a museum, 186, 192
of Herod Atticus, 131
Medici, 78
Villanova, necropolis discovered by Count Gozzadini, 181, 190, 201, 202
Villas of the Roman Campagna, 111–18
Viminal, the, 45, 64
Vitiges, King of the Goths, besieged Rome in A.D. 537, 20, 119
Vitruvius, Marcus Vitruvius Pollio, Roman architect and author, 38, 39, 172, 184; his description of an Etruscan temple, 187
Volsini, capital of the Etruscan world, 196–7
Volterra, 170, 173
Vulca, Veiian sculptor, 193
Vulci, 167; exploration of Etruscan tombs at, 175; disengagement of the Francois Tomb, 178–80, 186, 188

wall building, Roman techniques, 130
Warrior of Capestrano, Picenum—statue discovered in 1934, 244–6
Weber, Carl, Swiss engineer—*see* excavations at Herculaneum, 136, 139–44, 159
Winckelmann, 40, 136, 138, 141, 142, 143, 147, 169, 170, 172, 174, 175, 213, 216, 249

Zannoni, Antonio, his excavations at Felsina (1869), 181
Zanotti-Bianco, Umberto, founder of the National Association for the Promotion of the Interests of Southern Italy, and of the Magna Graecia Society, 232; his discovery of the Heraion of Paestum, 234–9
Zeus, Temple of, Agrigente, 216
Zeus Meilichios, Temple of, Selinonte, 220